Happiness in a North

CU00659747

Happiness in a Northern town

Edited by
Sandie McHugh
and Professor Jerome Carson

Whiting & Birch
MMXXI

© Whiting & Birch Ltd 2021
Published by Whiting & Birch Ltd,
Forest Hill, London SE23 3HZ

ISBN 9781861776297

Contents

About the Editors and Authors

Rosie Allen is a PhD student at the University of Bolton where her thesis is focused on understanding the short and long-term impacts of Covid-19 on university students' education and wellbeing. She also works part-time as a Research Assistant at the University of Manchester.

Reginald U Amanze is a final year PhD psychology student at the University of Bolton UK. Research interest includes; Forgiveness, Mental health and wellbeing, & hate.

Sarah Banks is an Assistant Psychologist living and working in the North West of England. Sarah has a Master's Degree in Positive Psychology and often applies aspects of Positive Psychology within her practice. Her research interests include Neurodiversity, with a particular focus on the empowerment of Autistic females. A member of The Board of Directors at Mhist in Bolton, Sarah begins a Doctorate in Education and Child Psychology at The University of Manchester this year.

Jerome Carson has been Professor of Psychology at the University of Bolton since 2012. Prior to this he was a clinical psychologist in the NHS. He lectured at the Institute of Psychiatry in London from 1992 to 2006. His research interests are mental health recovery and positive psychology.

Professor Sir Cary Cooper, CBE is the 50th Anniversary Professor of Organizational Psychology and Health at Manchester Business School, University of Manchester. He is a founding President of the British Academy of Management, President of the Chartered Institute of Personnel and Development (CIPD), former President of RELATE and President of the Institute of Welfare. He was the Founding Editor of the *Journal of Organizational Behavior*, former Editor of the scholarly journal *Stress and Health* and is the Editor-in-Chief of the Wiley-Blackwell *Encyclopaedia of Management*, now in its 3rd Edition. He has been an advisor to the World Health Organisation, ILO, and EU in the field of occupational health and wellbeing, was Chair of the Global Agenda Council on Chronic Disease of the World Economic Forum (2009-2010) (then served for five years on the Global Agenda Council for mental health of the WEF) and was Chair of the Academy of Social Sciences 2009-2015. He was Chair of the Sunningdale Institute in the Cabinet Office and National School of Government 2005-2010. Professor Cooper is currently the Chair of the National Forum for Health & Wellbeing at Work (comprised of 40 global companies including among others BP, Microsoft, NHS Executive, UK government (wellbeing lead), Rolls Royce, John Lewis Partnership. Professor Cooper is the author/ editor of over 250 books in the field of occupational health psychology, workplace wellbeing, women at work and occupational stress. He was awarded the CBE by the Queen for his contributions to occupational health; and in 2014 he was awarded a Knighthood for his contribution to the social sciences.

Chris Elliott was born in the East End of London. He spent thirty years working in Jobcentres. Early retirement saw him studying for a B.A. (hons) at Bolton University where he was introduced to The Happiness Project. He was the support act when the Project visited local communities, telling stories, the odd joke and singing the occasional song.

Ken Heathcote has had a lifetime in the fitness industry as both a provider and also a fitness fanatic himself. The author of six books on the topic, Ken is still very active today, though he has moved from marathons to swimming as his main fitness outlet. At the age of 82 he swam the length of Windermere, just over 10 miles. He continues to work with and inspire people of all ages.

Dr Chathurika Kannangara is an Assistant Teaching Professor and an Early Career Researcher at the Department of Psychology, University of Bolton, UK. She is also a registered Counsellor with BACP. Her primary research interest lies within the broad and developing domain of positive psychology applications in wellbeing.

Julie Levy is an Arts and Education Consultant and visual artist. Following 20 years in Education, Julie worked as a Senior Teacher Adviser for Lancashire County Council. Following this she moved to the private sector where, as education adviser, she helped to open almost 20 new schools and academies. Most of Julie's time is now spent volunteering and organising arts and cultural events throughout Bolton.

Elisabeth Long is co-founder and Chief Officer of 1point, a community benefit company offering talking therapy services free at the point of use to the people of Bolton since 2012. Originally working in the media, her experiences as a Relate volunteer led to second career as a counsellor, lecturer and social entrepreneur.

Paul Makin is a psychology graduate of Bolton university having studied psychology psychotherapy and counselling and is currently undertaking a master's degree in positive psychology and counselling. He has lived in the north all his life and spent many years in the hospitality industry. He is very passionate about the field of recovery post addiction after experiencing alcohol addiction himself

Sandie McHugh is an honorary research fellow at the University of Bolton.

Sandie has two Masters Degrees and an MPhil. She is both a historian and a psychologist. Her early research at the University of Bolton was with Professor Rob Ranyard on economic psychology. Since 2013 she has been conducting happiness research with Professor Jerome Carson.

Aashiya Patel started her academic career in 2019 as an Associate Lecturer at the University of Bolton. She is also a practicing counsellor and continues this practice alongside her teaching at the university with a particular interest in breaking down barriers to accessing counselling and supporting clients to overcome trauma.

Ian Platt is Project Co-ordinator for the Hummingbird Project at Medequip4Kids. He is also working on his PhD at the University of Bolton. Ian previously worked with adults recovering from depression and his particular area of interest is in improving mental health provision and access to higher education for children from underprivileged backgrounds.

Dr Julie Prescott is a Reader in Psychology and is the programme lead for the undergraduate Psychology, Psychotherapy and Counselling Programme at the University of Bolton. Julie is a Senior Fellow of the Higher Education Academy, a Chartered Psychologist, Associate Fellow of the British Psychological Society and holds APA membership. Julie's current research area focuses on technology and health/mental health, with a particular interest in young people and online counselling as well as how people gain support and use online technologies for their health and mental health support.

By the Grace of Allah, Dr Mohammed Sadiq is an assistant teaching professor and practicing accountant. I am pleased to share my personal experiences and do not do so as a religious scholar. I ask Allah forgiveness if I unintentionally offend or cause distress in any way. Allah is the greatest!

Aishath Shahama Shahaa is a Muslim student from the Maldives who is doing her MSc in Positive Psychology at University of Bolton. Her research is based on the relationship between religiosity and happiness. It is a project supervised by Prof. Jerome Carson and in partnership with Aashiya Patel. She is known to be a persistent night owl. Her interests lie in psychology research and education.

Robert Snape is Professor of Cultural History at the University of Bolton. He has published widely on the history of leisure in Britain as a field of voluntary association and social policy. He is the founder and Director of the University's Centre for Worktown Studies.

Kathryn Thomasson is a part time PhD student at the University of Bolton and a lecturer in English at Blackburn College. Kathryn's research is focused on exploring the influence of arts engagement on women's subjective wellbeing. She has been involved in several community arts projects in Bolton, working with local women's groups. Kathryn recently project managed the Cotton Queens project which brought together women from Bolton to explore the local Worktown archive and create a radio play based on the archive's observations of women enjoying their holidays in Blackpool. Kathryn volunteers for Bolton City of Sanctuary where she holds the role of secretary.

Michelle Tytherleigh After a first career working in industry, Michelle Tytherleigh has been a Senior Lecturer in Psychology and a Senior University Teaching Fellow for the Faculty of Social Science at the University of Chester since 2008. Having completed a PhD on stress and memory, her research interests have now taken a more 'positive' direction, and she is now interested in how the principles of positive psychology can be applied to empower individuals, and particularly in relation to their experiences of learning and teaching.

Dedication

To Cheryl & Geof for their support without which we would have been unable to edit this book.

Acknowledgements

Participants in our research studies, without whom this book would not have been possible. Our co-authors for their chapters. Professor Sir Cary Cooper for his continued support and encouragement and for writing the Foreword. The University of Bolton for the Jenkinson awards which helped to fund some of this research. Professor Patrick McGhee, Dr Gill Waugh, and Psychology Department colleagues. The Centre for Worktown Studies and its Director, Professor Bob Snape. Bethan Atkins, Ian Glover, Adrian Greenhalgh, Donna Zarei and Ian Harrison. Martin Guha and Emma Entwistle. Matthew Watson, Julie Lamara and colleagues at Bolton Museum and Central Library. Simon Fletcher and colleagues at Lancaster Library. Saiqa and staff at The Bolton News. Dick Perkins, Dave Burnham and the 'Live from Worktown' team. Jose Alexandre Vasco, Dr. Jerson Laks, Dr Vera Rita de Mello Ferreira and Gabriela Azevedo de Aguiar in Brazil. Professor Woody Cann, Professor Kevin Gournay , Professor John Haworth, Professor Samuel Ho , Professor Claire Langhamer and Professor Bob Stebbins.

Preface

In 1968, Bobby Kennedy gave a lecture at the University of Kansas when he was on the campaign trial for the Democratic nomination for President, in which he talked about the importance of Gross National Wellbeing as opposed to Gross National Product as a better indicator of a society's success. He said: "Too much and for too long, we seemed to have surrendered personal excellence and community values in the mere accumulation of material things. Our GNP is now over $800b a year, but that GNP, if we judge the USA by that, counts air pollution and cigarette advertising and the ambulances to clear our highways of carnage. It counts special locks for our doors and the jails for the people who break them. It counts the destruction of the redwood and the loss of our natural wonder in the chaotic sprawl. It counts napalm and counts nuclear warheads, and armoured cars for the police to fight the riots in our cities........Yet, the Gross National Product does not allow for the health of our children, the quality of their education or the joy of their play. It does not include the beauty of our poetry or strength of our marriages........it measures neither our wit nor our courage, neither our wisdom nor our learning, neither our compassion nor our devotion to our country, it measure everything in short, except that which make life worthwhile".

Happiness and wellbeing are not abstract concepts, they are the foundation stones on what we build individual and community resilience, and is more enduring than our politicians or particular products we produce or the transitory nature of social media. They are fundamental to a good quality of life, and sustainable community and interpersonal relationships.

This book is an outstanding example of what really matters, as we have learned from the pandemic and the various severe recessions we have experienced over the last decade and likely to experience post Covid. It is a glimpse into happiness in a community in the North of Manchester, and what it means for individual health and wellbeing. This is a must read for anybody interested in how we build happiness in our neighbours and communities. As Vincent van Gogh once wrote in one of his bouts of depression "I put my heart and soul into my work, and lost my mind in the process". And on a more positive note, Voltaire reflected "I have decided to be happy because it is good for my health".

Professor Sir Cary Cooper,
University of Manchester

Introduction
and summary of chapters

Sandie McHugh and Jerome Carson

Introduction

Are you interested in the subject of happiness? If so why is that? Assuming that you are interested in achieving a happy state, it is because it is preferable to being unhappy. Concern with happiness does not appear to be constant in individuals during their lives nor in countries. Sometimes happiness is very low on a list of priorities. Throughout history there has been a fluctuating interest by governments and societies in happiness. In times of relative peace and prosperity attention can become more focussed on happiness, whereas in times of war and turmoil where survival is at stake happiness is less important (Guha & Carson, 2017). Maslow (1943) explained this in terms of a Hierarchy of Needs in the shape of a pyramid. Happiness could be part of self-actualization, and self-esteem at the top of a sectioned pyramid, lower at the base level are human needs essential to survival; food, warmth, shelter, safety. An individual striving to attain these basic needs will be less concerned with whether or not they are experiencing happiness. In the present century most people in western democracies have their basic needs met, fuelling a contemporary interest in the state of happiness.

If having our basic needs met we are able to think about happiness, what do we actually mean? Can it be defined? Frey (2018) maintains that this is an open question, but that in our contemporary times it has individualistic answers. Much of our own research has involved asking participants what happiness is to them personally. Although there is no universal accepted definition by eminent psychologists there are some similarities. Ruut Veenhoven, (2012) views happiness as subjective enjoyment of life which has economic, social and health components. This enjoyment of life and wanting it to continue is a definition used by Layard (2006). A distinction can be made between overall satisfaction with life and momentary sensations such as eating, drinking, fairground rides and other pleasures. Kahneman states there is an important difference between people's moment by moment experience and their overall satisfaction with life (BPS, 2012). This is from the idea that we all have two selves, the experiencing self and the remembering self. The former is our moment by moment experience of pleasure and pain; the latter evaluates the experience, reflects on past experiences and makes future decisions. These two selves are connected with Kahneman's idea of people having two systems of thought for judgment and choice. These are system one, fast thinking, instinctive and almost effortless and system two, slower complex thinking requiring concentration and effort. System two, the conscious self makes choices, uses reason and beliefs. Both systems are recommended for happiness, one for experience and two for evaluation, storage of memories and to generate satisfaction (Kahneman, 2011).

Paul Dolan (2014) defines happiness as experience of pleasure and purpose over time. Including overall satisfaction with life in a loose definition, this happiness can be referred to as 'Eudaimonia' and is contrasted with the momentary 'hedonistic' sensational feelings. In this way, happiness is linked to overall well-being.

Twenty first century world interest in Happiness is illustrated by the United Nations (UN) declaration in 2011 that happiness was a fundamental human goal and a conference the next year declared 20th March each year to be World Happiness Day (United Nations, 2012). According to a press release from Globe Newswire in 2019, this day was celebrated by over seven billion people in the world through local, national, international events, social media and virtual events (AP News, 2019). One of the best known happiness movements founded around the time of the UN conference is Action for Happiness. Lord Layard from the London School of Economics, Geoff Mulgan from the Young Foundation, Nic Marks from the Centre for Well-being at the New Economics Foundation, along with Mark Williamson and Anthony Seldon set up the charity to help 'create a happier and more caring society' (BPS, 2011). It has nearly 176,000 members from 180 countries and in excess of over a million followers on social media. Its provision of calendars, postcards, guidebooks and other material free of charge has made it a popular focus point for knowledge and dissemination of happiness (Action for Happiness, 2020). Another focal point for happiness is Positive Psychology developed from humanistic psychology and founded in 1998 by Martin Seligman. This branch of psychology concentrates on the scientific study of what makes life most worth living (Peterson et al, 2008). Flourishing, flow, the PERMA model for well-being is only a few of the initiatives from Positive Psychology which have been developed from research and theoretical concepts (Ackerman, 2020).

With an idea of what happiness is, albeit remaining subject to an individual's definition, then how do we measure it? By the nature of happiness it has to be a subjective measure. There are several different methods of measurement: experience sampling; day reconstruction; time use surveys; evaluations; building of individual constructs and questionnaires to name just some. As Veenhoven (2019), Director of The World Database of Happiness indicates, there are 2200 empirical studies. Frequently used is the Ladder of Life Scale, used in Gallup World Poll, this has 11 steps of a ladder at the bottom the worst life and at the top step the best life. The

World Values Study has a question about satisfaction of life and feelings of happiness. A satisfaction with Life Scale containing five questions to agree or disagree with statements has been used since the 1980's (Garling & Gamble, 2018). The completion of self-report questionnaires has been the mainstay of happiness research in Bolton, although we have also more recently used the medium of recorded focus group, which is a general discussion about happiness with a group of people. As the authors of the World Happiness Report 2017 describe, it is left to individuals to evaluate their own well-being. Questions are often on a sliding scale between 0 (not at all) to 10 (completely), 'How happy are you with your life nowadays', questions in the present tense might read as an emotional report 'How happy are you now? (Helliwell et al, 2017). Since 2012 the UK's Office of National Statistics (ONS) has collected well-being data from four questions. These are 'How satisfied are you with your life nowadays?' 'How happy did you feel yesterday?' 'How anxious did you feel yesterday?' and 'To what extent do you feel that the things you do in your life are worthwhile?' These questions are rated on a scale from 1 (not at all) to 10 completely (ONS, 2016).

In 1938 Mass Observation following the receipt of letters from Bolton townsfolk on what was happiness, issued a questionnaire to gather further information. We replicated their study in 2014 by issuing the questionnaire virtually unchanged from that of 1938. An important part of this exercise is the ranking in preferred order by the participants of 10 given aspects of happiness: religion, knowledge, equality, action, economic security, politics, leisure, good humour, beauty and leadership. Questions on the frequency of happiness, the preferred time of week, and whether it was in Bolton or away from Bolton that people were happier, was accompanied by a question of whether luck was important to happiness and a request for further comments. These two databases from the same town, 76 years apart are as far as we know unique. They provide the individual components of happiness of people in Bolton. The questionnaire from 1938/2014 has been used as a template for further studies we have conducted in Brazil, Manchester and with Bolton Community Groups. We are at present planning further comparative exercises with the questionnaire template. This contributes to the build-up of an insight into happiness components over time. This will add to the desire for knowledge and understanding of happiness in contemporary times. It should inform policy makers and provide material for programmes of enhancement of happiness from Positive Psychology.

Chapter Summaries

Chapter 2. Happiness in Worktown. Past, present and future. Sandie McHugh and Jerome Carson

Sandie and Jerome outline the time Mass Observation were in Bolton (Worktown) between 1937-1940. The rich archive of data they collected was put to one side with the outbreak of the 2nd World War. The happiness material was examined in 2012 by historians Gazeley and Langhamer. In 2014 The Centre for Worktown Studies at University of Bolton in conjunction with The Bolton News replicated the Mass Observation Happiness questionnaire. This exercise provided quantitative and qualitative data from the same town 76 years apart during which time extensive technological, economic and social developments had occurred. The authors give details of the results from the two databases; some were similar such as the belief by 60% of both samples that luck had nothing to do with happiness. There were changes in 2014, the importance of weekends over weekdays had increased, and the majority stated they were happier away from, than in the town. Participants were requested to rank 10 Aspects of Happiness in their own personal preference order from the most to the least important. There were some shifts in the combined scores with religion moving from the top three in 1938 to the bottom three in 2014 with leisure and good humour moving up the scale being more highly prized in the twenty first century. Whilst levels of reported happiness were similar, the qualitative data revealed free style descriptions of happiness that were very different, with Contentment and Peace of Mind having the highest frequency in 1938 whereas it was free time Activities in 2014.

Sandie and Jerome's research continued with data collected in Brazil in 2017 to compare with a similar section of the Bolton database. This offered insights into the importance of national culture in happiness. The top three rankings for Brazilians were Knowledge, Religion and Action, completely different to the Bolton sample which was Leisure, Good Humour and Beauty. Personal Relationships and Activities were important to both groups, but family and friends were paramount to the Brazilians. Happiness Questionnaires were also collected during the 2018 Manchester History Festival. This illustrated that equality had moved up the rankings in the 10 Aspects of Happiness since 2014. In 2019 the research scope was extended by working with four different women's community groups in Bolton to gain a more in depth view of happiness. The happiness questionnaires were presented alongside the PERMA profile measuring positive emotion, engagement, relationships, meaning in life, amongst other well-being facets. A recorded focus group discussion on the subject of Happiness replaced the collection of free style comments. The findings are reported; although the frequency of happiness was similar across the four groups there are some differences in their general enjoyment of life. The chapter is completed with suggestions for future research into happiness.

Chapter 3. The role of leisure in happiness. Professor Robert Snape

Leisure and its role in happiness is the theme of Robert Snape's chapter, exploring the contribution of hedonic leisure to happiness through social association and conviviality in everyday life. At the time of the Mass Observation Worktown study (1937-1940) and throughout the inter-war period in Britain there were different views on working class leisure. Passive mass leisure could be seen as a way working class people could have some enjoyment in life, others feared that the cinema, dance and music halls would undermine civilization. They argued that leisure should enhance social citizenship, instil a sense of duty and educate people on how to use their leisure for personal development. Robert explores leisure through an Epicurean lens that it fulfils the need for happiness, and requires a minimal level of material prosperity. This emphasises the importance of contentment, and companionship which could be found in communal enjoyment in the pub. One of the institutions of working class life, pubs allowed people to be participators, providing a facility where their thoughts and activities were not arranged for them, but by them. A meeting place for many communal clubs and society. New housing estates denuded of pubs restricted opportunities for social leisure.

Holidays in Blackpool provided opportunities for hedonic leisure with sideshows, piers, pleasure beach, theatres and dance halls. During the Bolton wakes week, holidays at the resort were like a collective exercise of townsfolk. Alternative holidays in the countryside were viewed more favourably by commentators concerned about mass passive commercial leisure. Organizations like The Co-operative Holidays Association, Youth Hostel Association were formed in this period. Hiking or cycling and countryside appreciation were seen as a civilized form of leisure for enjoyment. Social friendship and conviviality were important aspects of everyday leisure in Worktown. This could be found in form of mutual support and with the voluntary associations that met in the pub. The pub, the outings and holidays in Blackpool suggest that a shared hedonic leisure experience can be a source of happiness. At the present time this is being seen in community drama projects with socially excluded women in Bolton. A contrast is the drift of leisure association to online platforms which can be a source of unhappiness. Relationships online can alienate rather than create the sense of cohesion that Worktowners experienced.

Chapter 4. Perceptions of happiness in three women's groups in Bolton: A qualitative study. Kathryn Thomasson, Sandie McHugh and Jerome Carson.

This chapter focuses on the community aspects of happiness and the perceptions of members of three different women's groups in Bolton. Kathryn starts by providing an outline of some of the theories of human flourishing which emphasize the importance of social factors in happiness levels. Strong communities and social networks are known to have a positive impact on happiness.

There is a concern that globalization of the economy has had a negative impact on some people's experience of well-being and sense of community. The benefits of globalization with WIFI connectivity have not removed the need for local social ties and community, especially important for those less mobile or affluent. Education, employment, social relationships, health and housing are key local services that affect residents' well-being and happiness. There are many thousands of community development organisations in the UK supporting people in the improvement of their local communities through collective action, empowerment, shared learning and engagement with partner agencies. Projects often identified by local people can provide community centres and a range of services. This in turn can lead to increasing social capital that brings access to resources and the advantages of being part of social networks. Social capital is thought to benefit individuals, their neighbourhood and society both socially and economically.

The foremost community development organization in Bolton is Bolton at Home; a housing provider and community benefit society that works to improve social capital as part of a borough regeneration scheme. It provides a range of social support services as well as affordable homes. Some community development is through The Percent for Arts Programme which aims to deliver quality arts services that contributes to the regeneration of neighbourhoods. Projects evolve from community consultation and encompass a wide range of arts formats and objectives usually with an aim of improving skills and well-being,

The chapter goes on to describe the authors' collaborative happiness research in three women's groups. Bolton as a City of Sanctuary has a group created by local volunteers to support refugees and asylum seekers arriving in the community and to promote inclusion. In partnership with other organizations, drama and creative writing was offered to women from this group who call themselves The Sanctuary Story tellers. The Wonder Woman group meet regularly in a community centre with a local project officer where they can enjoy social support, creative and learning opportunities. The Golden Oldies meet several times a week in their local community centre. This group offers excursions, creative activities, support and information for older people, reducing social isolation.

A qualitative semi-structured focus group design was used in each group. An overview of happiness studies in Bolton with an artist singing and storytelling was provided at the centres along with lunch. Focus group discussion on happiness was recorded and later transcribed. This was analysed using thematic analysis technique by Sandie and Kathryn. The coded results revealed that the women considered social ties to the community and relationships with family and friends important to their happiness. Extracts from the data collected and an outline of the similarities and differences between the three groups finishes the chapter.

Chapter 5. Happiness through enabling others. Julie Levy

Julie provides us with interesting examples of her experience in teaching children with Special Educational Needs in Devon and Wigan. As an artist herself she shows how art from amateur adults was displayed for mutual benefit as part of the opening of Bolton Station Platform buildings, a community project. Julie's first teaching job was at a residential placement boarding school for teenage boys with emotional, learning and behavioural problems. She connected with her pupils through art and pottery, getting them to become absorbed in tasks, to express themselves and to gain a sense of achievement through their own creativity. This could range from putting colour to popular cartoon characters, sewing a tapestry with football team colours, to directing Julie to use her skills to decorate a slip cast pottery ornament to their own design. Through their work with Julie they had been given choice and the opportunity to create something they prized. The process and the outcome could give much satisfaction and create a sense of achievement and pride.

Appointed as a Special Educational Needs and Disabilities Coordinator at a comprehensive school near Wigan, Julie set about improving school life and therefore the prospects for the children she was teaching. One of the key elements was to maximise the best use of the Teaching Assistant resources and to ensure that each child's needs were fully investigated so that a child psychologist, social workers, community police officers and medical professionals would be able to co-ordinate their actions with the school for the pupils' benefits. This co-ordinated approach and the exclusive use of some classrooms began to improve the school experience for the pupils. Julie set up Nurture Group, a learning environment that provides model behaviour and social interaction, assisting the pupils to internalise their sense of self to develop empathy, understand behaviour and to contribute to, but also listen to others. The self-esteem of the children began to improve as they experienced achievement, they became more aware of the needs of others, absenteeism declined, their behaviour improved and they appeared happier.

As a volunteer for Bolton Station Community Partnership Julie was one of the organizers for the opening in July 2019. An exhibition of Railway Workers Art displayed high quality exhibits. Some of exhibitors had spent years enhancing their creative skills in their leisure time outside railway work. Artists were able to discuss their work with local dignitaries, officials from railway companies, staff from the School of Arts and interested public. Julie noted that the exhibitors showed great pride in their work. They were able to make connections with others with whom they shared a common need to create. It gave them confidence and more impetus to continue. Enabling provides more opportunities, and this can enhance happiness.

Chapter 6. Exercise and happiness. Ken Heathcote

In this chapter Ken has chosen 3 people and along with his own experiences these suggest a link between exercise and happiness. The late Dr George Sheehan, runner, Doctor, Author and eminent Cardiologist lived in Boston USA. He was one of the pioneers of running for pleasure; it need not just be an activity only for elite athletes. Running could be fun; people could escape from life's pressures. Marathons could be for a wide spectrum of people, competitive runners, fancy dress runners, and for those motivated to raise funds for charity. The fun runner and the serious runner could be at one, happy with just running and being. Ken's friend Native American Bill Pearl is a philosopher, poet, writer, restorer of vintage cars and a 'weight man'. Bill has collected a multitude of bodybuilding titles, including four times as Mr. Universe, and used his expertise to train astronauts and athletes. His own workouts would provide a physical and mental high; bring a love of life, of relationships and a positive outlook and happiness. Ken's third nominee is Edward Taube a behavioural neuroscientist in Alabama, USA. He has developed Constraint Induced Movement Therapy which helps rehabilitate people suffering from neurological injuries. These sprang from his belief that the brain is not hard wired, and with physical exercise can be rewired to enable partial or full recovery and enhance happiness. These therapies also provide hope to diminish future mental and physical ill health as people age. Physical exercise can have a positive effect on reducing obesity and lead to a happier life.

Ken's own happiness through exercise is in swimming. In 1945 as a 10 year old boy his father encouraged him to swim in a cold, unheated pool when elite swimmers refused to participate. At the age of 82 he swam the length of Lake Windermere in atrocious conditions. He considers happiness to be a by-product of commitment. Exercise brings contentment, satisfaction, and a purpose which has a future

that can increase happiness. Memories of fulfilment are important as people are in the twilight of their lives. He suggests, that people consider their thoughts first, then their words, then action, and with practice and movement develop habits that can become destiny. 'If you think you can – then you can'. This was the motto that helped Ken build the first multi-purpose Health Club in 1960's Bolton. In addition to the facilities it provided people with a socialable atmosphere and friendships. It was an enjoyable time and happiness is a great legacy, with memories lasting longer than dreams.

Chapter 7. Happiness and freedom from alcohol addiction. Jerome Carson and Paul Makin

Jerome and Paul describe their personal journeys as they overcame alcohol addiction. They then go on to outline their research on flourishing with recovering alcoholics. Alcohol is part of many social events, the subject of extensive promotion marketing and readily available in supermarkets pubs and restaurants. Unfortunately a knock on effect from overindulgence is avoidable deaths, accidents, social and family problems. Jerome's father was an alcoholic and suffering from grief at his mother's death Jerome started drinking at age 16. Student social life comprised of hall of residence bars, student's union and local pubs; egging each other on, a popular pastime for male students was a pub crawl round the town centre. Married to a teetotaller Jerome drank alcohol infrequently but on the occasions he did consumption was excessive. Although monitoring his drinking, Jerome didn't want to control it until in middle age he gave up drinking, seeing abstinence as the solution. Jerome concludes that although recovering from addiction did not make him happier, it made him a better person.

Paul describes his childhood as good, but things began to go wrong when at 16 his parent's separated and he left school to go to college where he was bullied. Alcohol became an escape, making him feel more confident and assured. He undertook a succession of jobs and by 18 was primarily a barman. He was not happy, although he made new friends through bar work he was on a self-destruct path. Following the breakup of a relationship because of his volatile behaviour, he moved to Warrington where he had no support network from his family. Living alone and with increasing debts he came close to committing suicide. As he had no accommodation and was sacked from his job he moved back home where his family, the GP and a recovery centre assisted him to give up alcohol. Life as a recovering alcoholic was difficult for Paul; he needed a lot of support and had to set routines for his life. He found a course called 'Intuitive Recovery' which helped him control his thoughts and reject the bad ones, enabling his confidence to grow. He began working as a volunteer providing a purpose in his life. He started a college course and later went onto University. Reading psychology he trained as a counsellor as he wanted to have a career helping others. The subject matter in psychology helped Paul to become more self-aware and to develop into a positive person. He is now happy without wanting to drink alcohol.

Jerome and Paul collected data online from 140 recovering alcoholics using the PERMA profiler, and questions about their recovery process. They had a longer length sobriety and a shorter length sobriety group. The

PERMA provided scores on the level of flourishing. Confirming results from other studies, they found that people who had been abstinent in recovery for longer achieved higher flourishing levels, although this was below the normal population range. The importance of support networks, including counsellors and therapists was revealed in the recovery process findings. A positive outlook and determination to rebuild or develop life also resulted in higher flourishing levels. For the experience of happiness individual perceptions matter, some are content to stop drinking whilst others want to develop their lives. Whatever the vision of the final outcome, flourishing in recovery depends on perceptions of happiness and the individual.

Chapter 8. Faith and happiness. Mohammed Sadiq, Aishath Shahama and Aashiya Patel

This chapter explores faith and its relationship with happiness. Aashiya begins by exploring faith in the context of religiosity. She defines faith as a trust in God or the teachings of a religion. She considers the Office of National Statistics data which shows there was a decline in religiosity in Bolton from 2011 to 2018. She discusses the costs and benefits of belonging to a religion in the modern world, and the differences between intrinsic and extrinsic faith. It is suggested that a more intense religious faith or practice can enhance happiness and well-being. This link is supported by a view that happiness has two components: hedonistic which is pleasure seeking and avoiding pain; eudemonic having meaning in life, a sense of purpose. Recent literature identifies it is this sense of purpose which provides a link between religiosity and happiness.

Aishath discusses the empirical literature which explores the relationship between religiosity and happiness and she highlights its implications and possible uses. Many of the studies of Islam and Christianity show that religiosity had a positive impact on mental peace, health and happiness. She explores the reasons for this; these appear to be the sense of meaning, comfort and a social network provided by religion. Aishath examines results from empirical research in several countries and in different religions. She finds that the relationship between happiness and religiosity is also influenced by education, personality, attachment, social/economical level of a nation, intentional religious activity, attendance and group participation in religious groups. Having a religious identity or belief makes people more content with life and impacts on their well-being across religions and nations. Modern religious practices are mirrored in Positive Psychology, which recommends the benefits of giving (charity in religion), encouragement of feelings of gratitude, and the practice of mindfulness (prayer).

In the final section of the chapter, Mohammed shares a personal reflection on his relationship with faith and happiness and how the two have intertwined throughout his life. As a baby his father whispered the call of Allah in his ear. The risks of childhood, exploration into the unknown world, were minimized by the intervention of parents. Like most children he cried externally, but he learned by himself to cry internally, his thoughts were his own, nobody would know about them or interfere with them. This living inside his head increased sadness and unhappiness. At the school to teach the Muslim faith, the Madrasah, Mohammed learnt right and wrong and how to behave correctly. It was a strict discipline and he is aware that he didn't appreciate at the time how vital the knowledge being imparted would be in later life. As an adult to answer the question why he felt sad and unhappy he turned to God. He looked to the Quran and to prayer to ask the question why was he unhappy and sad? Mohammed draws an analogy between battles fought in a war, to a silent internal war in the daily lives of people. This takes away joy, happiness and control. Through faith and prayer, Allah calms the mind. Meditative recitations help bring thoughts into the present. He recounts his trials for his mind to remain in the present, he identifies the role of fear, useful to keep humans safe, but which can easily transcend into worry, anxiety, grief and sadness. To break the vicious cycle between thoughts and fear, he suggests all that is necessary is to let go. Prayer to commit to Allah and the recitation 'Alhamdhulillah' enables the experience of gratitude. This brings contentment with the present and a faith through Allah in the unknown. Mohammed describes happiness as a calm and happy heart, a clear mind that can be achieved by faith as the past is lost, hope is from the unseen and rejoice is in the present.

Chapter 9. Forgiveness and happiness. Reginald Amanze

Reginald explores the relationship between forgiveness and happiness; has forgiveness any link with happiness? Are forgiving people happier or are happier people more forgiving? He notes that there is more agreement about what forgiveness is not, than consensus about a definition. Forgiveness is different from reconciliation, pardon, forgetting and not denying or suppressing anger. Reginald suggests that forgiveness is a process that involves developing the capacity to give benefit of doubt so that the offended can come to terms with, and let go of hurt and negative affect, to gradually develop positive feelings towards the transgressor.

To answer the question why do we need forgiveness Reginald explains that negative emotions are harmful. They can prevent people living in the present and moving on with life. Research has linked unforgiveness with poor mental health. Wilfully engaging in forgiveness brings both physical and mental health benefits. Positive Psychology emphasizes that forgiveness is one of the virtues that can foster character strength. As with forgiveness there are different definitions of happiness, it is often seen as part of subjective well-being. Happiness can be hedonic, the experience of pleasure at the time, and eudemonic, the pursuit of personal growth and life meaning.

Reginald suggests that forgiveness has a positive association with happiness, both being involved in human development. Although there are only a few studies investigating forgiveness and happiness, those that exist suggest their association. He gives details of seven separate quantitative student studies by different research groups led by Malby; Shekhar; Chan; Rijavec; Sapmaz; Batik; Peterson and a qualitative study by Rana and Gull. Results from these studies were varied, but overall supported the positive correlation between forgiveness and happiness. If participants reduced negative affect, forgiveness was found to effect happiness levels directly in the Chan study.

Reginald asserts that because of the positive relationship between forgiveness and happiness, it would be very beneficial to develop and deliver forgiveness interventions. There could be a variety of programmes, to suit different situations; these would be especially helpful for mental health patients. Existing work has been dominated by student participants. He would like to see future research studies with larger sample sizes and a diversity of participants, along with more qualitative research. He suggests that The Bolton Forgiveness Scale developed by himself and Jerome Carson would be a useful framework. This identifies three dimensions of forgiveness; coming to terms and letting go; developing positive feelings; giving benefit of the doubt. Further exploration of forgiveness could consider other variables that affect happiness levels and the question of whether happier people are more forgiving than those that are unhappy. As forgiveness and happiness are positively related and mutually beneficial to each other, it is suggested that letting go fosters inner positivity, Reginald asks the reader to consider how forgiving they are and reminds them that forgiveness can set them free and make them feel happier.

Chapter 10. Happiness, music and the occasional creative. Chris Elliot and Kathryn Thomasson

Kathryn begins the chapter reminding us of the importance of music for human well-being. Music has had a powerful role throughout history as shown with examples from the Bible and Greek mythology. Recent scientific research has provided evidence of the benefits of music to our physical and mental health. Listening to music can provide positive emotional stimulation and expression. Performing music can be used in development of community activities and these have been shown to have a positive effect on individual participants' health and on community wellbeing. Music can also be used as a creative and arts-based research method. This is social research using arts as part of the methodology during data collection, analysis or interpretation/dissemination. Music and performance were used as part of the Happiness research in 2019 with women's community groups in Bolton conducted by Professor Carson, Sandie McHugh and Kathryn. Colleague and performance artist Chris Elliott wrote and performed songs to the groups. This would start the conversations with participants about happiness.

Chris Elliot is an actor and writer. The lyrics he used with the community groups posed a series of questions on whether possessions can create or contribute to happiness. The participants were to work out their own answers to these and other questions. Chris's material is based on Lancaster which like Bolton has an industrial past with a large working class and now with its own University and colleges has many students. Chris offers a series of stories from the 1920's to the present day and considers the economic and social changes from that time and the developments within his own family from his grandparents to his own life in retirement.

The world of work features a drayman at Mitchell's brewery, his son who was a marine engineer and in wartime worked in Liverpool repairing ships. Both men were proud of the work they undertook to earn their living. In sport and pastimes, Chris describes the importance of allotments not only for the produce they provided, but for men's time away from home. Cycling and competitive racing were popular. A competitive weekly activity for the women before washing machines was 'wash day', using a copper to boil the clothes, dolly tub and a mangle. There was pride in achieving high standards of washing on the clothes line and comparisons were made with neighbours. The arrival of washing machines ended the Monday ritual. Motor bikes and side cars were replaced by cars. Hire purchase made these possessions widely available. Letter writing declined as families had telephones installed, and the wireless was supplemented by television. The world seemed smaller with pictures of news and daily programmes brought into the living room, and as affordable package holidays to Spain became available. Chris asks have all the changes brought more happiness, or made it more elusive?

Chapter 11. A bit of grim makes us great up North. Elisabeth Long

Elisabeth Long a proud Boltonian dedicates her chapter to '1point network staff and volunteers' as an appreciation of their work. A journalist, teacher and counsellor Elisabeth co-founded the community-led organisation housed in a Regency mansion in Bradshawgate, Silverwell House. With the house as a timeline she seeks to explain the values and beliefs that have shaped Bolton in the past and will assist it to face the challenges from the 21st century. Interdependency and reliance on others from social networks, community-led support and friendships are a mind-set, part of the inherited social constructs in Bolton. In the 20th Century these were seen in the studies of Mass Observation and the plays of Bill Naughton. In earlier times they can be seen from the community spirit and the philanthropy of the town's leading and wealthy inhabitants. Humour plays an important part in this inherited culture, and binds communities together with the trials and tribulations of daily life often being seen with a comic slant, a coping mechanism. Elisabeth argues that Boltonians and northerners in general being more resilient than people in other regions may well be happier in their lives. The values of resilience and mutual respect binding communities together will be an asset as Bolton overcomes descriptions of it now being a 'nothing of a town'. A fire in 2019 at student accommodation illustrated the kindness and compassion of the townsfolk who responded quickly with empathy and practical measures. These attributes should help people keep cheerful, show resilience, compassion and creativity during and beyond the Coronavirus pandemic.

Chapter 12. Happiness and Wellbeing in High Schools: The Humming Bird Project. Ian Platt, Chathurika Kannangara, Michelle Tytherleigh, Sarah Banks and Jerome Carson

Ian, Chathurika, Michelle, Sarah and Jerome describe their happiness and well-being project in secondary schools from the early days of the scoping study and pilot, to the main study and their future implementation plans. A partnership between the Universities of Bolton and Chester and the charity Medequip4kids the project has attempted to provide a mental health intervention against the background of reductions in spending on specialist child and adolescent mental health services since the 2008 crisis in the financial sector. The scoping study used qualitative research methods to interview educators to gain insights and perspectives into child mental health. Telephone interviews were deployed and interviews at schools with head teachers or Special Educational Needs Coordinators. These revealed the important role of deprivation in mental ill-health among school children. Difficult family backgrounds, inadequate housing, low incomes and a myriad of other problems often affected academic performance. In the last decade research has indicated that mental health problems are getting worse. To tackle the issue however, children's opinions must be considered, they are very sensitive to stigmatisation of special treatment. The scoping study found that existing provision in schools was variable with some not having a formal mental health policy, but as awareness increased the provision for mental health was improving. A range of barriers including inadequate resources, lack of specialist workers and training of teachers were revealed in the interviews.

For the pilot project a Positive Psychology Intervention Programme for 90 students in two schools was created with eight one hour sessions covering different aspects of well-being. A pre and post evaluation took place to allow comparison of scores at the beginning and end of the sessions. This resulted in a shortening of the programme to six weekly sessions and removal of some material. The main study involved over a thousand students in 14 secondary schools. The results showed that there was an improvement in all the measured factors, including overall well-being, resilience and optimism. Although the programme was designed for universal intervention, some schools were selecting children with mental health problems as participants.

Future Hummingbird Project for the next academic year will be only as a universal intervention, a normal part of the school day. To further improve the programme, part will be rewritten and there will be more tasks that involve worksheets and class discussions. Although it was designed for high school, there is now a need to adapt it for primary schools where prevalence of mental health problems is also increasing. The authors conclude that the Hummingbird Project is a significant step forward in intervention in schools, with positive changes in flourishing for over one thousand students. In the next phase it will be looking for evidence that it also reduces mental ill-health. It will be encouraging more continuous self-management to improve the experience of the programme.

Chapter 13. Happiness: is there a North/South divide? Jerome Carson, Sandie McHugh, Julie Prescott and Rosie Allen

The chapter starts with the background to the decline of industrial activity in the North of England. After a rapid expansion in Victorian times when British industry lead the world and northern areas were vibrant attracting a massive influx of workers, it experienced structural decline in the 20th century. As it deindustrialized, new industries often went to the South of England, and large numbers of people found there were few jobs in their communities. The comparative deprivation and lack of opportunity in the North compared to the South was hastened by world economic events in the 1970's, 1990's and financial system collapse in 2008. The North South divide can be measured in terms of unequal investment; the North has lower levels in transport, infrastructure, job creation and secondary education than the South of England. The economic outlook is reflected in social disparities between the regions, with higher levels of income in the South and higher unemployment and poverty in the North. Alcohol consumption as measured by hospital admission, rates of suicide, and incidence of disease are higher resulting in health inequality, and a lower life expectancy in the North.

The Happiness web survey took place via Prolific on March 18th 2020. Participants completed five measures. These were: PERMA scale; Office of National Statistics (ONS 4) Well-being Questions; Clinical Outcomes in Routine Evaluation (Core 10); University of California Brief Loneliness Scale (UCLA3); Worktown 10 Aspects of Happiness. The latter were to be ranked in personal preference order from most important (1) to least important (10), the Aspects were economic security, knowledge, religion, humour, equality, beauty, action, leisure, leadership and politics.

It was predicted that people in the South would have higher levels of happiness than those in the North. This proved not to be the case; there were very small negligible differences between the two samples (total of 1,574 participants) in only two questions. These were self-reported lower levels of health in the North in the PERMA scale, and a higher incidence of reported sleep problems in the Clinical Outcomes (Core 10). These two results were just significant; in others results were very similar. The preference ranking of the Worktown 10 Aspects of Happiness was the same in both regions. We discuss the similarities of happiness in the North and South as measured by our survey, there may be other variables not part of the survey that predict happiness.

Chapter 14. Voices from the Past: A qualitative investigation of letters on happiness from 1930's Bolton. Sandie McHugh, Julie Prescott and Jerome Carson

In this chapter the authors analyse 226 letters written in 1938 by townspeople from Bolton, England, Mass Observation's Worktown. The Worktown researchers ran a competition to discover *'What does happiness mean to you and yours?'* To incentivize participants, they offered three cash prizes for the best letters. These letters, which are part of the Worktown Archive, offer an insight into what made people happy in 1930's Bolton. This may be one of the first empirical studies into the concept of happiness. The letters were coded independently by Sandie and Julie and five general categories were identified of what made people happy. These were Personal Attributes/Attitudes, Personal Relationships, Others, Money/Economic and Activities. Then 12 sub-categories were identified. The significance of this data source is that it gives a unique insight into perceptions of happiness just before the outbreak of the Second World War.

One of the aims was to use the knowledge from these happiness letters to inform current research and to contribute to Positive Psychology strategies of enhancing well-being. The findings suggest that the cultivation of a contented frame of mind and an appreciation of the many advantages and opportunities of twenty first century living is an important lesson from the letters. Another is to make more connections in local communities, and to help others. People in 1930's Bolton were happier with less in the way of material possessions and money; they valued contentment and peace of mind. Other factors found to underlay happiness are remarkably similar to those identified by the economist Lord Richard Layard. His categories overlap with those revealed by the study, with the single exception of personal freedom.

Chapter 15. Conclusions and the way forward. Sandie McHugh and Jerome Carson

In the conclusions Sandie and Jerome consider the chapters in the book and note how diverse they are in style and content and they try to bring themes from them together. The book starts by going to the beginning of happiness research with the Mass Observation project in the late 1930's. Bob Snape adds more substance with his description of Bolton pubs and time spent in Blackpool as examples of the importance of leisure to happiness in that era. Kathryn's research in collaboration with Sandie and Jerome in three female community groups in Bolton in 2019 provides valuable insight into the positive outcomes from the Community Action Groups in the town. The importance of nurturing and providing opportunities for self-expression and esteem is given by Julie Levy's case studies of her time in a Devon Boarding School for 'Maladjusted' boys and at a Special Needs department in a school in Wigan. Her work with retired workers at the Bolton Station Community Partnership showed how important this is for all age groups.

Ken Heathcote's chapter gives four role models for tackling challenges and achieving success. Amongst these are himself, the runner George Sheehan and the body builder Bill Pearl. Jerome and Paul Makin describe their journey to success at recovery from alcoholism. The importance of faith and prayer to reach happiness is outlined by Mohammed Sadiq in his journey from childhood into middle age, with Aishath Shahama and Aashiya Patel outlining the advantages and limitations of religiosity to happiness. Forgiving others and yourself is a valuable attribute to improve health and attain happiness. Reginald states that because of the positive relationship between forgiveness and happiness, it would be beneficial to develop and deliver forgiveness interventions. Chis Elliott writer and actor, provides some interesting scenarios of past lives and values, with Kathryn Thomasson reminding the reader of the importance of music to happiness.

Boltonian Elisabeth Long introduces the humour of the town, the resilience of the inhabitants and the culture that have produced some great comedians. Voices from the past illuminates the world of Worktown from the Happiness letters, where Contentment, Peace of Mind and Concern for others in the community were part of the value system that informed daily life in the 1930's. Examining a possible North/South happiness divide in contemporary times highlights the disadvantages experienced by the North which have not affected comparable happiness levels. The chapter by Ian Platt and colleagues describes the trial in high schools of the Humming Bird Project. This project aims to increase happiness and contribute to the prevention of mental ill health, drawing on the past, the present and progressing to the future.

References

Ackerman, C.E. (2020) *What is Positive Psychology and Why is it so important?* [Accessed 12th February 2020 at https://positivepsychology.com/what-is-positive-psychology-definition.]

Action for Happiness (2020). [Accessed 12th February 2020 at https://www.actionforhappiness.org/]

AP News (2019) TEN Steps to Global Happiness. United Nations International Day of Happiness (UNIDOHappiness) campaign launches today. [Accessed 20th March 2019 at https://apnews.com/Globe%20 Newswire/737a0e07a7f755f49fd02e9d37b70af7].

BPS (2011) Building a happier society. *The Psychologist*, 24, 6, 406.

BPS (2012) A journey in the fast and slow lane. *The Psychologist*, 25, 1, 14-15.

Dolan, P. (2014) *Happiness by Design. Finding pleasure and purpose in everyday life*. London: Penguin.

Frey, B. (2018) *The Economics of Happiness*. SpringerBriefs in Economics. Cham, Switzerland: Springer.

Garling, T. and Gamble A. (2018) Life satisfaction and Emotional Well-Being: Psychological, Economic and Social Factors in R. Ranyard, (Ed) *Economic Psychology*. Chichester, UK: Wiley (pp 406-420).

Guha, M. and Carson, J. (2017) Happiness Down the Ages: Theory and Philosophy in S. McHugh, (Ed) *The Changing Nature of Happiness*. Cham, Switzerland: Palgrave Macmillan (pp 17-30).

Helliwell, J., Layard, R. and Sachs, J. (2017) *World Happiness Report 2017*. New York: Sustainable Development Solutions Network. [Accessed 4th February 2020 at https://worldhappiness.report/ed/2017/]

Helliwell, J., Layard, R. and Sachs, J. (2018) *World Happiness Report 2018*. New York: Sustainable Development Solutions Network. [Accessed 2nd February 2020 at http://worldhappiness.report/ed/2018/]

Kahneman, D. (2011). *Thinking Fast and Thinking Slow*. New York: Farrar, Straus and Giroux.

Layard, R. (2006) *Happiness: Lessons from a new science*. London: Penguin.

Maslow, A.H. (1943). A theory of Human Motivation. *Psychological Review*, 50, 4, 370-396.

ONS (2016) Statistical Bulletin Measuring National Well-being Personal Well-being in the UK, 2014-2015. [Accessed 8th February 2020 at H:/LITERATURE/ONS%20&%20Misc%20Reports/Measuring%20National%20Well-being%20Personal%20Well-being%20in%20the%20UK,

Peterson, C., Park, N. and Sweeney, P.J. (2008) *Group Well-Being: Morale from a Positive Psychology Perspective*. [Accessed 3rd February 2020 at https://doi.org/10.1111/j.1464-0597.2008.00352.x]

United Nations (2012) N1147568 United Nationals Resolution 28.6.12 A/Res/66/281. 66/281

International Day of Happiness. [Accessed 17th April 2016 at http://www.un.org/ga/search/view_doc.asp?symbol=A/RES/66/281].

Veenhoven, R. (2012) Happiness: Also known as 'Life Satisfaction; and 'Enjoyment' in K.C. Land, A.C. Michalos and M.J. Sirgy, (Eds) *Handbook of Social Indicators and Quality of Life Research*. Dordrecht, Netherlands: Springer Publishers (pp 63-77). [DOI 10.1007/978-94-007-2421-1_3.]

Veenhoven, R. (2019) *Measures of Happiness*. World Database of Happiness. Rotterdam: Erasmus University [Assessed 8th February 2020 at http://worlddatabaseofhappiness.eur.nl/hap_quer/hqi_fp.htm]

Worktown, paſt, present and future

Sandie McHugh & Jerome Carson

Introduction

'Peace of Mind and contentment' followed by 'Giving to and helping others' were the most frequent explanations for happiness in the town of Bolton in 1938. In 2014 it was 'Activities' that were quoted most frequently as bringing happiness to the townsfolk. These 'Activities' were things undertaken by choice in free time and ranged from domestic activities such as gardening, home baking, entertaining, to holidays, active and spectator sport, visits to pubs theatres and the cinema. How do we know about this and what data offers this insight? We know this because Bolton is unique it has two happiness surveys completed 76 years apart.

Early happiness research

The first one, in 1938 was by Mass Observation, one of the many studies they conducted in the town during the period 1937-1940. The second was a replication by the Centre of Worktown Studies at the University of Bolton, and The Bolton Evening News. Mass Observation roots started in 1937 with a letter written by journalist and poet Charles Madge published in The New Statesman entitled 'Anthropology at Home' which attracted the attention of anthropologist Tom Harrisson who was in the process of observing the working classes in Bolton while he worked in a variety of casual jobs visiting pubs and clubs in the evenings. Mass Observation was founded by these two and artist Humphrey Jennings with a purpose to observe ordinary British people. The knowledge of and connections Harrisson had in Bolton meant that it became the representative of the industrial north and they called it 'Worktown'. For the next four years Bolton townsfolk were observed, interviewed and photographed by mass observation volunteers and paid workers (Hinton 2013). One of the many surveys carried out was 'The Happiness Competition' advertised in April 1938 in the Bolton Evening News and attracting a first prize of 2 guineas (£2.20). Two hundred and twenty six people wrote letters giving their views on what happiness meant 'to you and yours'. These letter writers were sent a questionnaire where they were required to rank in their preference order,

10 aspects of happiness, state the frequency, the time of week and the place where they were happiest. This valuable data was not analyzed at the time and the Worktown project ended during the Second World War. It was not until the next century when an initial analysis was carried out by historians Ian Gazeley and Claire Langhamer and their findings were published in 2013 in The History Workshop Journal.

Results from the two happiness studies

The Centre for Worktown Studies at the University of Bolton decided to replicate the 1938 Happiness competition in 2014 in conjunction with The Bolton News. Four hundred and eighty nine townspeople responded to the advertisements in the newspaper. The 2014 data provided quantitative and qualitative data that could be compared with the results of 1938. The 2014 questionnaire followed the format from 1938, with most questions exactly the same. One of these was 'How Often would you describe yourself as really happy?' The results were similar from both periods. Statements of happiness of 'everyday' as 25% in 1938 and 24% in 2014 for happiness defined as 'several times a week', the figures were 55% and 48%, so it could probably be argued that Worktowners were slightly happier. There was a bigger difference with the choice of happiness being 'few times a month' with 21% of 2014 residents opting for this choice with only 11% in 1938. The 'rarely happy' group was recorded 9% of the respondents in 1938 and 4% in 2014. Along with this frequency of happiness there was the question 'Is it easier to be happier at weekends, or weekdays or is it the same?' In 1938 a large majority (72%) stated it made no difference they were just as happy any day of the week. The result for 2014 showed that although a small majority (57%) were happy whatever day of the week it was, a sizable proportion (39%) were happier at weekends.

Mass Observation followed Worktowners on their day trips and holidays to the Lancashire seaside resort of Blackpool. At the time this was the main destination outside the town. It had a regular train service with 'specials' day or evening trips, combining the rail fare and entry into one of the ballrooms. Coach journeys were also a frequent method of transport and many children first saw the sea on a Sunday school day out. Mass Observation made a special study of Bolton folk at the resort and had an office in the town (Cross 1990). As part of the study of Worktowners in Blackpool, the happiness questionnaire posed the question 'Which is the easier place to be happy in Blackpool or Bolton', in 2014 with a myriad of national and international holiday destinations for Boltonians, the question became, 'Is it easier to be happy when you are at home in Bolton or when you are away from the town?'. There was a big difference in the preferences; in 1938 75% said they were happier in Bolton, whereas in 2014 the majority, 61% said they were happy *away* from the town.

The subject of 'luck', part of an interest in working class superstition was studied by Mass Observation both the legal weekly punt on the football pools and the illegal betting in the town, co-ordinated by the 'bookies runners'. The question posed was 'Is luck anything to do with happiness?' in the 1938 questionnaire was repeated in 2014, including the caveat 'If so, what?' On both occasions the majority, approximately 60% stated that luck had nothing to do with happiness.

Different results between the two databases are shown in the 10 Aspects of Happiness. Respondents were required to rank according to their personal choice which of the 10 aspects would be most important to their happiness (no 1) through to number 10 the least important. The main changes during the 76 year interval were the importance of religion which moved down the rankings and leisure which moved nearer the top. Whereas, Economic Security (having enough to live on) was number one in 1938 this was replaced by Good Humour in 2014. The following table shows the findings from both databases.

Table 1
Participants ranked (1-10) choice of 10 Aspects of Happiness in 1938 and 2014.

Aspects of Happiness in 1938*	Aspects of Happiness in 2014+
1. More Economic Security	1. More Good Humour
2. More Knowledge	2. More Economic Security
3. More Religion	3. More Leisure
4. More Good Humour	4. More Knowledge
5. More Equality	5. More Equality
6. More Beauty	6. More Beauty
7. More Action	7. More Action
8. More Leisure	8. More Leadership
9. More Leadership	9. More Politics
10. More Politics	10. More Religion

*1938 rankings Gazeley & Langhamer (2013) ⁺2014 rankings McHugh & Carson

The increase in leisure from position eight to third is a reflection of the higher proportion of residents in 2014 finding it easier to be happy at weekends and corresponds with findings in the qualitative data outlined below. Knowledge was harder to obtain in Worktown, public libraries, newspapers, the wireless and cinema would be the main avenues, whereas in 2014 the internet provides near instant access to information of all kinds. Knowledge moved down from second to fourth place, perhaps indicating that although easier to obtain in 2014 the sources may not be considered very reliable. Economic security – being able to pay your way, afford the essentials of life –was the only aspect from 1938 to remain in the top three in 2014. Not surprising when although standards of living are much higher in the 21st century, there is still insecurity for many people in low paid and/ or temporary employment. Bolton as many other towns has a food bank, indicating a struggle by some people to afford the essentials. Religion moved from third down to 10th between the two databases, reflecting a more secular society. The population increased by 63% (to 279.000) with 81 places of worship whereas in Worktown there were 200 churches and chapels. These were often social centres as well as being centres of worship. The top place in 2014 went to Good Humour, moving up from fourth, defined as smiling and laughter for myself and those around me. (McHugh and Carson 2017)

The qualitative data from 1938 and 2014 contained the free style comments from participants on what made them happy. These were analysed by computer software, NVivo for frequent themes from the discourse. The table below shows the seven most frequent themes in both periods. As can be seen it was only family that remained in the top three from both databases.

Table 2
The most frequent coded categories from the two databases

1938 *	2014 +
Contentment & peace of mind	Activities
Giving to and helping others (2nd equal)	Family
Family and Home (2nd equal)	Friends
Security and money	Personal Development
Health	Economic
Friends	Natural World
Religion	Community

*1938 Prescott, McHugh & Carson
+ 2014 McHugh, Entwistle & Carson

The majority of the comments came within the seven categories shown. There were very few pertaining to religion in 2014, insufficient to compose a category. In 1938 there were some references but these were less than expected in view of the third ranking given to religion in the 10 Aspects of Happiness. Some examples from 1938's most frequent theme:– *'My opinion of happiness can be summed up in three small words Peace of Mind'*. *'Happiness is contentment* with *your lot .... a contented mind gives true happiness'*. *'My creative hobbies like photography and woodwork'*, and *'watching films, TV and reading books'* were two of the comments on activities from 2014. The theme of Giving to and helping others, equal second in 1938 with Family and home, is illustrated by this comment *'We can create happiness every day of our lives by sacrificing little things for others that are less fortunate than ourselves'* and *'Helping others that is my idea of happiness'*. Such phrases were absent in 2014, with the comments on Community being more general *'To do something for the community'*.

The constant theme in the two periods was Family. From 1938 *'Happiness is marriage'*, and from 2014 *'Kids, wife, family and money to spend on kids and wife'*. There were numerous references to friends in 2014 which was not the case in 1938. *'Happiness is being with friends'*. References to friends in 2014 were more frequent than separate references to children or to spouse/partner. Taken together with references to parents, siblings and other relatives, family was the second most important category following Activities.

The continuity of the importance of family from the two databases, illustrates the essential nature of personal relationships to happiness. In 2014 this was also shown with the category 'Friends' and in 1938 with 'Helping others'. It would seem that happiness was more related to individual concerns and pursuits in the 21st Century, whereas it was more an attitude of mind and concern for others in the 20th Century. This is reinforced by the responses to the question 'Is it easier to be happier at weekends or in weekdays, or is it all the same to you?' Respondents in both questionnaires ticked one in a choice of 'weekends', 'weekdays', 'same'. Weekends afforded the time for leisure more than the working week. In 2014 39% of respondents were happier at weekends, whereas in 1938 it had been 26%. The percentages reporting that they were just as happy at weekdays as weekends dropped from 72% in 1938 to 57% in 2014. The question 'Which is the easiest place to be happy in Blackpool or Bolton', was changed for the 2014 collection of data to 'Do you find it easier to be happy at home in Bolton, or on holiday or staying away from Bolton?' No longer did the townsfolk only venture as far as Blackpool when away from the town, now many world destinations could be visited. Travel and holidays was an important part of enjoyable 'Activities'. The findings were reversed, 75% were happier in Bolton in 1938, with only 25% in 2014. Leisure activities and travel were possible in 2014 with the higher absolute standard of living the majority of townsfolk enjoyed providing them with opportunities of affordable travel not available in the 1930's. This changing focus in lives of Boltonians was reflected in their ranking of the 10 Aspects of Happiness. More religion was in the top three in 1938, not surprising as many of the descriptions of helping others were akin to Christian beliefs and attitudes. *'Happiness is the state of one's mind when you help others...loving one's neighbour as thyself'. 'JOY Jesus First, Others next and Yourself last'*. In 2014 Religion was ranked at the bottom, whereas Leisure had moved up from number eight to number three reflecting the importance of activities in free time. *'Walks and away days bring me happiness'*, *'My internet access to the world'*.

Work and Leisure were bound together in community bonds in the 1930's when virtually all of everyday life was lived in the town itself. The 300 pubs, 47 cinemas, 6 dancehalls and 200 churches and chapels provided essential social facilities connecting the people from the closely packed terraced houses. The pub served as a social centre for neighbourhood community, facilitating and nurturing collective leisure. Social life could thus be conducted with mates from the workplace; many of the mills had their own sports teams, ranging from bowls, football, to girl's rounders. Work patterns and organizations have changed, bringing a rise in commuting; a person's colleagues may now be from a wide area. In 1938 there had been overlapping communities of workplace and residence, which helped to create and maintain neighbourhood relationships. (Snape 2017) If people did not know everyone personally there was a strong sense of common identity, thus a concern to help others if they were in need. In 2014 with the increased preference for weekends, the importance of activities, there appears to be far less shared social identity, less cohesive society. The rise in car ownership, the opportunities to travel for shopping, days out, holidays mean that less time is spent in the town itself. When people are within the town there is more focus on the domestic life, standards of home comforts have greatly improved, technology has enabled the enjoyment at home of things that people previously sought in the town, such as cinemas. It would appear that people are increasingly staying at home for their leisure encouraged by television and the internet and also motivated by a desire to invest in homes by making improvements, DIY activities (McCormick 2003). Leisure is more individualistic, or conducted with friends and family rather than the community.

Bolton community groups

Noting the decline of the cohesive community suggested a new angle in contemporary data collection involving different groups within Bolton. In 2019 data collection of the Happiness Questionnaire took place in four different women's groups in the town. Instead of requesting written comments on happiness, recorded Focus Group interviews were conducted during which participants discussed the essence of happiness. In addition the PERMA profile questionnaire was also completed. This measures in 23 questions respondent's positive emotion, engagement, relationships, meaning in life, accomplishment, overall wellbeing, negative emotion and physical health, (Butler and Kern 2016).

The first of group was The Golden Oldies. These ladies met at least once a week at a community centre in Bolton, day trips and various activities were organized for them. The youngest was 63 and two were 90, the mean age was 77. It was anticipated that this group may be able to provide a view from their early life to contrast it with contemporary times. Research has found that it is usually between the ages 65 and 75 that many people experience more happiness in their lives than during any other adult age span, (The Economist 2016). The second group was called Wonder Women, their mean age was 45, and two of the members were under 30 and three over 50. This group were from another community centre and tended to have challenges in their life, including single parenthood, lack of employment skills, and low income. This was also a well-established group with a dedicated leader of several years standing who provided moral support, literacy training and advice if required. Some of the members of the group had faced difficulties in their lives, emotionally and financially which could affect their experience of happiness and well-being.

Young women with an average age 19 were the third group, and they were attached to a charity housing provision scheme. Many would otherwise have been homeless, or face problems continuing in education or seeking first experiences in the working world. As with the Golden Oldies, there has been some focus in recent times on the loneliness and isolation of older people and young people. Bolton is a 'City of Sanctuary' with a welcome policy to refugees. This group with an average age of 40 is led by several volunteers and meet weekly for mutual support and assistance. Many had been in the UK for only a short time, and it was hoped that a newcomer's view of happiness and community and a comparison with their previous experience might help illuminate the characteristics of happiness.

On the Happiness Questionnaire the space for comments on happiness was removed and for the 10 Aspects of Happiness, two of the previous categories Action and Leadership were replaced by Assistance and Independence. These were considered to be more appropriate for these participants than for a wider collection of data from the general public. The women were already in a structured group which was designed to provide them with support. Would this be more important to their happiness than other aspects? Independence, having more control over the organization of one's life and making decisions, like personal agency is considered to be important for well-being (Brenner 2014). This might be an important element for the participants in these groups, especially the young people in provided accommodation and the refugees. As the project was not a replication of the 1938 questionnaire, the format could be varied.

The four groups were found to have differences in their views on happiness. For the top three ranked aspects of happiness the Wonder Women and the Golden Oldies chose Good Humour as number 1. This was the same result as for the 2014 Bolton residents, for the young women and the City of Sanctuary group, Equality was important, being number 2 for the latter and number 1 for the former. Equality was a feature for the Golden Oldies, at number 3. Politics and religion came in the bottom two for all four groups. The ranked order of the 10 Aspects of Happiness is shown in table 3 below.

Table 3
Ranked order of the 10 Aspects of Happiness for the 4 community groups

Golden Oldies	Young Women	Wonder Women	City of Santuary
Good Humour	Equality	Good Humour	Knowledge
Economic Security	Independence	Knowledge	Equality
Equality	Leisure	Assistance = with Leisure	Economic Security
Leisure	Economic Security	Leisure = with Assistance	Independence
Independence	Knowledge	Equality	Good Humour
Knowledge	Assistance	Independence	Assistance = with Beauty
Assistance	Good Humour	Economic Security	Beauty = with Assistance
Beauty	Beauty	Beauty	Leisure
Politics	Politics	Politics	Religion
Religion	Religion	Religion	Politics

All the groups rejected the notion that wealth and possessions could make them happy, the majority answered 'no' to the question. 'Do you think that your happiness is directly related to the material possessions and wealth that you have?' It was different for the City of Sanctuary Women with the question, 'Do you think that your happiness is directly related to the amount of money you have each week or month to live on?' where six out of the eleven thought that happiness was related to the amount of income to live on. For the Wonder women the figures were six out of thirteen. This probably reflected low income and/or debt experiences of some of the members. The importance of having enough to live on was reinforced by views expressed in all four focus groups. It was wealth by itself that was not regarded as bringing happiness. For the Golden Oldies nine out of the 13 stated that neither wealth nor income would influence happiness.

These ladies in their Focus group expressed their concern about younger people being wasteful and replacing consumer durables before they were worn out, to keep up with fashion. *'I think money today seems no object. The younger ones they have everything on credit'.* They reported that they were accustomed to saving up for things they wanted and were wary of getting into debt. *'They (young people) don't want to save up for it or do without'. 'We had to save up until you got enough.........if you can't afford it you can't have it'.* All groups agreed that it was important to have enough income. As a Golden Oldie remarked *'As long as you can eat and pay your bills'.* One of the Wonder Women exclaimed *'You have got to live..... you don't have to worry about your bills'.* And from a member of the City of Sanctuary group *'money is important – enough to buy food'.*

The Happiness Questionnaire explored the frequency of happiness with the question 'How often are you really happy?' Respondents choose one from four options:- 'Everyday', 'Several times a week', 'Few times a month' and 'Rarely'. The groups had similar results. Nine of the 12 young women were happy either every day or several times a week. For the Golden Oldies, 11 of the 13 were happy either every day or several times a week, with four stating they were happy every day. Six of the women in City of Sanctuary reported they were happy every day, making 10 out of the 12 being happy at least several times a week. Of the 13 Wonder women nine were happy at least several times a week. On the question 'Is it easier to be happy at weekends, in weekdays or is it all the same to you?' the choice was 'weekends', weekdays' and 'same', it was only the Young Women with 5 of the 12 who preferred weekends; the other groups reported it made no difference. In answering the question 'Is it easier to be happy when you are at home in Bolton or away from Bolton?' the Golden Oldies and the City of Sanctuary were united that it was easier to be happy in Bolton than away from the town. For the Wonder Women, nine of the eleven preferred to be away from Bolton and the Young Women's preferences were equally split.

The respondents were asked to state 'Yes' or 'No' to the question 'Has Luck anything to do with happiness?' The majority of Golden Oldies, Wonder Women and Young People answered 'No', whereas for the City of Sanctuary women, eight out of 11 said 'Yes' Luck did affect happiness. This is possibly a reflection of their circumstances in gaining entry to the UK. The women were asked to rate on a scale of 1 (not at all) to 10 (completely) how much in general they enjoyed their daily life. The young women reported the lowest mean at 6.25 for enjoyment with the City of Sanctuary Group and Golden Oldies recording 7.36 and 7.31 respectively. The Wonder Women were slightly above the young women with 6.54, and as fewer of their members reported being happy several times a week it suggests there were lower levels of happiness in this group compared to the other three.

The Community Groups project was the first time the PERMA Profiler had been used alongside the Happiness Questionnaire. The analysis of this Profiler showed a significant difference between the young women and the other three groups in the Engagement category. This is a combination of three questions, and refers to being absorbed, interested, and involved in an activity or the world itself. The young women scored the lowest in this area, being less engaged the lower the score, compared to the other groups. (Young women mean 18, Wonder Women 21, City of Sanctuary and Golden Oldies 23). The question on loneliness was 'How lonely do you feel in your daily life?' the replies were on a scale of 0 (not at all) to 10 (completely. The Golden Oldies were the least lonely, with a mean rank of 4, followed by the young women with 5. The Wonder Women reported experiencing the most loneliness at 7, more than the refugees whose mean rank was 6. This finding is counter to the recent national study where loneliness was found to be more pronounced in older age groups and younger people (Office of National Statistics 2018). The Bolton community groups studied were small, a larger scale town study would be required to further investigate this area and to establish if Bolton did not experience as much self- reported loneliness as other areas. It also needs to be borne in mind that the young people are resident in a charity based housing facility and other young people and support workers are around. They may experience less loneliness than young people living in a family home. The Golden Oldies group was well established and their conversations gave indications that contact with each other could extend outside their regular meetings.

Happiness in Rio de Janerio and Bolton

One of our happiness studies was across national lines when data was collected whilst Sandie McHugh was on a visit to Rio de Janerio in 2017 presenting a paper at an International Conference. The Happiness Questionnaire was translated into Portuguese and data collected from 37 members of the public. This was then compared with a similar sample in age and gender from Bolton. The Brazilians provided comments on what made them happy and these were subject to qualitative analysis by the authors, so that they could be compared with the comments from the Bolton participants.

On the question 'How often would you describe yourself as really happy?', over half of the Brazilians were happy every day or several times a week, for Boltonians this was only 38%. The preference for weekends was more marked in Bolton, in answer to the question 'Do you find it easier to be happy at weekends, weekdays or is it all the same to you?' ten preferred weekends whereas only four Brazilians opted for weekends, with 33 of the 37 sample stating they were just as happy regardless of the day of the week, making a significant difference between the two countries. Continuing the findings of higher levels of happiness in Brazil, the question 'How much in general do you really enjoy your life?' (1 not at all) to (10 completely), more Brazilians choose 8, 9 or 10 on the scale. This gave a mean rank of 8, whereas for Bolton it was 7. The majority of participants from both countries answered 'no' to the question 'Do you think your happiness is linked to the amount of money and possessions that you have?'

The ranked order of the 10 Aspects of Happiness do show differences, with significant results between the two samples on Leisure, Good Humour, and Knowledge with a near significant on religion. The ranking for all 10 aspects for both countries is shown in the table below.

Table 4
Ten Aspects of Happiness ranked in preference order for the two databases (37 participants for each country)

Bolton Aspects of Happiness	Rio Aspects of Happiness
1. Leisure	1. Knowledge
2. Good Humour	2. Religion
3. Beauty	3. Action
4. Equality	4. Leadership
5. Economic Security	5. Politics
6. Politics	6. Economic Security
7. Leadership	7. Equality
8. Action	8. Beauty
9. Religion	9. Good Humour
10. Knowledge	10. Leisure

The difference between the two countries is surprising, and provides an example of the importance of cultural differences for happiness. As shown above in the results from the survey questions, Brazilians appear to enjoy life to a greater extent, and experience happiness more frequently. Perhaps leisure is a more integral part of their lives? It is not expressed as an important separate aspect of happiness, as in Bolton, where the most frequent comments on what made people happy was 'Activities' they could choose to take in their own free time, and where Leisure was the top aspect of happiness. These considerations will be reported elsewhere.

The qualitative data, the free comments on Happiness and Luck from the questionnaires were coded by the authors into categories and the frequency of words noted. Participants had been asked what Luck had to do with happiness. Two major categories emerged that of 'Personal Control' and 'No

Personal Control'. The Rio participants had sub categories 'chance, fate' and 'religion' whereas these did not emerge in the coding for Bolton. The Bolton participants were more likely to think it possible to make their own luck, and that they could make the most of opportunities. Making own luck - *'I work hard to make my luck'. 'I think you make your own luck'. 'it is the paths we choose in life'* and *'you can influence how often things happen'*. There were no Brazilian comments about making their own luck; the closest was the comment, *'When happy you attract luck'*. Whereas there were seven comments about optimism, positiveness and happiness being part of personal control, *'a happy person is naturally lucky'. 'Happy people attract good things, like good luck'*. In the Bolton group there was only one comment.

Both groups recognized the importance of circumstances and opportunities. From Bolton, *'being in the right place at the right time and knowing the right people - luck!* A Brazil comment *'Sometimes you have to be in the right place at the right time'*. On the subject of opportunities, from Bolton *'It affects your circumstances, the opportunities you have to do the things that make you happy'*. Brazilians appear to consider that their inheritance, parents and their country could dominate their life chances, *'the family you are born in, economic conditions, genetics', 'Economic conditions'. 'Lucky people with work and career tend to be happy'. 'person who is born into comfortable situations is more likely to be happy'. 'Luck to have been born and live with a family of value, ethical, respectful and encouraging'*. There were no comments about inheritance or parents among the Bolton sample, there was one that referred to *'Health is often down to luck'*. There were comments about the country and the economy from both groups. From Bolton - *'one might become unemployed or financially insecure'* and the importance of *'job opportunities'* was recognized. From Brazil opportunities and economic conditions were mentioned. There were no comments on the role of chance, fate and religion in Luck from Bolton, whereas there were a few from Brazilians *'God grants us both (Luck)'*. On the role of chance *'it is a part of life and can influence for good and for evil'*, and luck is closely connected to well-being *'it brings something good unexpectedly'*, and it is *'part of life and can influence for good and for evil'*. Interestingly there were no comments from the Bolton or Rio respondents that referred to money lotteries.

'What are the things in your life that give you the most happiness and/or give you the most enjoyment?' This question gave participants' an opportunity to explain in their own words what was important to them. The happiness comments from both countries could be sorted under the main headings Personal Relationships, Activities, Economic, Personal Development, Attitudes and Community Involvement. For Bolton there was an additional category Natural World, encompassing comments on the sea, sunshine and the countryside, which did not feature at all in the Brazilian comments. For Boltonians and Brazilians Personal Relationships and Activities were important. In the case of the Rio participants the frequency of Personal Relationships was higher than for Bolton, with Activities attracting about half the number of references, whereas for Bolton, the number of references to Activities was very similar to that for personal relationships. There were twice as many references to Economic factors in happiness in Rio than in Bolton, for the former there were 13 references to work and four for the latter. Personal Development attracted 16 comments from Brazilians and nine from Bolton. In the Attitude category, for Bolton freedom and Humour were mentioned but not in Rio, whereas the importance of safe environments, justice and passion did not occur in Bolton. 'God' and 'my faith' were stated in Bolton, with 'Loving God and my neighbour as myself', and spirituality in Rio. A small number of comments on community involvement were made by both sets of participants, 'Volunteering to help the needy' in Bolton and from Rio, 'Volunteering and co-operation'.

Similar things make people happy across the two cultures, for the Brazilians, Personal Relationships and Work featured more frequently, with no references to the Natural World. It is suggested that this is taken for granted in Rio, the climate is warmer and sunnier and there are large expanses of accessible beeches and sea. This may explain why a higher proportion of the Brazilian participants reported being happy more often than those in Bolton and have a higher level of enjoyment.

The happiness questionnaire was based on self-report of happiness levels from a small number of participants. A national collection of data looking at other elements of happiness and well-being, the 2017 World Happiness Report ranked the United Kingdom 19th; Brazil not far behind at 22 out of 53 countries (Helliwell et al 2017). This was on a combined basis of GDP per capita, social support, healthy life expectancy, freedom to make life choices, generosity, and perceptions of corruption. The Happy Planet Index in 2016 measuring sustainable well-being (well-being, life expectancy, inequality of outcomes, and ecological footprint) showed Brazil at number 23 out of 140 countries, with UK lagging behind at 34 mostly explained by a higher ecological footprint (NEF 2016).

Manchester Histories Festival

In 2018 the Happiness research was presented at the bi-annual Manchester Histories Festival, in June. A programme of events including talks, walks, music, performances, stalls and debates around the theme of democracy, freedom of speech and protest. The study focussing on ordinary people in Worktown and Bolton was welcomed for presentation as a package 'Spinning Dreams, Performing Worktown and Meanings of Happiness in inter-war Bolton'. In addition to power point presentations, theatre studies students gave dramatic performances on the Worktown Happiness Letters. During the two day run of the Spinning Dreams Package, Happiness Questionnaires were collected from members of the public.

The question on happiness in Bolton or away from Bolton was removed from the questionnaire as it was anticipated that most participants would be from the Manchester area. It had been considered that the question on materialism and happiness should separate living costs and regular income from material possessions and wealth. Contentment and achievement could come from owning a house, having a financial portfolio may enhance happiness by giving a sense of economic security more than a weekly or monthly income. To test this, the previous question on materialism became two: - 'Do you think that your happiness is directly linked to the amount of money you have to spend'? And 'Do you think that your happiness is related to the material possessions and wealth that you have?' (eg. home ownership, investments and savings). Both required either a Yes or No reply.

A total of 91 questionnaires were collected, 65% of the participants were female. The largest two occupational groups were those employed at 45% and retired at 37%. Ages ranged from 16 to 88, the two largest age band groups were those participants between ages 56-65 and 66-75. Seventy five per cent of the participants reported they were happy at least several times a week. Eighty two per cent stated they enjoyed life on 7 or above on a scale of 1 (not at all) to 10 (completely) giving a mean of 7.29. On the two materialism and money questions, 60% agreed that happiness was not related to material possessions, and a higher percentage, 68% agreed that happiness was not related to the amount of money they had to live on. The preferred order for the 10 Aspects of Happiness is shown in the table below.

Table 5
Manchester Histories Festival 10 aspects of happiness

10 Aspects of Happiness	Ranked order (81)
Good Humour	7.79
Equality	7.00
Knowledge	6.75
Leisure	6.32
Economic Security	6.23
Beauty	5.57
Action	5.52
Leadership	4.16
Politics	3.49
Religion	2.54

Since 2014 it appears that equality has become more important. It was ranked 5th in 2014, with the Manchester data it is 2nd and it was high ranked in the top three with three of the community groups in Bolton.

Conclusions and future research

A number of databases providing findings on the same questionnaire have been outlined above, the first one collected by Mass Observation in 1938, replicated by the authors in 2014, and in 2019 four separate female Community groups in Bolton were studied with the addition of the PERMA questionnaire and a recorded Focus Group. The project comparing Rio and Bolton was a small cross cultural study and a group outside the town at the Histories Festival provided another dimension.

The City of Sanctuary group mainly Christian African refugees and Asylum seekers were the only community group to refer to God or to Jesus in the Focus Groups. Yet they did not rank religion high in their 10 Aspects of Happiness, but the comments suggested it might be an integral part of their values and beliefs. In the large 2014 database there had been no test for ethnicity or religion and as Bolton has a higher than average Asian population (Bolton Council 2011) with 80% white, 13% Asian, 2% African and others, for England and Wales it is 86%, 7.5% and 3.3% respectively (UK Gov 2018) it was decided that a study with the Bolton Asian Community would be a valuable insight into the importance of religion in the 21st Century. A researcher is presently conducting such a study and it is hoped that results will be available later this year.

The use of Focus Groups where happiness is discussed and the direction of conversation follows the participants' inclination or the comments people put to the open question 'What makes you really Happy?' gives a voice to the respondents. Their own words convey the meaning of happiness more than a questionnaire can do so. This qualitative data has shown changes over time and differences between groups. Future research into different age groups could assist in providing knowledge for Positive Psychology interventions, to enhance happiness and increase well-being.

There are plans to develop the line of research to specific age groups and to develop interventions to tackle loneliness and enhance happiness. These include looking at younger members of society and those in older age. Letter writing is not a popular form of communication nowadays, but e mail, or messaging is widely used. One possible research project would be to offer cash or voucher prizes to Secondary School children in Bolton. They would give their views on what made them happy by e mail. The provision of some information from happiness theories could be an introduction to the topic with a few of the 1938 letters.

Another research project would be a study with older people. The Golden Oldies small scale study showed that they reported frequent happiness and an enjoyment of life. The ages 60-75 can be the happiest in a life span, but recent concern had been on the loneliness of older people, especially as society has become more individualistic and there has been a decline in community life (Age UK, 2015). Some commentators have described loneliness as an epidemic with young people and older people being particularly vulnerable increasing the risk of mental illness. The UK Government created a new post Minister for Loneliness (Gov.UK Press 2018; Campaign to End Loneliness 2019).

A larger sample of older people from Bolton, that may not belong to a community group could complete the template questionnaire and with Focus Groups gather suggestions on practical action to improve their happiness and well-being. The Schools project could raise awareness of possible personal interventions to improve happiness. Results could assist in designing Positive Psychology interventions, and provide input for policy makers and service providers.

References

Age UK Loneliness Evidence Review (2015). Susan Davidson and Phil Rossall. [Accessed 15th January 2020 at https://www.ageuk.org.uk/globalassets/age-uk/documents/reports-and-publications/reports-and-briefings/health--wellbeing/rb_june15_lonelines_in_later_life_evidence_review.pdf]

Bolton Council (2011) *People in Bolton. 2011 Census Factfile population and households. Communicating research and sharing knowledge Bolton Council.* [Accessed 29th December 2016 at http://www.bolton.gov.uk/sites/DocumentCentre/Documents/Census%202011%20People%20in%20Bolton%20factfile%20population%20households.pdf]

Brenner, A. (2014) 6 Ways to take Control. *Psychology Today June 2014.* [Accessed 24th January 2020 at https://www.psychologytoday.com/us/blog/in-flux/201406/6-ways-take-control]

Butler, J. and Kern, M.L. (2016) The PERMA-Profiler: A brief multidimensional measure of flourishing. *International Journal of Wellbeing.* 6(3), 1-48, doi:10.5502/ijw.v613.526

Campaign to End Loneliness (2018). [Accessed 15th January 2020 at https://www.campaigntoendloneliness.org/about-the-campaign/]

Cross, G. (1990) Worktowners at Blackpool: Mass Observation and Popular Leisure in the 1930's. Abingdon, UK: Routledge.

Gazeley, I. and Langhamer, C. (2013) The meaning of happiness in mass observation's Bolton. *History Workshop Journal*, 75, 1, 159-189.

Helliwell, J., Layard, R., and Sachs, J. (2017) World Happiness Report 2017, New

York: Sustainable Development Solutions Network. [Accessed on 4th February 2020 at https://worldhappiness.report/ed/2017]

Hinton, J. (2013) *The Mass Observers: A History 1937-1949*. Oxford: Oxford University Press.

McCormick, J., (2003) *Contemporary Britain*. Basingstoke, UK: Palgrave Macmillan.

McHugh, S. and Carson, J. (2017) Happiness Perceptions- A comparison 1938 and 2014 in S McHugh, (Ed). *The Changing Nature of Happiness*. Cham, Switzerland: Palgrave-Macmillan (pp 69-85)

NEF. The Happy Planet Index 2016. A global index of sustainable well-being. [Accessed 28th June 2017 at https://static1.squarespace.com/static/5735c421e321402778ee0ce9/t/57e0052d440243730fdf03f3/1474299185121/Briefing+paper+-+HPI+New Economics Foundation www.neweconomics.org]

Snape, R. (2017) Leisure in Worktown in S. McHugh, Ed. *The Changing Nature of Happiness*. Switzerland: Palgrave Macmillan (pp 87-102)

Office for National Statistics (2018). Loneliness What Characteristics and Circumstances are Associated with feeling lonely? [Accessed 24th January 2020 https://www.ons.gov.uk/peoplepopulationandcommunity/wellbeing/articles/

The Economist (2016) *Why people get happier as they get older* [Accessed 23rd January 2020 at https://medium.economist.com/why-people-get-happier-as-they-get-older-b5e412e471ed]

UK Gov Press Release (2018) *PM Theresa May launches Government's first loneliness strategy* [Accessed 15th January 2020 at https://www.gov.uk/government/news/pm-launches-governments-first-loneliness-strategy]

UK Gov. Ethnicity Facts and Figures. UK Population by Ethnicity. Population of England and Wales (2018) Office for National Statistics. [Accessed 15.2.19 at https://www.ethnicity-facts-figures.service.gov.uk/uk-population-by-ethnicity/national-and-regional-populations/population-of-england-and-wales/latest]

The role of leisure in happiness

Robert Snape

Introduction

David Cameron's survey of happiness, launched shortly after becoming prime minister in 2010, presented an opportunity for a national discussion on the relationship between leisure and happiness. Unfortunately, but perhaps not surprisingly, this did not happen. As long ago as 1933 the Liberal historian John Lawrence Hammond (1933) observed the absence of a tradition of common enjoyment in leisure in England; the English had lost their sense of leisure and had, perhaps, never really had one. Leisure is arguably one of the most misused and least understood words. Some of this misunderstanding is semantic; 'leisure' is derived from Latin 'to be allowed' but the best philosophical ideas of leisure were formed by Plato and especially Aristotle in fifth century Athens. Aristotle made clear distinctions between leisure, entertainment and relaxation and would not understand our use of 'leisure' to denote an industrial sector, watching television or shopping, none of which seem to lead to true happiness. However, a recent turn to the history of emotions has created new interest in narratives that might enhance our understanding of cultural practices and social institutions (Boddice, 2018). This is of particular relevance to leisure, a universal cultural sphere in which people seek happiness within a socially structured world.

Happiness too is a slippery word. Jeremy Bentham found it impossible to establish a quantitative means of measuring it. However, statistical research has since found both positive and negative associations of leisure with happiness (Wang and Wong, 2014). It has been suggested that happiness can be hedonic on a short-term basis and eudamonic in the context of longer-term subjective well-being (Maltby, Day & Barber, 2005). Fave et al. (2011) support this view, but note that although hedonic happiness derives from transient experiences and positive emotions, most measurements of happiness are quantitative and do not allow for participants' comments. It was this latter restriction that Mass Observation avoided in its innovative 1938 survey of happiness in Bolton, a cotton spinning town in the north-west of England, by asking people to 'write down what you think' happiness means for you (Mass Observation, 1938). This investigation was undertaken as part of Mass Observation's 'Worktown' study of a northern industrial town, for which Bolton had been chosen. Tom Harrisson, anthropologist, co-founder of Mass Observation and the leader of the Worktown project, had previously published the results of his immersive study of Malekula in the

New Hebrides (Harrisson, 1937) and applied the same technique of detached observation to Bolton. Harrisson was dismissive of sociology's preference for scales and graphs and the Worktown project's inclusion of qualitative data allowed insight to the everyday experience of leisure. While respondents were asked to complete a hierarchical scale of factors of happiness, they were also encouraged to comment freely on the relative importance of these. Drawing from Mass Observation's Worktown' study, this chapter explores the contribution of hedonic leisure to happiness through social association and conviviality in everyday life.

Theorisations of leisure in inter-war Britain

Leisure and happiness were important to social policy makers concerned with post-First World War social reconstruction. Reconstruction, according to Bertrand Russell (1916), had to be spiritual as well as material in order to bring a unifying integration of individual and community life and a sense of wholeness. Debate on reconstruction consequently focused not only on economic recovery but also on an enhanced quality of life. Leisure was conceptualized as a sphere of human welfare through which working-class people would have democratically distributed opportunities for personal development and the enjoyment of life. Social policy discourse was heavily influenced by a resurgence of social idealism and the social thinking of the Oxford philosopher Thomas Hill Green. Green's ideas drew from Plato and Aristotle, promoting the idea of the community as a *polis* and the political obligation of the citizen to its maintenance. In a society facing radical re-building, the importance of leisure to social service became widely recognized. Several commentators, notably the social idealist Bernard Bosanquet, the classicist Ernest Barker, and Cecil Delisle Burns, Stevenson Lecturer in Citizenship at Glasgow University, wrote and lectured on the use of leisure and its relationship to happiness, which was widely understood to imply flourishing and well-being in both individual and social contexts. The devotion of leisure time to voluntary social service, for example helping to run a lads' or girls' club, was considered a virtuous use of leisure (Snape, 2018).

Leisure, according to Delisle Burns, was the most valuable product of modern social organization, containing the capacity for a wider democratic culture. New forms of hedonistic leisure, for example the cinema and wireless, were not agents of alienation or totalitarianism but widened peoples' cultural horizons (Burns, 1932: 13); the Lynds, in their Middletown survey, similarly noted how they provided ordinary people with new opportunities for enjoyment (Lynd and Lynd, 1929). Conservative critics, however, feared popular leisure, especially that mediated through the new means of mass communication. The literary critic F. R. Leavis (1930) saw mass culture to be inimical to civilization; the cinema, for example, was not a source of happiness but an unprecedented use of applied psychology and a surrender to a hypnotic receptivity. Whereas progressive thinkers, notably John Hobson (1914), argued for a more democratically distributed leisure and equality of leisure opportunity, Clive Bell (1929: 205-8) believed civilisation could only be maintained by preserving a leisure class on the grounds that to be properly civilized was to experience the most intense and exquisite states of mind. As an aim of social reconstruction was to enhance social citizenship through leisure, many critics turned to Aristotle's linking of non-hedonic leisure to social duty. To Aristotle leisure was a necessity, both for growth in goodness and for the pursuit of political activities, while happiness was virtuous activity with the active life being best for both the individual and the whole community (Aristotle, 2009; Barker 1946). A wide range of institutions adopted these arguments to promote leisure as a sphere of social citizenship and to educate people in its 'right' use. Civic Societies proliferated after the War, seeking to regenerate of the idea of citizenship and energize the civic and cultural life of the community (Branford, 1921) and as several respondents to Mass Observation's (1937) survey of happiness in Bolton reported, happiness could be equated to service to others and to the wider community. Interest in the differing natures of eudamonic and hedonistic leisure-time activities were not confined to social philosophers. This was particularly the case in associations devoted to young people's leisure which experienced strong competition from the nascent cinema and dance halls. To many voluntary youth social workers, the passive leisure of the music hall and cinema were considered anathema and even, in some cases, a form of juvenile delinquency. In their place, youth leaders sought to encourage active leisure as a means of character building by instilling a sense of social citizenship, recognition of collective responsibility and the qualities of leadership (Snape, 2018).

Although Aristotle (2009) considered amusement and relaxation different to leisure because they were a means to an end rather than ends in themselves, he nevertheless acknowledged their importance. However, the social importance of amusement and relaxation has not received the same degree of attention in leisure historiography as Aristotle's concept of leisure. This chapter accordingly explores leisure in inter-war Britain through an Epicurean lens. As Karl Spracklen (2011) notes, Epicureans considered good leisure to be that which fulfilled the need for happiness. A useful distinction between the hedonic and eudaemonic constructs of leisure is that the former is concerned with the subjective happiness of the individual while the latter involves the actualization of human potential (Lopez et al., 2016). More simply, as Guha and Carson (2017) note, while Aristotle emphasized virtuous activity as the basis of happiness, Epicurus saw happiness as the result of passive virtue, or *ataraxia*. Mass Observation's study of happiness in Worktown revealed that although the peace of mind derived from economic security was most highly valued, people also valued their holiday week in Blackpool (McHugh and Carson, 2017). Epicurus' understanding of hedonism was not that of Jeremy Bentham. While pleasure was a good, it remained subordinate to peace and freedom from anxiety, and not all pleasures were desirable (McMahon, 2006). Epicurus was not a philosopher inter-war social reformers often referred to; Aristotle's association of leisure with personal development and citizenship seemed more appropriate to the needs of social reconstruction and a new community. However, Epicurus' writings on happiness emphasize the importance of contentment, an ability to distinguish desirable from undesirable pleasures, companionship, and the mental relaxation of freedom from worry, all of which bear a close relationship to leisure and its use. In some aspects this brings to mind William Morris' ideal of a collective leisure in a collective life, with a communal hall (Morris, 1984a). Although this utopian state of affairs did not exist in Bolton, its desirable characteristics of communal enjoyment and a communal space were present in the form of the pub.

The pub

Although originally undertaken as a study in social anthropology, the archive of the Worktown project now constitutes an internationally acknowledged historical record of everyday life. In the history of the everyday, as John Brewer (2010) notes, historical figures are actors and have agency, motives, feeling and consciousness; they become the subjects, not the objects of history. The emphasis is thus on forms of interdependence, interiority, intimacy and emotional responses related to leisure and happiness. The everyday also affords closer access to the social associations and cultural institutions of a neighbourhood and their role in creating spaces and facilities for leisure and thus essential to happiness. Such associations abounded in Worktown, many being found in the pub, a building described by Mass Observation (1987) as one of the basic institutions of working class life. There were three hundred pubs in Bolton, patronized by both genders but mainly by men. As Mass Observation (1987) perceptively commented, the pub was the only kind of public building used by large numbers of ordinary people where their thoughts and actions were not being in some way arranged for them; in the other kinds of public buildings they might be audiences, spectators of dramatic and cinematic productions, religious sermons or sports, but in the pub, men and women were participators. The pub had both alcoholic and social functions. Working-class people rarely met in each other's homes in the way the middle classes did. Most drinkers lived within a short walk from the pub, from which Harrisson deduced that choice was largely a result of being familiar with its regular customers. The pub effectively served as a 'home from home'; it was an institution to which patrons felt they belonged (Mass Observation, 1987). The main social activity of all drinkers was conversing with other patrons, nearly all of whom would share important aspects of identity of place, work, interest in sports and dialect language. The pub also served as a communal venue for neighbourhood associations, for example savings clubs, picnic clubs, secret societies including the Ancient Noble Order of United Oddfellows, the Royal and Antediluvian Order of Buffaloes, Ancient Order of Foresters, trade unions, wedding parties, pigeon racing, bowling and fishing clubs, and canine societies. In addition to drinking, the pub provided social interaction, conviviality and various forms of pleasure. The social sharing of leisure rather than the consumption of alcohol was the more important to happiness; as Humphrey Spender observed, 'When you were in a pub, there was a kind of community feeling, the feeling of a lot of people who knew each other, and who were happy to know each other' (Mulford, 1982, 6).

The significance of the pub to leisure and happiness became starkly evident by its absence on the new inter-war housing estates, which rarely provided any places of commercial leisure. Although estates were imagined as ideal communities of social integration and cohesion, their planners, according to Harrisson, had little understanding of the community value of the pub to the nurturing of fraternization and democratic feeling (Mass Observation, 1987:202). While the physical conditions of estate life were generally superior to those of the slum housing they replaced, they fragmented previous community and family structures. As the Coles (1937, 181) noted, instead of developing a new community, estate dwellers were often compelled to travel to the town centre for amusement and social intercourse. Mass Observation's study of Bolton's 'Top' o th' Brow estate provides much evidence to support this comment. Living on the estate did not imply a higher living standard; 25% of its children qualified for free school dinners and 33% for free milk (Mass Observation, 1937a). Bus fares to the town cinema were expensive, limiting women to one cinema visit a week (Mass Observation, 1937b). Opportunities for social leisure were thus restricted.

Closer to the centre of town, a working-class man, although living in poorer housing, could visit a pub several times each week; on the estate, this was no longer possible. A street dweller had a regular pattern of leisure: he could, for example leave home around 6.30 p.m. to 'walk to Merehall Bowling Green; stroll at same speed at 9.00 pm to Alexandra Hotel in Meadow Street for a pint or two and a game of dominoes and walk home' (Mass Observation 1937a). Such ritual had a 'definite-ness about it', each night's performance varying only in minor detail. On the estate, however, the cordiality and community spirit of the pub were absent, forcing men to walk considerable distances to visit pubs in their former neighbourhoods. Women too had few opportunities for social leisure, although gardening became a summer time occupation for outdoor conversation with neighbours. The one fixed time of the week for communal entertainment was Saturday night when estate residents travelled *en masse* into Bolton town centre. It was, in Mass Observation's estimate, as if the sociability of the estate was transplanted to the town at weekends only to drift back into the estate to take up its routine until the following weekend when the process was repeated. The bus became the connecting link between two worlds of the town and the estate and the scene of more exchanged intimacies than any other place. In this respect, it effectively took the place of the absent pub as the 'meeting place' of the estate with the bus stop at the estate shopping centre rather than the pub becoming the hub around which the estate revolved. The last bus back from town on Saturday night, although noisy and jovial, was never argumentative but created the feeling that 'everybody's happy' (Mass Observation 1937a). Inter-war social service organizations faced the problem of creating social cohesion on new estates. Although the National Council of Social Service's (1937) New Housing Estates Committee promoted the building of community centres to develop a spirit of social life, these rarely fulfilled such expectations (Durant, 1932). Middle class people who could spare an evening two or three times each month were exhorted to educate estate populations in leisure activities and unlike the pub, estate community centres, staffed by a warden, were places that *did* arrange the thoughts and actions of their members. Estate planning, in effect, failed to understand the social function of the pub in terms of community cohesion and agency in leisure organization.

Holidays

In a town dominated by work, the annual wakes week holiday occupied a unique position in people's pursuit of happiness. For those Worktowners who could afford a holiday, this implied Blackpool, the largest resort on the Lancashire coast. In the first year of the Worktown study a week's holiday often meant the loss of a week's pay; only with the Holidays with Pay Act of 1938 were wage regulating authorities able to direct provision for holidays and holiday remuneration for workers. An annual holiday therefore depended upon careful stewardship of the domestic budget and planned saving. However, poverty denied many Worktowners the opportunity of a holiday, and even those who could afford one found it challenging. As respondents to the Worktown study commented, in phrases resonant of Epicurus' emphasis on the essentiality to happiness of peace of mind, concerns about the financial implications of a holiday diminished happiness:

"No-one can really enjoy their holiday and get the best out of it unless they have no worries, if a holiday means facing a week without wages on returning home, this cannot be the case.'

'I find it impossible to leave home for a holiday; I must remember the half-empty wages packet that will leer at me after the holidays. I can only hope that some day, Holidays with Pay' will be more than a pious idea' (Mass Observation 1937c).

The link between security and the ability to afford a holiday remains a relatively under-estimated factor of in happiness. As Juliet Gardiner (2010, 585) comments, having time off was not necessarily the same as being able to take a holiday. One elderly lady explained to Mass Observation she had no change of underclothes, obliging her to stay indoors while these were washed and that

'We never get no tasties or nothing'. Husband can't afford tobacco. 'We've been away to Blackpool one day in fifteen years' (Mass Observation, 1937d).

Most working people therefore developed strategies for saving through savings clubs organised by employers, banks and religious organizations. In June 1937 Bolton Savings Bank paid out £100,000 in the fortnight prior to holidays (Mass Observation, 1937b).

Over the course of the nineteenth century, Blackpool grew from a small coastal village to a town designed to make commercial profit from its expansive industrial hinterland of coal mining and textiles industries. To Worktown's cotton operatives, it was Lancashire's 'Mecca' (Mass Observation, 1937e). Blackpool's raison d'etre was to guarantee the maximum opportunity for hedonic leisure. Although developed primarily to attract working-class people, Blackpool town council also sought to appeal to middle class visitors through a spatial segregation of the social classes. The north shore was subject to planning restrictions on commercial development but south of the north pier, the town was devoted to hedonistic leisure with sideshows, two further piers, pubs, fish and chips cafes and the pleasure beach. Like other Lancashire cotton towns, Bolton had an annual wakes week during which the cotton mills closed. Holiday-making was consequently a collective exercise in that Worktowners left for Blackpool on trains and buses in each other's company. Although people went there to 'get away', many holidaymakers found themselves sharing accommodation with other Boltonians. Home town affinities were important; Worktowners tended not only to prefer to drink with other Bolton people but to do so in pubs selling beer brewed in Bolton. The Bolton observer Walter Hood, for example, was able to direct southern observers to those Blackpool pubs frequented by Boltonians. Leisure behaviour was marked with coarseness and drunkenness:

'At one side of room two girls in black coat and skirts and white silk blouses are singing loudly a dirty song, encouraged by a group of men at a table in the middle. Song is about Old King Cole and the people he called for; the chorus of each verse contains a repetition of all the others. Magees pubs the only ones observed with singing tonight. At Concert Inn the lounge is densely crowded. Obs[erver] thinks them all Bolton people. At one table 7 men and 7 girls, all pretty drunk, ordering Crown ales rapidly, singing Victorian music-hall songs, noise deafening, considerable erotic squeezing, one girl, blonde, very young, (about 17 has long kiss with youth lasting nearly a minute). Most of the people seem pretty drunk after a while and most join in with the songs' (Mass Observation 1937f).

This hardly constitutes an example of an Epicurean temperate life; nevertheless, the observers felt this was much like the ordinary weekend pub behaviour in Bolton. However, as J. B. Priestley (1934, 267) noted when visiting Blackpool on his tour of England, this aspect of the resort appealed to 'less intelligent and enterprising' young people. Most people, he believed, preferred to spend their leisure in the quiet countryside, cycling, walking and playing games in the sun.

By the late nineteen- thirties the countryside offered an alternative and non-commercial holiday of rambling and cycling in the countryside. Following centuries of land enclosure and privatization, the countryside was gradually becoming more accessible to town dwellers, though it required the mass trespass of Kinder Scout in the Derbyshire peak district in 1932 to secure the introduction of national parks after the Second World War. Left wing organizations contributed to the growth of a countryside leisure culture, notably through the politically radical Clarion movement and the Fabian Co-operative Holidays Association [1893] and Holiday Fellowship [1912]. The latter two were both formed by Thomas Arthur Leonard, a Congregationalist minister in the Lancashire cotton town of Colne, to provide rational and wholesome alternatives to resorts like Blackpool. These were essentially collective holidays, with people living together cooperatively in guest houses, enjoying rambles and visits to places of interest in the daytime and making their own entertainment in the evening. As a Bolton respondent to a Mass Observation survey noted 'I would like to spend my vacation at one of the Holiday Fellowship Centres in Yorkshire. Our evenings would be spent in entertaining each other, singing songs and melodies that we know' (Mass Observation 1937g). The Co-operative Holidays Association (CHA) had been supported in Bolton by Annie Barlow, a family member of one of Bolton's large industrial employers. The emphasis of both the CHA and the Holiday Fellowship was on simplicity and comradeship. Leonard was averse to displays of conspicuous consumption and left the CHA to found the Holiday Fellowship (HF) when he perceived an unhealthy middle-class element to be dominating the former. A symbolic interpretation of the landscape was essential to the enjoyment of the holiday (Snape, 2004). Happiness in leisure in the countryside was interpreted in Ruskinian terms in which the materialistic urban leisure of balls, assemblies and idle occupations were contrasted with the wholesome enjoyment of the natural landscape (Ruskin, 1856, 310). An important feature of both organizations was their network of local branches which organized walks and rambles throughout the year. In the winter months, leisure association was maintained by social meetings, New Year reunions and the formation of choirs, maintaining a culture of co-operation and creative leisure that was non-alcoholic, non-material and mainly Christian in outlook. The Bolton CHA Rambling Club, for example, was founded in 1905 while the Bolton Holiday Fellowship Walking Club was formed in 1922; both remain today. In Epicurean terms these organizations emphasized a leisure grounded in contentment with simple things and the enjoyment of companionship.

The cultural construction of the countryside as a leisure space became more marked after the First World War. The establishment of the Youth Hostel Association in 1929 reflected a growing demand for simple and affordable accommodation in the countryside and was instrumental in democratizing access to the countryside. The leisure it represented was not that of blood sports, the traditional pastime of the leisure classes, but that of the enjoyment of the landscape and the company of fellow hikers and cyclists. To Cecil Delisle Burns (1932, 77) the countryside offered a new and alternative escape from the town marked by quiet rather than excitement. Hiking and rambling, he argued, required the capacity for enjoying one's self rather than being entertained by others and represented a mode of leisure necessary to a civilized life. Moreover, both had expanded spontaneously and were not the product of the youth organizations of late Victorian and Edwardian Britain. Other young people's organizations included the Kindred of the Kibbo Kift, founded in 1920, by John Hargrave, formerly a senior member of the Boy Scouts, and the Woodcraft Folk, founded in 1925 by two young socialists, Leslie Paul and Sydney Shaw. Like the CHA and HF, the Kibbo Kift emphasized communitarianism but in the context of a spiritual and pagan relationship with nature. Its dress code was drawn from that of the American Indians. With its utopian idealism and blend of world peace, handicrafts and camping (Pollen, 2015), its leisure culture reflected what Burns (1932) identified as a 'revolt of youth' through which a new generation was rejecting the values of their forefathers to work towards the establishment of a new kind of community. Like the Kibbo Kift, the

Woodcraft Folk represented a breakaway movement from the Boy Scouts that modelled itself on William Morris' (1984b) utopia News from Nowhere. One of the first youth associations to promote a mixed gender membership it gained a much wider membership than Kibbo Kift by working through local Clarion groups and co-operative societies. Unlike the CHA and HF it promoted family holidays, using leisure to develop values of equality, justice and peace and, unlike the short-lived Kibbo Kift, it has survived into the twenty-first century.

Conclusion

Leisure acquired an important social significance in inter-war Britain, not only for its potential as a sphere for community building and training in social citizenship but also because leisure was itself undergoing seismic change, with new technologies with unprecedented reach being feared for their potential to erode social and cultural norms and values. In a period that sought greater social democracy in the face of populism and a growth of fascism, leisure could, it seemed, have a Janus-faced nature. Social philosophers often turned to the philosophers of ancient Athens in their effort to articulate a philosophical grounding for a new and modern leisure. Clearly, given the acceptance of slavery as a norm and the exclusion of women from civic life in Athens, there could be no simple transfer of a Greek leisure to the modern developed world. Nevertheless in Plato and Aristotle, reformers found accounts of leisure and happiness that could be re-interpreted to articulate, in Cecil Delisle Burns' term, a leisure for the modern world. Many found Aristotle the most useful to the task of social reconstruction. From a historical point of view, however, Epicurus' focus on pleasure, in both its eudamonic and hedonic forms, widens the scope of investigation. In their everyday consumption of leisure, people made moral decisions, seeking or rejecting balances between pleasure and pain, indulgence and restraint, and thrift and debt. The above account highlights the importance of leisure as a sphere of social friendship and conviviality and the ways in which this was an essential aspect of the everyday leisure of Worktowners. This reflects Epicurus' (2012: 177, 183) assertion of the acquisition of friendship as the single most important thing for happiness. Recent commentators have noted the importance of this to current debate on well-being; Long (2006), for example, suggests that Epicurus implied friendship to be not only a means of pleasure but to be in itself a pleasure. The value of friendship in terms of mutual support and protection is evident in the accounts of the voluntary leisure associations of the holiday savings club and working-class secret societies that met in the pub. Not the least important of Epicurus' theories of happiness to the modern world was the assumption of a minimal level of material prosperity for happiness; as we have seen in the straitened circumstances of Worktown, this assumption was not the experience of a significant proportion of the population.

This historical account suggests ways in which Epicurus might be re-visited by policy-makers concerned to understand leisure as a means to enhanced subjective well-being. It shows how association in a shared hedonic leisure experience can itself be a source of happiness. This is evident in work currently being undertaken by Kathryn Thomasson in the Centre for Worktown Studies at the University of Bolton in the use of community drama based on the Worktown Archive, which engages women in writing and performing short plays in leisure time. Although built around drama, these workshops are mainly valued for their friendship, mutual support and the sense of security they offer. However, interventions of this nature have been subject to severe reductions in public sector spending and throughout Britain many working families struggle to afford the happiness of a holiday. Furthermore, as the drift of leisure association to online platforms has become a significant source of unhappiness, particularly amongst young people, 'real world' leisure association presents itself as an ever more desirable social good. If, as Gutenschwager, (2013) suggests, emotional development is age related, the necessary social conditions need to be present. Particularly with young people, this does not appear to be the case. Recent resesarch has shown a significant decrease in children's happiness with friends (Children's Society, 2019) and a UNICEF (2016) investigation has reported the United Kingdom sixteenth in the world in terms of children's well-being. 'Friend', in the online world, does not have the materiality of friendship in the real world and appears to tend towards alienation and individualism rather than the maintenance of a sense of cohesion. Although, as Bergsma et al (2008) note, friendship should imply personal security, support and assistance, public spaces for young people, for example youth centres, sports fields and social areas, and the youth leaders to organize these, have been much reduced under David Cameron's and subsequent governments. Even though Epicurus did not involve himself in politics, his notion of the essentiality of material prosperity to happiness rather suggests that politicians would be better informed if they understood this relationship.

References

Aristotle (2009) *Nichomachean Ethics. Book 1 The Good for man*, 6, 1176. Oxford: Oxford University Press.

Barker, E., (1946) *The Politics of Aristotle*. Oxford: Clarendon Press

Bell, C. (1929) *Civilization: an Essay*. London: Chatto and Windus

Bergsma, A., Poot, G. and Liefbroer, A.C. (2008) Happiness in the Garden of

Epicurus. *Journal of Happiness Studies* 9, 397–423. https://doi.org/10.1007/s10902-006-9036-z

Boddice, R. (2018) The history of emotions in S.Handley, R. McWilliam and L. Noakes (Eds) *New Directions in Social and Cultural History*. London: Bloomsbury (pp 45-64)

Branford, S. (1921) Citizenship and the Civic Association. *Sociological Review* 13, 4, 228–234

Brewer, J. (2010) Micro-history and the histories of everyday life. *Cultural and Social History*, 7, 1, 87-109

Burns, C. Delisle (1932) *Leisure in the Modern World*. London: George Allen and Unwin

Children's Society (2019) *The Good Childhood Report* [Accessed 18th June 2020 at https://www.childrenssociety.org.uk/sites/default/files/the_good_childhood_report_2019.pdf]

Cole, G. D. H, and Cole M. I. (1937) *The Condition of Britain*. London: Gollancz

Durant, R. (1939) *'Watling': a Survey of Social Life on a New Housing Estate*. London: P.S. King

Epicurus (2012) *The Art of Happiness*. London: Penguin

Fave, A.D., Brdar, I., Freire, T., Vella-Brodrick, D., and Wissing, M. P. (2011) The Eudamonic and Hedonic components of happiness: qualitative and quantitative findings. *Social Indicators Research*, 100, 2, 185–207

Gardiner, J. (2010) *The Thirties. An Intimate History*. London: Harper

Guha, M. and Carson, J. (2017) Happiness down the ages in S. Mc Hugh (Ed.) *The Changing Nature of Happiness. An in-depth Study of a Town in North-West England 1938-2016*. Cham, Switzerland: Palgrave Macmillan (pp 17-30)

Gutenschwager, G. (2013) From Epicurus to Maslow: Happiness Then and Now and the Place of the Human Being in Social Theory. *CADMUS*, I, 6, 66-90

Hammond, J. L. (1933) *The Growth of Common Enjoyment*. London: Oxford University Press

Harrisson, T. H. (1937) *Savage Civilization*. London: Gollancz

Hobson, J. A. (1914) *Work and Wealth. A Human Valuation*. London: George Allen and Unwin

Leavis, F. R. (1930) *Mass Civilization and Minority Culture*. Cambridge: The Minority Press

Long, A. A. (2006) *From Epicurus to Epictetus: Studies in Hellenistic and Roman Philosophy*. Oxford: Oxford University Press

Lopez, M. P. , da Palma, P. J., Garcia, B. C. and Gomes, C. (2016) Training for Happiness: The impacts of different positive exercises on hedonism and eudaemonia. *Springer Plus*, 5, 744

Lynd, R. S. and Lynd, H. M. (1929) *Middletown: a Study in American Culture*. New York: Harcourt Brace

McHugh, S. and Carson, J. (2017) Happiness Perceptions – A comparison 1938 and 2014 in S. McHugh (Ed.) *The Changing Nature of Happiness: An in-Depth Study of a Town in North West*

England 1938-2016. Cham, Switzerland: Palgrave Macmillan

Mcmahon, D. M. (2006) *Happiness: a History.* New York: Grove Press

Maltby, J., Day, L. and Barber, L. (2005) Forgiveness and happiness. The differing contexts of forgiveness using the distinction between hedonic and eudamonic happiness. *Journal of Happiness Studies,* 6, 1–13

Mass Observation (1937a) 'Social Conditions and Housing' Worktown Collection Box 44A

Mass Observation (1937b) 'Savings Clubs' Worktown Collection Box 33B

Mass Observation (1937c) 'Holidays Questionnaires' Worktown Collection Box 46

Mass Observation (1937d) 'Household Budgets' Worktown Collection Box 28B

Mass Observation (1937e) 'Holiday Town' Worktown Collection Box 63A

Mass Observation (1937f) 'Pubs and Drinking' Worktown Collection Box 55

Mass Observation (1937g) 'Holiday Competition' Worktown Collection Box 46

Mass Observation (1938) *Happiness* Topic Collection no. 7

Mass Observation (1987) *The Pub and the People.* London: The Cresset Library

Morris, W. (1984a) 'How we Live and How we might Live' in *William Morris. News from Nowhere and Selected Writings,* ed. Asa Briggs, London: Penguin, 1984 pp. 158-178

Morris, W. (1984b) 'News from Nowhere' in *William Morris. News from Nowhere and Selected Writings,* ed. Asa Briggs, London: Penguin, 1984 pp. 183-304

Mulford, J. (ed.) (1982) *Worktown people: photographs from Northern England 1937-38.* Bristol: Falling Wall Press

National Council of Social Service Community Centres and Associations Committee (1937) *New Housing Estates and their social problems,* 4th edition. London: NCSS

Pollen, A. (2015) Utopian Futures and Imagined Pasts in the Ambivalent Modernism of the Kibbo Kift Kindred in David Ayers, Benedikt Hjartarson, Tomi Huttunen and Harri Veivo De Gruyter (Eds,) *Utopia: The Avant-Garde, Modernism and (Im) possible Life.* Boston: Walter de Gruyter

Priestley, J. B. (1934) *English Journey.* London: Heinemann

Ruskin, J. (1856) *Modern Painters Volume Three.* London: Smith, Elder and Co

Russell, B. (1916) *Principles of Social Reconstruction.* London: George Allen and Unwin

Snape, R. (2004) The Co-operative Holidays Association and the cultural formation of countryside leisure practice. *Leisure Studies,* 23, 2, 143-158

Snape, R. (2018) *Leisure, Voluntary Action and Social Change in Britain 1880-1939.* London: Bloomsbury

Spracklen, K. (2011) *Constructing Leisure. Historical and Philosophical Debates.* Basingstoke: Palgrave Macmillan

UNICEF (2016) *Fairness for Children A league table of inequality in child well-being in rich countries.* Florence: Unicef.

Wang, M and Wong M.C. (2014) Happiness and Leisure Across Countries: Evidence from International Survey Data. *Journal of Happiness Studies,* 15, 85–118.

Perceptions of happiness in three women's groups in Bolton: A qualitative study

Kathryn Thomasson, Sandie McHugh and Jerome Carson

Introduction

Happiness studies have focused on how people can support and improve their own wellbeing, within the context of their life circumstances, the local area and community they live in, being an important part of how they feel. Whilst several key thinkers in the area of wellbeing research have proposed different theoretical models of human flourishing (Diener, 1984; Keyes, 1998; Ryff, 1989; Ryan and Deci, 2002; Seligman, 2002), they all share the importance of social connections and relationships to our happiness levels. Perhaps one of the most thorough investigations into the root of happiness in social science research has been conducted by Richard Layard (2005). Layard investigates the social factors that affect happiness and argues that unless you are very poor more money will not help you become happier. He proposes seven key factors that affect happiness in adult populations: financial situation, family relationships, work, community, friends, health, personal freedoms and personal values (Layard, 2005:63). Layard suggests that the key to happiness for the widest range of people is determined by the quality of the society they live in and happy societies are built on family collaboration, trust, altruism, and good quality social relationships. He proposes The Big Seven, the key factors that support happiness in a society. In Layard's analysis happier societies are those that involve people working together to provide better working conditions, strong family relationships, good financial situations, work opportunities, good quality communities and friendships, support good personal and physical health and promote and protect personal freedoms. Local communities and these societies are the ones where people thrive when there is a commitment to providing more equality in these areas.

Strong communities and social networks can have a significant positive impact on our wellbeing and our happiness levels (Diener and Seligman, 2002). People who have strong and satisfying relationships report feeling happy more frequently and have fewer periods of experiencing sadness. However, whilst our understanding of the influences of happiness and the importance of the social ties we have with our friends, family and community is growing, at the same time much has been written in the last few decades about the loss of community and the implications this has for our civil society (Putnam, 2000). Globalisation has had an impact on economic, political and social relationships at a local level. Advances in communication technology have changed the way that people communicate, offering new ways for connection between people with shared interests. Global companies now move their capital and workforces around the world to take advantage of the most profitable places in which to conduct their business, and people migrate to take advantage of job opportunities. All these facts combine to change and reduce the sense of community that people have in physical places (Robinson and Green, 2011). However, whilst social media has expanded the range of social communications, people remain connected to local social ties and attachment to place. Although they may not be restricted to local place-based communities, the structure of these and their services: education, employment, social relations, health and housing are still key support systems for resident's wellbeing and happiness. The need for community development work to support local people to improve their local communities in building a stronger and happier life for themselves still generates interest (Green and Haines, 2007).

Community development work is focused on improving the quality of society by working with people in local communities to build wider friendship networks, new and better access to activities and facilities, better connections with economic opportunities and the ability to overcome poverty, improve health, wellbeing, and the physical environment. The concept of community participation is at the centre of community development practices and planning, based on the premise that local people are best placed to know what is needed in their area and how those needs can be met. At the heart of community development work are the principles of collective action, participation and social justice through emancipation and empowerment, shared learning, accountability and good governance through development programmes and critical engagement with the state (Eversley, 2019: 9). Community groups are at the centre of these activities. They are groups of local people who identify the needs of their local area and work together to find long term solutions, often with the support of partner agencies.

Community development organisations (CDO'S) are a primary vehicle for development in low income neighbourhoods and areas of social and economic deprivation (Gittell et al, 2000). Evolving from local needs they are led by local people addressing issues in their own community and neighbourhood. Community development is the way in which stronger ties in a community can be formed. People coming together can improve their own lives through the processes of initiating social action to drive change and deliver positive social outcomes (Phillips and Pittman, 2009). Projects provide highly localised support for communities because they are grass roots initiatives run by people who are well-placed to identity local community needs, focusing on issues that are of concern to local people without the distraction of centrally identified priorities (McCabe and Phillimore, 2012). Key objectives commonly include building safer communities, improving the local physical landscape, enhancing health and wellbeing and building trusting relationships. People involved in community development stress the importance of engaging with members of the community throughout the programme, from initial consultation to the development of long-term project outcomes and their achievement. This is based on the belief that residents are not passive consumers of the services being developed in their area, rather active collaborators working towards long term sustainable solutions. Community groups are a key part of this approach. They can be formally constituted groups with their own agreed constitution policies and procedures, aided by local supporting organisations, part of Non-Government Organisations, or part of the smaller local networks of friends and shared interest groups that are not formally recognised. There are many of these unofficial groups in the United Kingdom, perhaps as many as six to nine hundred thousand, (Community Development Fund, 2014) and the vast majority are operating on very small financial budgets of under two thousand pounds a year. They also provide a wide range of services including activities that meet the interest of their members, advice and information, advocacy and planning, education and lifelong learning services and personal support. Community groups also provide a vital link for connecting to people who may be less visible in society for public and private sector services (Community Development Fund, 2014). In the last decade a growing volume of research has shown that being part of a social group and the access people have to wider social networks are an important predictor and protector of health and wellbeing (Jetten et al, 2017). A major link between happiness and social integration is social capital. People who are members of groups and have strong social networks that provide networks of trust and reciprocity enjoy high levels of social capital (Halliwell and Putnam, 2004). Social capital benefits individuals both socially and economically. Having higher levels of social capital means that people find employment more easily, have higher earnings from employment, better access to useful information, better social safety nets and more social control and influence (Appau et al, 2019). Just as importantly social capital provides social support which helps people have better quality social relationships. Good social networks also provide a buffer for people against the stresses and strains of life, giving them more resilience and reducing stress (Diener and Seligman, 2002).

The efficacy of neighbour based social networks on people's evaluation of their life satisfaction differs from person to person. For some people the strength of their neighbourhood's social capital makes no difference, for others their local neighbourhood still plays an important part in their daily lives (Howley, Neill and Atkinson, 2015). It can depend on a person's levels of social connections outside of their immediate neighbourhood (Freiler, 2004) or the amount of time spent within their neighbourhood boundaries (Henning and Lieberg, 1996). People who are less mobile and less able to travel are more reliant on social capital for this reason, so that the impact of the local community social capital levels can be particularly important to people who are less affluent, with fewer opportunities to travel, or have monetary restrictions, such as people on low incomes, the elderly or the disabled. Community development programmes are frequently strategically planned to support and engage with local neighbourhoods and communities that are in some way disadvantaged, be that socially or economically. They are a social process, and in being so support the development of social capital, with the implicit value of bringing people together from all backgrounds to take part in activities that are designed to improve their own quality of life (Robinson and Green, 2011).

This chapter explores what group members who are participating in community groups in their local area in Bolton consider to be the most influential factors for their happiness. Three women's groups: Wonder Women; Sanctuary Story Tellers and the Golden Oldies, formed in response to community development programmes and strategies. We asked each group key questions about what makes them happy: the importance of their social relationships with family, friends, neighbours; their faith; working life; education; the impact of their economic conditions, and their personal values. Additionally, the discussions also focused on what people would change to improve their happiness if possible. The study finds that local social conditions in the participant's community are still considered to be important in helping them achieve a happy life; of most importance are their social relationships with friends, family and neighbours..

Community development in Bolton

There is a diverse range of practicing community groups in the Bolton area. The funding and organization vary widely: some are led by individual practitioners who respond to perceived local needs and apply for funding from local and national funding organisations: including local authority grants, private business grants and national bodies such as the Arts Council and National Lottery. Others are Non-Government Organisations (NGO's) created locally and self-constituted, run by group elected committees and officers. Many of these groups work in partnership together to strengthen their delivery and funding efficiency.

Bolton at Home

One of the key supporting organizations in Bolton's community development work is Bolton at Home, a registered housing provider and community benefit society, and an exempt charity (Bolton at Home, 2017; Bolton at Home, 2019). The organization was initiated as an arm's length management company responsible for the council's housing stock. Additionally, and somewhat uniquely, Bolton at Home was also given the responsibility for delivering borough wide regeneration in both the public and private sector (Creative Options Consultancy Ltd, 2010). It is a not for profit organization that currently provides housing and support services to more than eighteen thousand homes across the Bolton borough (Bolton at Home, 2017; Bolton at Home, 2019). In addition to providing affordable homes they also provide a range of social support services to their customers, including money advice, employment support, signposting to services, and independent living support. There are drop in centres and services available through a network of Urban Community and Neighbourhood Centres or UCAN's (Bolton at Home, 2019) throughout the borough.

Bolton at Home's key work in community development is through its Percent for Arts Programme. The service is located within Bolton at Home and is also a part of Bolton Community Homes, an umbrella partnership of nine housing associations working in the Borough (Bolton at Home, DU). Initially launched in 1997, the scheme was established with the intent that social landlords should engage with local communities and encourage ownership at a local level (Bolton at Home, 2003). The programme aimed to use art as an agent for social change (Lewis and Caswell, 2001) and has the core key objectives: To help improve the physical and social fabric of communities, develop opportunities with local cultural industries, encourage closer links between artists, residents and the professionals that shape the environment and work in partnership to develop Borough wide arts and culture projects (Bolton at Home, DU). The range of projects is diverse, but all have the aim of offering creative solutions to neighbourhood problems. The key principles established by Percent for Arts is to deliver a quality arts service that meets customers' needs and contributes to the regeneration of Bolton at Home's neighbourhoods (Bolton at Home, 2011).

Projects evolve from a variety of outlets, including community consultation and partnership working, and encompass a wide range of art formats including visual, performance based, film, music and crafts. Initiatives have a wide range of aims and objectives including skills development, improved well-being, community cohesion and advocacy, celebratory events, environmental projects and enhancements to the physical environment which includes streetscaping. This ongoing programme gives Bolton at Home the unique position of being the only service of this type offered by a housing organization that is known in the United Kingdom (Bolton at Home, 2017).

The Percent for Art initiative

The Percent for Art initiative currently runs several women's groups in some of the most deprived areas in Bolton. Women who attend the group can experience a range of social and economic disadvantages including marginalisation, social exclusion, heavy caring responsibilities and disempowerment within their homes and communities as well as social isolation, low self-esteem, stress, anxiety and depression. They also have limited incomes and social networks. Bolton at Home's women's projects aims to empower service users so that they can regain control over their lives (Bolton at Home, 2017). Two of the focus groups, The Wonder Woman and The Golden Oldies are supported through Bolton at Home community development work.

City of Sanctuary Bolton

City of Sanctuary Bolton was created in 2016 and is part of the wider National City of Sanctuary network. Bolton takes an active role in the Gateway Resettlement Programme, which is the UK's contribution to the United Nations High Commissioner for Refugees (UNHCR) global resettlement programme (Refugee Council, 2018). Greater Manchester, which includes the town of Bolton, is a dispersal area for resettlement, and the North West is currently home to a quarter of all people in receipt of section 95 housing support, many of whom are living in the Bolton area (Dearden et al, 2015). People who have come to live in Bolton and are currently asylum seekers or refugees can have a complex range of needs covering their physical and mental health, social provision and general wellbeing. Many asylum seekers have already experienced trauma in their home countries and in their flight to a safe country and common health problems include diabetes, hypertension, dental disorders, anxiety, depression and post-traumatic stress (Dearden et al, 2015). Understanding and accessing health care facilities and support services can be difficult as many refugees and asylum seekers face language barriers and a limited understanding of support services that are available. They can also lack the social networks that can provide additional support and information leaving new arrivals feeling isolated (Mateo, 2017). City of Sanctuary Bolton was created by a group of local volunteers to support people arriving in the community and to promote inclusion. They are a constituted voluntary group who support local communities and voluntary organizations in welcoming and assisting refugees. They also run several projects aimed specifically at women as they often face additional challenges when arriving in a new community. Asylum seekers and refugee women have been consistently considered one of the most vulnerable groups. Many are young women with small children or infants. Single women often lack financial and family support, they are at risk of gender-based violence and exploitation and as women in their host countries, they are expected by their communities to embody all the reminiscences of the country of origin, being the primary care giver and homemaker, which can impact on their own integration in their new communities and leaves women more at risk of isolation. Their isolated status is impacted further by the loss of the family and friends support network left behind when moving from their country of origin. This makes women's support services that actively encourage community participation an important element to foster community integration and cohesion (Sansonetti, 2016).

Wonder Woman

The Wonder Woman group is a Bolton at Home led group that meets weekly at a local community centre that serves the area in Bolton of Tongue Moor and Hall 'i' th' Wood. It was established in 2012 and constituted in 2018. The group was set up and is still led by a local project officer who has a strong working knowledge of the area and long-term relationships with many of the participants. The group provides arts interaction, creative activities, and social support, learning and engagement opportunities for local women. Over the length of the group's existence it is estimated that over seventy women have attended (Awards for All, 2017), some accessing the group on an infrequent basis, others attending regularly. The group provides an opportunity for women to meet, share time together away from the often-demanding responsibilities of their home life and engage in creative activities across a wide range of areas in arts and crafts. The group has also worked in outreach activities and community projects in their own area, including commemorations of local people in the First World War in 2017 and a celebration of prominent local women living in Bolton in the 1920's and 1930's, who were involved in the suffragette movement, education and women's sport. Most recently the group took part in the University of Bolton's conference celebrating the work of American poet Walt Whitman (1819-1892) when they performed a variety of poems from his work *Leaves of Grass* (1855 [2005]).

The Golden Oldies

The Golden Oldies meet several times a week at their local community centre, Meadowside. The group is self-constituted and led by local retired women who run the group in a voluntary capacity. It is supported by Bolton at Home's Big Local initiative, but the projects and programs that the group engage in are self-selected and funded by individual grants and awards that are applied for by the committee and chair. The Big Local initiative is funded by the National Lottery, with grants of at least one million pounds being awarded to one hundred and fifty communities across the United Kingdom. The initiative focuses on long term community development that is resident led and flexible (Oxford Consultants for Social Inclusion, 2019). The group has been operating for over ten years, during which time it has enjoyed a strong membership. Members are generally older and retired people living locally but this is not exclusive, and they welcome everyone. They have an established core membership, and this provides a good centre of local support and advice for older people in the local vicinity, providing a friendship and activity based local group for older people who may otherwise be at risk from social isolation. They also offer support for older people across a wide range of areas including health and budgetary advice, creative activities, exercise classes and regular excursions. The Golden Oldies often engage in projects as advocates for older people's rights and concerns and have worked frequently on projects funded through Ambition for Ageing (2020) in partnership with the Big Local and Bolton at Home.

Sanctuary Story Tellers

The Sanctuary Storytellers women's group originated from the women's theatre group that was originally formed under the partnership of the City of Sanctuary, Bolton, The Destitution Project, Bolton and the community engagement team at The Octagon Theatre. These partner agencies offer a drama group for women asylum seekers and refugees to support social cohesion and integration in Bolton, giving participants individual support to improve their confidence, English language skills and provide opportunities to be more active in their local community. The group ended in the summer of 2018 and restarted in October of the same year. Many of the women who attended the group missed the social aspects that they had gained from their participation during the summer months. As a result, the arts organising committee members at City of Sanctuary created a women's creative writing group as an interim project and donated space for the group to meet in Bolton Central Library. The group proved a very popular initiative and continued to run, becoming one of the key community arts projects now led by Bolton City of Sanctuary. The aim of the group is to provide a space and opportunity for women to engage in arts practices in creative writing and to widen their social networks in the area beyond the asylum seeker and refugee community. The group is open to all women to attend and is not exclusively for refugees and asylum seekers.

Method of data collection in the community groups

A qualitative semi-structured focus group design was used to capture the opinions and beliefs of the group participants. The study was conducted under the guidance of the University of Bolton ethics framework for research and ethical approval for the study was obtained from the University ethics panel. All participants that took part in the study gave their approval prior to the focus groups and provided written consent. For each group an overview of happiness studies in Bolton was given, along with a short performance from a local visiting artist of singing and storytelling. Each session lasted approximately two hours with a lunch provided. Group leaders and facilitators were present with the authors. Professor Jerome Carson and Sandie McHugh have been studying happiness in Bolton since 2013 (McHugh and Carson, 2016). As the focus group was semi structured, nine main questions were asked to each group, but the participants were encouraged to develop their discussions with everyone taking part. We asked each group: What was a time in your life when you were really happy? Do you think money is important to your happiness? If you could change anything in your life to make it happier what would that be? Do you think you can control what makes you happy? How important are study and work to happiness? How important are friends in terms of your happiness? How important is family in terms of your happiness? How important are religious beliefs or personal values to your happiness? How important is health to your happiness? The questions were designed to help participants explore the concept of happiness in relation to their own lives and experiences.

Each focus group was recorded and then transcribed by Sandie McHugh verbatim. Analysis began at the end of the data collection using inductive and deductive phases. The data was read carefully to analyze the way in which the participants viewed happiness and the factors that they felt influenced and supported their own personal feelings of happiness. The transcribed data was analysed using a thematic analysis technique by two of the researchers, Kathryn Thomasson and Sandie McHugh. Working independently the researchers initially analysed the data using an interpretative approach to form a codebook. They then compared their coding and agreed the codebook before commencing with further analysis. To manage the data the QSR International software package NVivo was used (NVivo 10, 2020).

Findings

The analysis from participants in each group identified six main themes that influenced happiness, these were: education, faith, family and friends, money, personal values and work. Whilst all the groups demonstrated many similarities in their responses there were notable differences in some areas. Across all three groups the most significant factors identified for happiness was family and friends and personal values. This was followed in the hierarchy by faith, work, money and education. Two themes did not consistently appear across all three groups. Noticeably, faith was most strongly present as a theme in the discussions with the Sanctuary Story Tellers, was mentioned only briefly in the Golden Oldies group and was not mentioned at all by the Wonder Women group. The theme of education was also only present in two groups, Sanctuary Story Tellers and Wonder Women. Other notable differences were with Work, which appeared to be of most significance to the Golden Oldies and was barely mentioned in the focus group with the Wonder Woman whereas Money was most discussed by the Wonder Women group and appears very little as an emerging theme with the Golden Oldies.

Discussion

Friends and family

The influence of friends and family on happiness was the most important theme across all three groups. Immediate family, parents, partners, children and grandchildren and the time spent with them were frequently mentioned. Key moments in family life, marriage and having children were some of the happiest moments for many participants, particularly for the Golden Oldies who were predominantly reflecting on past times and highly valued time spent with close family members. Family were also seen as a strong support structure for group members, providing support and help in difficult circumstances and offering emotional support. Friends were also considered a key component of a happy life to all groups. However, there were some noticeable differences between the older members of the Golden Oldies and the younger women in the other two groups. For the Golden Oldies, they felt that the quality of neighbourhood friendships had diminished in more recent years and they felt that there had been a decline in social networks in their local areas.

'You did in the past you were a similar age and they had children of a similar age. You were very friendly.'

'As my children grew up – I've got grandchildren and great grandchildren. When our neighbours had children similar to me, it was 'Oh can you get such a body off the park – tell them to come home- anybody else wants their children? Get mine, get everybody else's. Come on your wanted home.'

The Golden Oldies group participants suggested that the changes to working and leisure patterns may have made a difference to the strength of friendships in their local area. They commented on younger people at work during the day involved in their own activities at home, not engaging with neighbours.

'they are younger and always out at work. You don't see them. Only to say Hello, Goodbye and that's it. You don't have a proper conversation with them.'

The result of the changes to these social conditions for this group meant that they felt their neighbourhood was less safe and not as friendly as it had been when they had young children at home. They suggested that the change in the relationships in the local area had caused a decline in the support that local neighbourhood friendship networks had previously provided:

'Your neighbours. I remember my mum, if someone was sick in the street, and she was making a potato pie for us, she would make one for them as well. They don't neighbour the same as they used to do.'

The community group membership of the Golden Oldies provided them with key social contact that they might not otherwise have had and prevented some members who did not have the benefit of close family relationships with a remedy to social isolation. Friendship also provided feelings of self-worth and membership of community groups also provided social support:

'You make friends and it makes you feel you are worth something'.

'If anything there, we are all for each other. We help when we can.'

'..and I see each other every morning, and we will have a chat for about half an hour. If they want anything and I am going out I will get it. She does the same for me. We just keep in touch with each other, don't we?'

Both the Wonder Women and Sanctuary Story Teller's group felt that friendships groups were important to happiness; however they also mentioned that the quality of friendships is very important:

Wonder Woman: 'Surrounding myself with good people, people that I like, doing things with people those.'

Sanctuary Story Tellers: 'If I am happy and people around me are not happy what use? So most times things are affect me are the things that affect people around me'.

'It's choice of people you know. You know people choose what makes them happy.'

Participants from Sanctuary Story Tellers also felt that family were more trustworthy than friends in most circumstances and were more important for social support.

'It is really necessary that you can have some people in your life that are very close to you and trust you. They must be able to because there are friends that are there when you are OK, but when you are not good they disappear. So when time is of hardship when you determine who are the true friends. Um, so it's good to have friends.'

Personal values

Across all the groups the most important aspect of happiness under the theme of personal values was finding contentment in day to day activities, situations and experiences and remaining thankful for them. The Wonder Women and the Sanctuary Story Tellers had a similar position on the need for a positive outlook when dealing with problems, and this was achieved by not dwelling on past events and getting through difficult times one day at a time. Participants in the Sanctuary Story Tellers noted that:

'You have to say that everything will be fine. I know like Nothing lasts forever.'

'I choose to live life is what today brings. I try to live my life today and then tomorrow comes it has its own problem.'

The Sanctuary Story Tellers also expressed the importance of strong moral values; these were both linked to religious teaching as well as how people can make personal moral choices. They felt that living in a society that gave its citizens free speech and personal freedoms for religious choices was very important for happiness.

Faith

Only members of the Sanctuary Story Tellers discussed the importance of faith to happiness. The group suggested that prayer supports happiness because it is a mechanism to deal with problems and difficult life circumstances. They also felt that religion contributed to moral guidance which was important in how people evaluated their own life. Following the teachings of their chosen religion is something that makes them feel happy.

Some group members discussed finding happiness in the freedom to openly engage in and practice their religion. The acceptance of religious beliefs and cultural diversity was also discussed as something that contributed towards personal happiness.

Health

Across all groups good health was thought to have an impact on happiness although there was some variation between the groups about how this happens. The Golden Oldies group focused on the access and quality of health care and how it is important to be able to find remedies to health problems such as pain relief. They also felt that not having local doctors that they knew and who would visit them at home impacted on the stress they experienced with health issues. Both the Wonder Women group and the Sanctuary Story Tellers discussions were more focused on how the health of other people such as their parents and children, affected their happiness, with both groups agreeing that the health of family is important to them. Both the Sanctuary Story Teller group and the Wonder Women group include women who have caring responsibilities for children and older relatives, whilst the Golden Oldies no longer have these responsivities, which is perhaps why their focus was on how they can find solutions to their own health problems which they seem to accept is inevitable at their age. The Golden Oldies also value health service provision which is patient friendly and accessible and discussed the importance of services that include people who know them and their personal history, which influenced their evaluation of the quality of the health care provision that they receive.

Money

For all three groups money was only considered to be important if they had enough to cover bills and provide them with some basic financial security. Happiness was having enough without worries and stress around paying bills and buying food. Out of the three groups money was the most discussed topic by the Wonder Women group, followed by City of Sanctuary and with the least discussion from the Golden Oldies. Some of the Wonder Women group participants had experienced financial stress and this had impacted on their happiness:

'I've been on the other side of the fence as well when you didn't have the money and you couldn't pay your bills – if you didn't have the money you couldn't be.'

They expressed that trying to find a way to live within their financial budgets would be more inductive to their happiness that having a higher income:

'now I think it is – you learn to live within your means –you learn to do what you have to do, it is not to do with that money that makes you happy. It is like you are content, you can live with what you have got – and learning to make the most of what you have got.'

The Golden Oldies felt that in previous years or their younger lives there was less comparison amongst people regarding money and not the same pressure to own material goods. They commented that their neighbourhoods felt stronger because everyone was in the same situation with money and that no one had a great deal.

'Everybody was in the same boat then. If you understand what I mean. Your neighbours didn't have anything more than you had.'

They also commented on the change of culture that credit has brought to how people use money and felt that the traditional value of saving for what you want rather than instant access to credit was better for contentment and happiness.

The Sanctuary Story Tellers were the only group to mention that money provided safety regarding health and access to medical care if required. As discussed earlier, many of the participants in this group originate from countries that do not provide access to free health care and this was a significant part of the advantages of having money, being able to access health. This group also expressed the importance of money for basic needs of living and accessing travel to come to a country where they could find asylum. For them money provided additional safety and security to their personal freedom and health. None of the participants across any of the groups felt that having a lot of money or a large increase in income would provide happiness.

Work

While working did not factor significantly in any groups assessment of importance to their happiness levels, both the Golden Oldies and the Sanctuary Story Tellers discussed work in the context of the friendships and social relationships that working offered, and how having a steady income provided for financial security and independence. For some members of the Sanctuary Story Tellers work provided a sense of accomplishment and fulfilment and independence through financial security.

Education

Education was the least covered theme across the focus groups. Most of the group members in all three groups have not been in education for some time or have not experienced higher education. When education was mentioned, two participants with experience of higher education commented that education brought them happiness with it's sense of accomplishment. One participant stated they enjoyed the active process of learning. What is notable by its absence is any mention of the community group activities currently engaged in, based on lifelong learning activities, enhancing happiness. Perhaps this is because of how the group participants conceptualise education and study, considering it to be only notable if formal or structured.

Conclusions

The aim of this study was to identify what women who are actively engaged in groups that are part of community development initiatives perceive is important to their happiness. Each group felt that the provision of local community services had an influence on their happiness level. Social capital featured significantly in the discussions amongst all three groups, with the importance of their social ties to the community and their relationships with close family and friends being of importance. The people living in their local area also were of importance, with several focus group participants from across the groups mentioning the significance of being surrounded by 'good people'.

For the Golden Oldies a safe and friendly neighbourhood with good social ties is important along with access to good quality healthcare provision in the local area. The Golden Oldies felt that their neighbourhood has lost its friendliness, and this was in part due to modern working patterns and local people not spending as much time at home. Their community group has offered some of the friendship and social support networks that they feel may be missing from their traditional local community, and for some members it is their main source of social interaction.

For members of the Sanctuary Story Tellers personal freedoms, accessible healthcare, social inclusion and religious tolerance were all aspects of their life that they felt were contributors to their happiness. Living in a community and wider society that provides strong leadership and a stable democracy is important to them. The United Kingdom provides them with personal freedom and religious tolerance that may have been lacking in their lives when living in their countries of origin.

For the Wonder Woman group the quality and goodness of the people living in their local area and their connection to their community is important to their happiness. Traditionally the area in which the Wonder Woman group is situated has suffered from severe economic disadvantage, high crime rates and local doorstep credit companies. Being able to manage a household on a limited budget without experiencing any significant hardship is an important aspect of their happiness levels.

What are significant in these findings are how these groups of women coming from social backgrounds where they are more tied to their local community and area, value the social structure that is part of Layard's framework for the promotion of happiness. Whilst many theorists have suggested that sense of community in local neighbourhoods is in decline, for many people from more disadvantaged social and economic backgrounds, thriving communities can be a key factor in supporting them in living happy and fulfilling lives.

References

Ambition for Aging [Accessed 22nd June 2020 at https: www.ambitionforageing.org. uk/bolton]

Appau, S., Churchill, S. A. and Farrell, L. (2019) Social integration and subjective wellbeing. *Applied Economics*, 51, 16, 1748-1761

Awards for All (2017). *National Lottery Awards for All Application Form: Wonder Woman.* Unpublished

Bolton at Home (2003) *Housing Percent for Art Strategy Document, March 2003.* Bolton Metropolitan Council: Unpublished

Bolton at Home (2011) *Housing for Art Six Months Development Review Report.* Bolton Metropolitan Council: Unpublished

Bolton at Home (2019) *Our Plan: April 2019 to March 2024. Five-year strategic programme.* [Accessed 24th October 2019 at https://www.boltonathome.org.uk]

Bolton at Home (2017) *CVS Zine project bid.* Bolton at Home: Unpublished

Bolton at Home (DU) *A Working Guide to Percent for Art.* Bolton Metropolitan Council: Unpublished

Community Development Fund (2014) Tailor-made: How community groups improve people's lives, *Trust for London.* [Accessed 29th June 2020 at https:// www.trustforlondon.org.uk/publications/tailor-made-how-community-groups-improve-peoples-lives/]

Creative Options Consultancy (2010) Housing Percent for Art – A retrospective Evaluation, Bolton at Home. *Stafford, Creative Options Consultancy Ltd.* [Accessed on 28th October 2019 at http://map.poortheatres.manchester.ac.uk/Content/ Uploads/M00085/PercentforArtRetrospective%20Evaluation-Final%20Report. pdf]

Dearden, S., Bailey, S., Arnall, S. and Worthington, E. (2016) *Briefing on Issues Affecting the Health of Refugees and People Seeking Asylum.* [Accessed 17th July

2018 at https://councildecisions.bury.gov.uk/documents/s10628/Briefing%20 on%20Health%20Issues%20Affecting%20Refugees%20and%20People%20 Seeking%20Asylum.pdf]

Diener, E. (1984) Subjective well-being. *Psychological Bulletin*, 95, 3, 342– 57

Diener, E. and Seligman, M. E. P. (2002) Very Happy People. *Psychological Science*, 13, 1, 81–84. https://doi.org/10.1111/1467-9280.00415

Eversley, J. (2019) *Social and Community Development, An Introduction*. London: Red Globe Press

Freiler, C. (2004) *Why Stronger Neighbourhoods Matter: Implications for policy and practice*. Strong Neighbourhoods Task Force, Toronto [Accessed 13 March 2020 at http:// www.urbancentre.utoronto.ca/pdfs/curp/SNTF_Why-Neighbourhoods-Mat. pdf]

Gittell, M., Ortega- Bustamante, I. and Steffy, T. (2000) Social capital and social change. Women's community activism. *Urban Affairs Review*, 36, 2, 123-147

Green, P. G. and Haines, A. (2007) *Asset Building and Community Development*, 2nd Edition. Thousand Oaks, California: Sage Publications

Helliwell, J. F. and Putnam, R. D. (2004) The social context of well-being. *Philosophical Transactions of the Royal Society of London. Series B. Biological sciences*, 359, 1435- 1446. https://doi.org/10.1098/rstb.2004.1522

Henning, C. and Lieberg, M. (1996) Strong ties or weak ties? Neighbourhood networks in a new perspective. *Scandinavian Housing and planning research*, 13, 1, 3-26

Howley, P., Neill, S. O. and Atkinson, R. (2015) Who needs good neighbors? *Environment and Planning A: Economy and Space,* 47, 4, 939–956. https://doi. org/10.1068/a140214p

Jetten, J., Haslam, S. A., Cruwys, T., Greenaway, K. H., Haslam, C. and Steffens, N. K. (2017) Advancing the social identity approach to health and well-being: Progressing the social cure research agenda. *European Journal of Social Psychology*, 47, 7, 789-802

Keyes, C. L. M. (1998) Social well-being. *Social Psychology Quarterly*, 61, 2, 121–140. [Accessed 30 June 2020 at https://doi.org/10.2307/2787065]

Layard, R. (2005) *Happiness: Lessons from a new science*. London: Penguin

Lewis, B. and Caswell, G. (Eds.) (2001) *Creative Solutions. The Use of the Arts in Regeneration, Bolton*. Bolton Metropolitan Borough Council: Available at https:// fliphtml5.com/wyhs/lbet

Mateo, A. (2016) Health needs assessment of asylum seekers and refugees in Lancashire. *Lancashire County Council* [Accessed 18th July 2017 at http://www.lancashire.gov. uk/media/902306/hna_asylum-seekers-and-refugees_lancashire.pdf]

McCabe, A. and Phillimore, J. (2012) *All Change? Surviving Below the Radar: Community groups and activities in a Big Society*. Birmingham: University of Birmingham

McHugh, S. and Carson J. (2016) Happiness then and now, looking back. *The Psychologist*, 29, 12, 406-407

NVivo 10, QSR International [Accessed 29th June 2020 at https://www.

qsrinternational.com/nvivo-qualitative-data-analysis-software/home]

Oxford Consultants for Social Inclusion (2019) *Local Trust. Left Behind? Understanding communities on the edge.* Creative Commons [Accessed 13th March 2020 at https://localtrust.org.uk/wp-content/uploads/2019/08/local_trust_ocsi_left_behind_research_august_2019.pdf]

Phillips, R. and Pittman, R. H. (2015) A framework for community and economic development. An introduction to community development. in R. Philips and R.H. Pittman (Eds) *An Introduction to Community Development.* (2nd ed.) New York: Routledge. (pp 3-19)

Putnam, R. D. (2000) *Bowling Alone: The collapse and revival of American community.* New York: Simon & Schuster

Refugee Council (2018) *Gateway Resettlement Programme.* [Accessed 20th February 2020 at https://www.refugeecouncil.org.uk/latest/projects/gateway-protection-programme/]

Robinson, J. W. Jr. and Green, G. P. (Eds.) (2011) *Introduction to Community Development: Theory, practice, and service-learning.* London: Sage

Ryan, R. M. and Deci, E. L. (2002) Overview of self-determination theory: An organismic-dialectical perspective in E. L. Deci and R. M. Ryan (Eds.) *Handbook of Self-Determination Research.* Rochester: University of Rochester Press (pp 3–33)

Ryff, C. D. (1989) Happiness is everything, or is it? Explorations on the meaning of psychological well-being. *Journal of Personality and Social Psychology,* 57, 6, 1069–1081. [Accessed 1st July 2020 https://doi.org/10.1037/0022-3514.57.6.1069]

Sansonetti, S. (2016) *Female Refugees and Asylum Seekers: The issue of integration. A report commissioned by Policy Department.* Citizen's Rights and Constitutional Affairs, EU Parliament. [Accessed 18th July 2017 at http://www.europarl.europa.eu/RegData/etudes/STUD/2016/556929/IPOL_STU(2016)556929_EN.pdf]

Seligman, M. E. P. (2002) *Authentic Happiness: Using the new positive psychology to realize your potential for lasting fulfilment.* New York: Free Press

Whitman, W. (2005) *Walt Whitman's Leaves of Grass: The first (1855) edition.* New York: Penguin Book

Happiness through enabling others

Julie Levy

Introduction

Julie Levy qualified as an art teacher in 1980 having previously achieved a BA in Fine Art (Sculpture) at Liverpool Polytechnic. Her career started in a challenging residential school and over the next 20 years she went on to teach a wide range of children and young people of all abilities in both special and mainstream secondary schools, using art and creative writing to engage with them and help them to achieve their potential. Julie was awarded a National Teaching Award for her work with children with Special Educational Needs in 2003 and she went on to become a Senior Teaching Adviser for Lancashire, travelling all over the UK training teachers how to teach and assess the progress of individual pupils who are performing outside normal parameters. During this period Julie was also writing and delivering a modular BA course for Edge Hill University, including the most recent research and innovation in this field into the course content.

By invitation Julie eventually went on to work in the private sector, acting as an education advisor to several IT companies, and as a specialist advisor to architects designing schools under the Building Schools for the Future scheme. She was heavily involved in the designing of Darwen Vale School and Pleckgate School, both of which utilised the latest creative design features. For this part of her career, Julie had to learn about construction techniques, architectural and furniture design, and IT systems and how they worked. The latter was the most challenging as Julie only had day-to-day computer skills but she progressed so much she was able to design the entire IT infrastructure for a new school in Birmingham. Over the next few years Julie helped to open 18 new academies and studio schools and eventually started her own business in 2010. Ten years later, Julie is currently working in the arts as an independent Arts and Education Consultant, across many organisations in Bolton town centre. These include the University of Bolton, Bolton Council, the Bolton Hindu Forum, the Market Place Shopping Centre and Bolton Railway Station where she is heavily involved in the creation of an arts and culture community centre in the old station buildings.

Happiness through enabling

Enabling is defined in the Collins dictionary https://www.collinsdictionary.com/2020 as follows. *'If someone or something enables you to do a particular thing, they give you the opportunity to do it.'* It's not always an easy thing to do, in many cases it takes a long of time to really understand what a person is trying to achieve and what is required to allow that to happen. In the words of Sam Johnson, Head of the School of the Arts at the University of Bolton, it is the 'Greenhouse Effect' - but this one has nothing to do with climate change, and all to do with the particular conditions you need for achievement to happen and happiness to grow.

Boarding school in Devon

My first case study goes back to my very first teaching job at a school in Devon where I was employed as an art teacher. The school no longer exists, but when I was there from 1983 to 1987 it was a 52-week placement boarding school for teenage boys, meaning the students never returned home, or if they did, it was for a weekend visit only. Occasionally parents came to visit them, and whether it was this, or a home visit, it caused a lot of emotional trauma for them both before and after. The school was quite spartan; the dormitories and communal areas were housed in a Tudor mansion which was not very warm and had stone floors. It was a strange combination, this historic and dignified setting and teenage boys who in most cases had quite severe emotional and behavioural difficulties rattling around inside it. They mainly came from Bristol and London and there was an almost half-and-half mix of black and white ethnic backgrounds which made things even more volatile, as it was the time of the race riots in the cities and some of the students had recently been involved in them.

The reasons for the boys' placement there were varied and generally quite complex. Some had been treated badly as children, whilst others had spent time in a Young Offenders Institution mainly for the crime of TWOC which I soon learned was stealing cars. They were young men who mainstream schools were unable to manage. Nearly all had behaviour and learning difficulties and at the time were referred to in documentation as being in the Special Educational Needs and Disabilities (SEND) category of 'Maladjusted'. Terminology in those days was quite harsh, and, as a teacher, I always avoided it whenever I could. It is a sad fact of our education system however that if you want to access funding for supporting children with additional needs; you need a label to describe them. I knew nothing about these students prior to working with them as the management had a policy of a 'fresh start'. This was fine in principle, but in practice it meant that staff were having to try and assess the students' needs whilst teaching them. No mean feat!

There was little evidence that Art was taught there until I arrived – there were certainly no displays of it in the corridors and classrooms which surprised me. I knew from my teaching practice how proud students felt to have their artwork on display, and yet here there was none. The teaching spaces were single storey classrooms out in the yard behind the house and again, were very bleak. There was very little in terms of equipment, although there was a kiln, so I knew that ceramics was an option. Prior to completing my PGCE, I had studied for a degree in Fine Art and had worked in ceramics, and, in particular learned about mould making for a year, so I felt fairly confident I could tackle some basic techniques with them.

From our conversations (usually held whilst they were occupied with a fairly simple activity like colouring in) I started to learn about the students' lives, their hopes, their families and their aspirations for the future. I also learnt some colourful language including swear words in Jamaican patois which, once I had learned them, I would admonish them for using. On the whole they treated me nicely. I heard more than once the words *'Don't diss Miss. She's a lady.'* [*Diss*: If someone disses you, they *criticise* you unfairly or speak to you in a way that does not show respect. https://www.collinsdictionary.com/2020.] Unfortunately, this sentiment did not extend to their behaviour towards each other. Tensions ran high most of the time, and fights were common. The daily regime included frequent breaks on the cold fields next to the classrooms where students were encouraged to play football in the hope of using up their excess energy, but even there, aggressive physical contact was frequent.

The students were very keen to colour in the hand-drawn popular cartoon characters I created for them and I quickly learned that this was a way of establishing some kind of order in the classroom. They would not engage with printed material, the cartoons had to be drawn by me to their satisfaction. Disney characters were highly prized as were the superheroes they chose from my own sons' comic books that I brought into school from home. I realised that I had to reach these students from the learning and developmental stage they were at; they were not going to respond to drawing from observation or painting landscapes. These cartoon characters are what they admired and colouring them in carefully gave them some pride in their achievements, and admiration from their peers.

I observed a strange phenomenon in terms of a few of the students' reaction to praise. These tended to be the boys with the most severe learning difficulties. In hindsight, I think a lot of them had dyslexia but I was not aware of the condition at the time, and as I had not been allowed to read their notes I had no real understanding of their needs apart from through trial and error in the classroom. As a reaction to praise, these particular students would angrily throw away the piece of work you had just praised them for. They did not rip it up but would screw it into a ball and throw it in the waste paper bin, usually exiting the classroom afterwards in a rage. This surprised me at first but I always retrieved the work from the bin, took it home, ironed out the creases and put it on display in the Art Room where the student would not comment when they saw it again. I instinctively began to 'tone down' my praise for good work where a violent reaction would follow. In some cases a discreet thumbs up sign was enough.

Over 20 years later when I was a Senior Teacher Adviser for SEN I heard a lecture by the inspirational behaviour expert Sir John Jones which gave a possible explanation for this. To paraphrase his words, he suggested that mental conditioning from many years of failure and negativity makes some students seek out the situations that will provide this. They are familiar with these feelings and it reinforces the mental model they have of themselves. If you praise them, they do not know how to react because it is something they are unfamiliar with. The example he gave was that if a dog over a period of time sleeps on a rough floor with a nail sticking into its side, eventually it will be the normal way it sleeps, and moving it to a place where there is no nail will make it unsettled (Jones 2020).

Several of the students were respected by their peers, either for their physical strength or their mental superiority, though in the latter case this had to be grounded in knowledge of 'the street' i.e. urban culture. Although in their teens, a lot of the students were the size of adult men with strength to match and were proud of this. I knew from talking to them that as well as street culture including fashion, music and popular imagery they valued their football teams. Rather than drawing outline letters for them to colour in, I decided to try them with sewing and bought some large-weave tapestry canvas and coloured wools. Once the students who were respected started to learn to sew, the others followed and they quickly took to tapestry. We would create the names of their football teams in cross stitch and, strangely, not one of them complained it was not a manly thing to do. I still recall the day one of the senior staff came into my room with a look of incredulity on his face when he found us all quietly sitting around a big table sewing.

Despite being badly treated by their parents, in most cases these young men all had a fierce loyalty to their mothers or 'My old girl' as they liked to describe them. It was common practice for one student to goad another by making some derogatory comment about their mother. This would result in a furious outburst of emotion, usually with aggressive actions and words towards the perpetrator who, if he was wily enough, would alert a member of staff that the student was out of control, resulting in punishment for the victim of the goading. Apart from this quite regular occurrence, I could see they genuinely were fond of their mothers who they hardly ever saw. I think the image they had of their mother had perhaps been idealised in their absence but in any case, I wanted them to be able to make something in the Art lessons that they could give to their mother when they saw her. It had to be of an acceptable standard, something that would be admired and something they could be proud of. I imagined much of the contact these parents had already had with schools was quite negative and thought this would be a way of giving them positive feedback through a tangible manifestation of a creative action.

The students loved this idea and we started to think what might be the best thing to make. At this point they started to look at the kiln and considered making pottery or, more specifically, an ornament they could give to their mother or other significant family member (in some cases grandmothers had taken the place of their mothers). I knew that hand making pots would not give them the quality of product they were expecting so we looked at moulds for slip casting*, and I had a catalogue with some examples in it. Slip casting would allow the students to produce a high standard of finish that looked very competent. [*Slip casting is a method of making a ceramic object by filling a plaster mould with a liquid mixture of clay and water called slip, letting some of the water be absorbed by the plaster leaving a layer of clay on the mould and then pouring out the excess liquid. The cast is then left to dry before opening the mould. The object can then be fired in a kiln.]

I decided to buy a selection of moulds for them to choose from and they picked things like a seated cat or dog, and also one of a house. All these models were very traditional and, in my eyes, quite kitsch - but to them they were highly desirable and so these are what we made! Making the slip was a task I could give to a student who needed something calming to occupy them. It proved strangely popular, as did sharpening all the coloured pencils in our pencil tray. There must have been a hundred of them, but some students would come in and ask me if they could do that so I let them as it was satisfying and gave them a repetitive task they could do that would sooth them. To make slip a quite a large piece of clay had to be repeatedly squeezed between fingers in a bucket of water until there were no lumps - just thick, creamy, liquid slip.

We often had art lessons where students were all doing different things. It was harder to organise but lead to better outcomes if there was an element of choice. I think it would be called 'personalisation' now but back then it was the way I was learning to teach this group of highly emotional and volatile young men (Department for Education and Skills 2004). And so, we began the production of our ornaments. I made several myself beforehand to ensure I gave them the instructions that would result in success as I knew the importance the ornaments had for them. Soon a selection of unglazed ornaments started to appear which helped them to decide which one they wanted to make. We could only produce 4 or 5 at a time as we only had that many moulds but they were happy to take turns and we soon had a production line started. I had already decided that glazing the pots was too risky. There was a higher chance of failure and my skills were not up to the standard they needed to be for intricate glazing, so I decided to help them paint and then varnish the fired pots. After firing, the base colour was put on by the students, but the fine detail I completed for them to their instructions. It seems strange, but they did not mind me finishing things off for them. As long as it was to their satisfaction, it was as if I did not exist as a person, I was just a facilitator to help them create something they really prized. The concentration on these ornaments was intense. They were the first things they wanted to see when they came into the classroom and had to be regularly viewed to satisfy themselves they were of a good enough standard. I did not let the ornaments go out of the room because I knew exactly what would happen in the communal areas of the school, and I wanted to make sure they had their work intact to take home or present to their family on the rare occasion they visited.

One student in particular showed real promise and I felt sure he would be able to take a qualification in Art. I made enquiries with the local comprehensive school and had arrangements made for him to submit work as an external General Certificate of Secondary Education (GCSE) candidate. He needed a lot of encouragement and support, but did gain a grade in Art and Design producing his coursework mainly in my classroom when it was a quieter time. Many years later I was teaching in Exeter and he knocked at my classroom door. I was amazed he had found me and even more amazed when he told me he was now a policeman and had wanted me to know. Although it was extremely challenging working at the school, I will never forget my three years there and I am confident the students remember those times too. To finish this case study I have included a quote from an email I received in 2014 from a man, now 48, who was one of my students. He had tracked me through my business website even though I had a different surname by then. I cannot begin to describe how humbled I felt when I received it. *'I still have a clay house I made in your class and we baked it and glossed it, I still have it lol. You know a lot of us had troubles and there wasn't many staff we trusted, but you was cool like you let us be creative and weren't a nag lol.'*

Special needs co-ordinating at Wigan

Twelve years later I stood at the gates of a secondary comprehensive school near Wigan ready for an interview for the position of SENDCo (Special Educational Needs and Disabilities Coordinator). Upon entering, it was obviously lesson changeover time where pupils must move from room to room, and I was struck by the apparent chaos in the corridors, with groups of pupils shouting, pushing and generally bursting through the throng.

Like many schools in the area, the school had formerly served mining and mill communities and with the decline of both of these industries there were inevitable high levels of unemployment, with some families into the third generation who had never had paid work. The immediate area was dominated by a large council estate where, at that time, levels of poverty were deemed to be among the worst in Europe. Drug use was common, as was alcohol abuse and ill health. It was in effect a 'challenging' school, so challenging in fact that one of the candidates for the post left before the end of the interview. I however was made of sterner stuff, and having secured the job, I started to look at the data held on the pupils and in particular the Special Needs Register. Here it became apparent that over a quarter of the school population had been identified as SEN for either learning or behaviour. This was a staggering number of pupils who would require a great deal of extra help and support. The staff I had available to deploy across the whole school amounted to two Teaching Assistants (TAs), who were fortunately very knowledgeable and experienced. My first job was to get the register into some kind of order so I could identify who were the most needy children, what the types of learning and behaviour needs were, and how I could begin to organise the right levels of support. Astonishingly although there were so many pupils on the SEN register, only two had Statements of Special Educational Needs, which meant they had been assessed by a child psychologist as being of a severe level of need that required extra provision in school which was different from that being made for the other children. This came with an amount of money which could be used to partly employ a Teaching Assistant. One pupil had been allocated a full time TA, a valuable third person who at the time I arrived spent all day sitting beside this pupil helping him to access the curriculum and manage his behaviour. He had complex and challenging behaviour needs which I quickly discovered were exacerbated by the close proximity of the TA, who wrote lengthy observational notes about him which she passed to me every day. Eventually, I managed to persuade his mother and school staff this was not in fact the best way of supporting him and I formed a small group of pupils within the class who all had SEND, using the TA to work with all of them and decreasing the pressure on the one student.

I had just spent two years working for a most wonderfully talented SENDCo in a large comprehensive in Knowsley so I felt confident that I could make inroads here and improve school life and, hopefully, prospects for a lot of these pupils. I worked hard to involve parents in their child's education and started to hold meetings exclusively for the parents of SEND pupils. These became opportunities to learn more about the circumstances and lives of my pupils, building my understanding of what help was required. In some cases this was family support, in addition to support at school, and I found myself getting a real picture of how life worked for many of the local families. It was little wonder the pupils with behaviour difficulties acted as they did in school with, in many cases, such chaotic and deprived lives outside. I realised I had to look much deeper into the situation of my SEND pupils to really respond to their needs.

It took me about a year to wrestle the SEND register into a manageable working document, with some pupils removed, as their difficulties were general and amongst this particular school population did not rate highly enough to warrant extra support. Reading ages were generally low, and I discovered the reading test used only covered reading ages of nine upwards, so many of the pupils were recorded at a reading age of below nine. I introduced a wider range of tests, including one for dyslexia, and gradually untangled the web of SEN that spread through this school, working closely with both the child psychologist, a behaviour advisor from the Local Authority, social workers, the local police and many other specialist educational and medical professionals who were involved in the lives of the pupils and their families. Nearly every child I formally referred to the psychologist was awarded a SEN Statement with funding, and a large cohort was also awarded funding to support their behaviour in school. By this time, I had been put in charge of both learning and behaviour support and had a team of ten TAs to deploy across the school. In addition I had created a large inclusion unit known across the school as 'Room 2' to avoid any stigma of going there. It was strictly timetabled. Pupils were allocated slots according to their needs and the classes available each day. Multi agency staff from outside the school worked with targeted groups of pupils covering topics which responded to their needs both inside and outside school. This included a group for children who were in care, another for boys at risk of offending, a third for young women who needed sexual health instruction, and a fourth for pupils who had been the victims of bullies. It was very wide-ranging. I even had a community police officer stationed in the school for some of the week and a social worker available most days.

As part of my preparation for the next year's intake, I would visit the local primary schools where most of the pupils came from. The knowledge I gleaned from these meetings was invaluable and meant I could prepare for these children in an appropriate way. I became aware of the most vulnerable children from the primary SENDCos, and started to see a pattern emerging that was in many instances very worrying. Many of the children they were most concerned about when transferring to a secondary setting seemed to have developmental delay in addition to learning needs, presenting as much younger children. In the primary setting this was dealt with effectively by things like placing the child for part of the day with a class of younger children or giving them 'time out' to play with toys. In some cases these were designed for very young children including in one school, a 'Wendy House' (a small model house for children to play in) normally found in nursery schools catering for under-fives. The environment these children were going to move into did not provide opportunities for this kind of individualised and specific provision, and I started to understand why we were getting some quite alarming responses from pupils in Year 7, the intake year, which usually manifested in outbursts of aggressive or inappropriate behaviour punished by school sanctions and, in some cases exclusion from school. It was also seen as 'fair play' for some of the older pupils to goad the younger and, especially more vulnerable ones into misbehaving for their own amusement, or to bully them both in the school yard and outside school. Although staff were on duty in the school grounds they could not be everywhere and, sadly, there were enough older pupils and even peers willing to mistreat immature, younger ones to make their lives very unhappy at school. I needed a solution.

I then discovered Nurture Groups. These are specially designed learning environments that support children who need a completely different emphasis to their personal curriculum. The Nurture Group Network, a national body who set out the recommendations for the setting up and running of such groups describe them in the following manner:

'Nurture groups were originally developed in 1969 in London by educational psychologist Marjorie Boxall who saw that a large number of children entering school arrived with severe social, emotional and behavioural needs. These students were unable to form trusting relationships with adults or to respond appropriately to other children – in effect, they were simply not ready to meet the social and intellectual demands of school life.' (Boxall and Lucas 2002; Boxall Principle 2002).

Children are usually placed in a Nurture Group in a primary school. It provides an immersive environment which focuses on accelerating the child's emotional and social development in addition to catering for their learning needs. Two adults are always present in the room and model the kind of behaviour and social interaction the children are encouraged to adopt; they verbalise their actions and are very polite in their exchanges. The room is set out partly as a learning space, whilst other parts of it contain essential elements for delivering the 'nurturing' experiences. During a school day the children will have opportunities to learn together, eat and drink together, play together and are always encouraged to respect and support each other, including in the playground (Nurture Groups 2020). The original primary model did not quite fit a secondary school, so I had to develop a model that followed the principles but responded to this very different environment. I wrote a short paper outlining my ideas which I had to present to my line manager the Deputy Head, and the Head Teacher. They were initially sceptical, but allowed me to then explain my ideas to the school governors. They, surprisingly, seemed to agree to all my proposals and to the very modest budget I asked for. Over the school holidays I worked hard to create my

Nurture Group. Building works were needed to block the windows onto the school corridors. I did not want my pupils to be observed as 'specimens' by the others. However, I was aware how curious they would be and made sure there were prearranged opportunities for older pupils to visit the room during the first term. I had to provide information and the timetable to the rest of the staff and the parents of the pupils identified as needing this provision, and get them to support the venture if it was to succeed. I identified a suitable classroom right at the front of the school, next to Room 2. My Nurture Group room contained four rows of ordinary school desks with a teacher's desk at the front and a whiteboard behind, a dining table big enough for all the pupils and staff to sit around, a large sink, a full length mirror, a huge settee that could seat about eight of us, some bean bags, books and toys like Lego and construction kits, board and card games, and a portable music player. I also had four computer stations set up at the very back of the room. I trained one of my more experienced TAs in the routines we needed to follow with the pupils and made sure my teaching timetable permitted me to be with them every morning. The other subject teachers agreed for at least the first term to come to the room to deliver their lessons, meaning that the Nurture Group could stay in this special environment designed around their needs for as much of the day as possible. I made sure they had a safe place to be outside and obtained permission for them to use the courtyard garden at the centre of the school with break times different from that of the rest of the school. As far as I could anticipate, we were ready for the first intake.

And they arrived. I think I started off with eight or nine, but this quickly built to thirteen as further pupils were identified who had been put into other classes and were suffering as a consequence. The profiles of SEND across the group varied enormously from developmental delay, general and specific learning difficulties, including dyslexia, dyscalculia (similar to dyslexia but with numbers) autism, medical needs, mental health needs and general behaviour needs across the board. Reading ages varied from about 5 to 13. One of my pupils could not even manage to sit on a chair when he arrived and sat or lay underneath his desk on the floor instead for the first few weeks. I had arranged the desks in 3 rows with 4 seats in each row, and the dining table doubled up as a further working space. Interestingly the children wanted to be in the seats next to my teacher's desk, and so I ended up with all of the front row desks butted up to mine. Our day was closely in line with the rest of the school in that we had registration, lesson times, break times and lunch times. However, the flexibility came when I had the group to teach. This is when the TA and I could concentrate not only on raising their academic skills but also improving their social and emotional skills and most importantly, their general understanding of how their community, families and the school setting had to work collaboratively. The full-length mirror in a Nurture Group room is designed to assist this process by showing the children how they appear to other people. Many of the children in the group still internalised their concept of 'self', seeing the world in terms of their needs. So, in effect, the viewing of themselves is a step towards being outside themselves and a step towards developing empathy and an understanding of the behaviours needed to successfully integrate with their peers, and ultimately, the wider school community and the world outside school.

We spent a lot of time learning turn-taking, developing the patience to wait, learning how to deal with losing as well as winning, and the concept of conversation being 'speaking but also listening'. The TA and I modelled formal conversational exchanges e.g. '*Good Morning Miss*'. *Isn't the weather lovely today?*' '*Good Morning to you too Miss. Yes, it's a lovely sunny day.*' [In the school the female teachers were all referred to as 'Miss'. All the male teachers were called 'Sir'.] Gradually we noticed the children copying us, and they also started to speak more freely to each other. Every day we started with a speaking and listening session with the children sitting at their desks, covering subjects as broad ranging as pets, home settings, grandparents, allotments, meals and, sadly, with bereavement. At least one of the pupils had lost a parent and some of them had already lost grandparents, as life expectancy in the area was generally low. During these sessions each child was allowed to contribute while the others had to listen. I had to respond in an appropriate manner, guiding the conversation with questions where necessary and not showing an emotional response to the sometimes very graphic and colourful things that came up. We learned manners. We learned 'Please', 'Thank you', 'Could you please pass?' and 'Excuse me' and we learned to stand when a member of staff came in, until told to sit down. Their manners developed quite quickly once they realised certain actions and words elicited praise from the staff and even from their peers. Some of the subject teachers who came into the room to teach started to tell me how they looked forward to the lessons as the pupils were so well behaved, a fact I shared with the pupils and which surprised them very much. They were used to thinking of themselves as not very able, low attaining and in receipt of negative comments so this was a big change. I worked hard to build their self-esteem at every opportunity for example, in our English lessons when we were looking at adjectives I would create sentences on the board that included every member of the class in a positive way; Michael is marvellous, Susan is sensational, George is great! To supplement group learning, the TA would work on individual or small group learning targets. We read together to give the weaker readers confidence. I had purchased some 'Big Books' or oversized reading books with large print designed to be read by a group of children, usually in primary school. I would read to them pointing to the words as I spoke them. This was no mean feat as the book was standing on my desk and I was reaching over from behind, reading it upside down. They loved these books and the stories and poems. We read them over and over until they knew them by heart and they loved speaking together as a group. Their confidence grew across the board. They started to care for each other with the more socially able ones becoming nurturing themselves towards the most needy. They became more emotionally aware and started to show curiosity about the rest of the school. And above all they were happy! Instances of absenteeism had plummeted; behaviour was greatly improved and this had happened not just in the Group but across the school. Amazingly, it seemed that having a Nurture Group in the school had made the whole place more aware of the needs of others.

One day near Christmas we were making paper chains to decorate the classroom. This involved cutting coloured paper up and then fixing each loop with tape. The next loop was then formed through the previous one making a chain. This exercise was keeping everyone occupied and thinking about numbers whilst they conversed in an appropriate manner. We were working as a team and everyone was making sections, and then joining them to the main chain to lengthen it. Very soon we had a chain that reached around the whole room, so we made it go around again until the bell rang for change of lesson. They were so disappointed! We had all been so engrossed it the activity we had not seen the time passing. I had the children for the next lesson as well and so I made the decision to carry on for another hour. Their delight was plain to see. I waited until the rest of the school had started the next lesson and then I opened the classroom door. 'Come on', I said. 'We're going to take it right down the corridor'. And that is exactly what we did! We took it along the corridor past several classrooms, and then round the corner along the next corridor. The children were amazed at the end of the lesson at what we had achieved and I can honestly say they didn't stop talking about it for months. I think what was interesting was they felt they had been allowed to do something very special; not just by carrying on an activity they were really enjoying but also by temporarily taking possession of a space that could normally be seen as a place of potential threat to them i.e. the school corridor.

In the New Year I started to let those who wanted to go outside in the yard at breaktime do so, but with the proviso that they were not alone as I knew they would be vulnerable. Initially the TA went to look after them but I was pleased to see on a day that I was covering supervision duty for the whole school that my Nurture Group children were moving together like a small pack. No-one was pushed aside or excluded, and I think they had realised that together they were too big and visible a target for the bullies to take on. In fact, they seemed to develop somewhat of a celebrity status within the school and other pupils in other years became quite proud of them, and used to come and play games and read with them in the Nurture Room. I even successfully included a very intelligent school refuser who was 14 and experienced Asperger's syndrome (high functioning autism). He had been out of school for a very long time and when he visited with his mother he went around the school holding on to the walls as he was so overwhelmed. In the Nurture Group structured routine he was treated just the same as the other pupils and was expected to join in with appropriate responses, which he gradually learned to do. Years later I found out that my school refuser had not only gone on to successfully pass his exams, but in fact he was studying for a degree at University, something both he and his mother had never thought possible.

Bolton Station community project.

My last case study is set more recently in 2019. By then I had pretty much finished working for a salary other than a few specialist projects which I chose to complete, mainly in the Arts field, and was working as a volunteer for Bolton Station Community Partnership. We very much wanted to open a gallery in the station platform buildings, and with the help of many other volunteers and the support of the University of Bolton School of the Arts, Network Rail and Northern we managed to achieve this in July 2019. One of the first exhibitions we scheduled was of Railway Workers Art and for this there was a national call-out for submissions. In the end I had only eight participating artists but the quality and variety of the work was astounding.

The artists were required to drop off their work and so in this way I met them all and heard their stories. All of them had full time jobs in railway stations, but also had a passion for producing art which motivated them to work long hours being creative. Some of the work was railway related photography, whilst some was painting and drawing. It covered a very wide range of subject matter from portraiture to landscapes, both real and imagined. One artist in particular visited the gallery many times, and we talked in depth about his artwork and about the book he had written which complemented the themes within his work. None of the artists had shown their work in a gallery before. Every one of them accepted the space I had created was indeed a gallery although some of them remembered its former use as a mailsack sorting office and pointed out the markings on the floor where the sacks had been piled up. I had tried to keep some of the history of the space so people could relate to it as part of the railway station but also make it neutral enough to let the artworks really stand out. I had four large display columns built from sheets of MDF, in fact the whole gallery had been put together for a few hundred pounds and many hours of volunteer work.

The pride the artists had in seeing their work hung in the gallery was evident. I curated the exhibition myself, giving each artist the best possible exposure I could, and we held a preview to which they were encouraged to invite their families and friends. We also invited local dignitaries and people from senior managerial posts in the railway companies and the School of the Arts. It was a joyous occasion! The artists were able to talk about their work both to the guests, from whom they received compliments and praise, and to each other. They were exploring techniques and exchanging ideas and it struck me at that point that in the main these men had worked for years on their art in solitude. They had all read about other artists but had not actually spoken to any. Most of them worked at home and although some of them had sold work, it was not sales that motivated them. They were united by a common need to create.

The exhibition attracted many visitors who were curious to see what was happening in the station buildings. Both the general public and railway workers came to see the exhibition and without exception everyone found something they could respond to. The work had a certain quality about it, being very accessible and commenting on aspects of life that immediately engaged the viewer. Many tales were told of days gone by and memories of the railways from years ago – it made me realise just how important railway stations were and are to people still. They are places of great emotion, of arrivals and departures that in some cases mark points in time that are followed by feelings of great sorrow or feelings of great joy. They are places of movement and energy punctuated by periods of stillness and waiting but, above all, they are places that belong to the community.

To conclude this case study and this chapter, the artist who had written the book actually resigned from his job at the railway station and set up his own business. He told me it had been a turning point for him and made him realise what he really wanted to do with his life. He just lacked the confidence to make the move. I am happy to report he now paints canvasses for residents in care homes who apparently engage with him as he works in a very positive manner.

Some have dementia and are not usually communicative but watching him paint seems to trigger their memories, and he is receiving very positive reviews from his employers. He also has an artist's studio where he continues to work but now in the daylight and not just at night. He says he has never been happier.

References

Boxall, M. and Lucas, S (2002) *Nurture Groups in Schools: Principles and Practice.* London: Paul Chapman

Boxall Principle (2002) Measure children's emotional, social and behavioural development in Nurture Groups. [Accessed on 23rd June 2020 at https://www.nurtureuk.org/introducing-nurture/boxall-profile]

Collins online dictionary [Accessed 23rd June 2020 at https://www.collinsdictionary.com/]

Department for Education and Skills (2004) *Personalised Learning.* [Accessed on 23rd June 2020 at https://dera.ioe.ac.uk/5932/1/personalisedlearning.pdf]

Jones, J. (2020) Welcome - Sir John Jones contains videos of lectures [Accessed on 23rd June 2020 at https://sirjohnjones.com/]

Jones, J. and Fallon, M., (2011) *The Magic Weaving Business. Finding the Heart of Learning and teaching.* Ireland: Leannta Publishing.

Nurture Groups [Accessed 23rd June 2020 at https://www.nurtureuk.org/nurture/what-nurture-group]

Fitness and happiness

Ken Heathcote

Introduction

Choosing four individuals was probably one of the easiest choices of my career. Bill Pearl lives on the historic Oregon Trail in Southern Oregon and has been a friend for over fifty years. We have had many conversations about life, cultures, bodybuilding, running and writing books, this left no doubt in my mind that we shared a similar philosophy, together with the love of exercise.

'Life is movement and all movement is life' were the words of Eugene Sandow, the father of physical culture over a hundred years ago. Exercise is simply a controlled expression of Sandow's beliefs and take on life (Sandow, 2012).

My choice of Dr George Sheehan, Runner, Doctor, Author, Cardiologist, his eloquence brought poetry to running when everyone just saw it as being about blood, guts and dedication. Overnight people saw the re-invention of a sport into a hobby and pastime with fun being the operative word.

My third choice is Edward Taub and the only one who is not sports related, but he brings happiness to millions. He is a Behavioural Neuroscientist who through a physical exercise programme called constraint-induced movement therapy treats stroke victims or people with brain disorders helping them cope with the challenges in their lives.

For me, I just loved to work-out and compete. My first love was weight-lifting and body-building, but outgrowing my potential I found a new love of running and finally swimming. Like Sandow, my life was movement and all of that movement brought happiness.

Dr George Sheehan

The late George Sheehan, Runner, Doctor, Cardiologist, Philosopher and Author lived in Boston USA. His passion in life was running and it was his books on running that would change the face of running forever.

Prior to 1975 running was for athletes who ran to compete. Sheehan changed that concept with his first book in 1975, Sheehan on Running ironically it was his second book Running and Being (1978) that became the Times best seller; selling over 1 million copies; a huge success fifty years ago. Many more millions would embrace Sheehan's philosophy. He saw the value of just running for pleasure; the struggle was not against others, but one's self. The experience was the ultimate feeling, body, mind and the challenge of being the person you wanted to be. He believed the reasons for running exceeded the numbers of days in his life. 'The more I run, the more I want to run' [accessed 12.6.20 at George Sheehan Quotes, https:// allauthor.com/quotes/92424].

He would say, he found freedom in his daily run, creativity and an escape from the pressures of life. He also found solace through the pain and challenge. His words still ring clear from half century ago when he said:

> 'Live if you like a life without risk. Avoid the fire, the forge and the flame, but know that joy and happiness and the good life come only as unexpected interludes in the endless stressful, tense and restless journey to become the person you are.' [Accessed 12.6.20 at Dr Sheehan On Running, Input the Output, https://thinkfastwaitrun.blogspot.com/2014/09/].

Sheehan clearly struck a chord with so many people. This would be the start of running for fun! His love for the Boston Marathon would be the subject of his entire book; the challenge was there in his own city. The cult following would demand something more in towns and cities across the World. Fun runs would be the norm; everyone across all ages would be doing 10'ks, half-marathons and marathons. The commercial side of this would create this concept into mass marathons across the Planet. In the footsteps of Sheehan's Boston; New York, London, Paris, Rotterdam, Berlin and many more would expand the running world to unprecedented heights. The fun would follow with the comic figures running in Mickey Mouse suits, Superman outfits, the Incredible Hulk and everything the imagination could conjure up. Charities would catch on to this and in time push the boundaries to bike rides, park runs and anything to raise money for the needy. The focal point of the charities would first, transform a hobby into a sport and then sport into a hobby. Serious runners and world class runners would be tempted to run in fun runs and the connection merging a seamless transition from serious to fun and back again.

Happiness however, comes with many faces; the serious runner, like Sheehan, seeks solace in pain; the challenge, the stress, the fire, the forge, the flame. It is not enough to take part, but to win, to exceed the person I can be with my own fastest time; to flog the others. For the competitive runner it is war; in their world it is about winning medals, trophies, awards and podiums. There is no give or take, no Mickey Mouse! The Superman is I. The intensity is depleting, destructive and debilitating to the point of collapse. The war is both external and internal; it is I against the world, self-brutal, unforgiving, and unrepentant when measuring against oneself.

I guess Sheehan's philosophy was as near to the serious competitive runner you could possibly get, but his genius was to write it with the rhythm of a runner in the zone in the feeling that I have mastered myself. To write it in such a way that the fun runner and the serious runner were really of one; whatever the reason, it worked. For all of us and them, or them and us were happy just running and being.

Bill Pearl

Bill Pearl is a Native American and a collector of cars. At the age of 12 Bill was delivering papers to a customer and in the backyard overgrown with grass and sinking into a boggy part of the garden he saw what was to become his first car financed with money saved from his paper round. This car, a much desired Ford Model T purchased nearly eighty years ago would be the first of his twenty five vintage cars. His collection includes a Ford Mustang, Lincoln Continental, Rolls Royce and practically every major car manufacturer in the USA; all painstakingly renovated and in mint condition by Bill himself; a grand total of twenty five cars.

Bill now 89 years of age is a remarkable man. His hobby of finding cars that could only be described as wrecks is just one of his many talents. Bill and his wife Judy have been friends of my wife and me for over forty years. Their fairy tale ranch in the hills of Southern Oregon is on Mockingbird Lane and the town is appropriately called Talent. This is almost symbolic of his wide range of skills, and yes Talents.

He has eight books to his name, three of which are best sellers; his collection of vintage cars is matched with his collection of vintage push bikes and his collection of trophies is even more surprising, when we realise that Bill Pearl, a Northern American Indian, is a four times Mr Universe. Yes, Bill is a bodybuilding icon. In addition to his four times Mr Universe he holds the title of the World's Best Physique. He is a Mr America, Mr USA and Mr California; these are only a part of his multitude of bodybuilding titles. He has trained Astronauts, world class athletes and was the senior judge for the Mr Olympia and the only bodybuilder to beat Arnold Swarzenegger. Bill Pearl's Pasadena Health Club was considered to be one of the best gyms in the World before he retired nearly forty years ago (Pearl, 1986).

Bill would say to me many times 'I am never more happy.' He would also say the same about his hobby of renovating cars. Brenda and I have seen Pearl on more than one occasion with delight on his face beaming at an item from a scrap yard; an engine part, petrol pump or a pair of wing mirrors; the promise of making it work, bringing it to life for something that otherwise would be condemned to the crusher! I am just happy to be a muscle head he would say. His knowledge and lifelong occupation would say different! Pearl loved to train; his visits to our club in Bolton would speak volumes for his reputation. Over the years hundreds would turn up when it became know that Pearl was in town; his obvious joy of working out with others, together with their privilege of sharing some time with an icon of bodybuilding worldwide.

Like George Sheehan, Bill Pearl is a philosopher, poet and writer; Sheehan was a runner, Pearl, a weight man. Both sharing an inner peace, both icons in their own right, comfortable in their own skims and no wish to be anything other than what they are. Bill said to me quite recently,

'While I never felt the euphoria described as 'runner's high' I always felt better physically and mentally after a workout. Moreover, everything I love, everything own, everything I have accomplished in life can be attributed to my weight training. The relationships and long time friendships with people I treasure are all directly related to weight training. I believe it has added tremendously to my quality of life and positive outlook. It is something that can be shared and paid forward.'

Jonah Barrington

Another icon Jonah Barrington (A legend in Squash in the 1970's) was another, who like Pearl and Sheehan was only happy with his chosen sport. I had the good fortune of bringing these two remarkable people together in 1982. I had brought Bill over to the UK to tour the country promoting his book, Keys to the Inner Universe, (Pearl, 1979). He would on my behalf appear at three seminars, one of these was in Birmingham and the home town of Jonah Barrington. Two icons, two articulate men, sharing their own particular areas of expertise; two entirely different sports, one all movement fast and slow; two different physiologies and two different psychologies, two people from entirely different backgrounds living two countries apart, both with one common denominator. Both masters of their own talent, energies and expertise; opposites with an understanding of the others commitments and what it took to win. The three of us would stand in the grounds of Barrington's home; the symmetry of their conversation was electric. How people so far apart could be as one, was for me a moment of sheer magic. They were both happy to share this exclusive private conversation with no reservations, and no one happier than me to experience being a part of this.

The word happiness is in itself subjective; it is transient, fleeting and in Sheehan's words contained in those unexpected interludes. Those interludes on the lawn of Jonah Barrington's home were everything that Sheehan described; for me, and I think for them too, moments to be remembered to this day, nearly 40 years ago.

Ken Heathcote – exercise and happiness – swimming

The year was 1945 and to be more precise May 8ᵗʰ and to be even more precise, 3 o'clock in the afternoon. The time Winston Churchill announced the end of WW2. It was said that the whole of the British Isles would come to a stop and you could have heard a pin drop in the factories, on the streets, in the offices and homes across the country. Churchill would speak of a better future; it was time to celebrate, a time to allow ourselves a brief period of rejoicing; hope was heavy in the air with the promise of enlightenment that hostilities would end and it would be the start of a new beginning - *Happiness alongside relief for all*. Along with my Mother I would listen to this momentous time in our lives. I was just a few weeks from my 10ᵗʰ birthday. Our council house was full of friends and neighbours and just three miles from the pit known as Newtown Colliery in Swinton. At the precise time of 3.15 Churchill was speaking of a brighter future when a thousand feet down and a mile into the coal face Joe Heathcote, my Dad, was picking away and loading coal onto the conveyor belt that would take the coal to the surface. There would be no warning, just a crack and the coal face would collapse bring down tonnes of earth and rock breaking my Dad's back in three places.

He always said that he was lucky! The three fractures allowed the spine to survive and Joe Heathcote would walk again and a burning ambition would be achieved. At the age of 8 Joe Heathcote would watch a close friend drown in a pond near his home and the guilt would live with him because he could not swim. This guilt would manifest itself in being driven into making sure that his children would not lack this skill. I would be the first of his children to be taught the skill and art of swimming the crawl; something I would cherish for the rest of my life.

It would take 8 months for Dad to recover and his first foray into normality would be to take me to the local swimming baths. This incredibly important day in my life was the Friday before Christmas and Friday was club night at Farnworth Baths. We trudged through the snow on a bitterly cold night for swimmers. From the street we went straight to the changing cubicles, into our trunks and straight to the poolside. It was here we discovered Dad and I were the only ones who had changed for swimming; everyone was stood around the pool fully dressed and with no intention of entering the water.

The reason for this was there had been no delivery of coal to heat the pool. The rationing of fuel alongside other things, petrol, fruits from abroad and even sweets. The water was like a sheet of glass, we were told later it was only 4 degrees; any colder and it would probably have frozen over! Seeing all my idols, first team trainers and senior members, the elite of our club, all stood fully clothes, arms folded, looking miserable and also looking straight at Dad and me. Without any hesitation Dad turned to me, he raised one finger and said, 'come on Kenneth, let's just do one length.' This was not an order or even a request, it was just something we needed to do and we did. I still believe to this day that this was the fastest length I have ever swum.

Walking back past all of my heroes he turned and very quietly said 'you have just beaten this lot tonight Kenneth – you have to be in it to win it.' Now at the age of 84 I ask myself how much those few minutes in time affected the rest of my life. Perhaps in part this was answered 72 years later when I challenged myself at the age of 82 to swim the 10.5 miles of Lake Windermere. The conditions that day were atrocious, heavy rain, low cloud, choppy water and a force six wind blowing in my face for the durations of the swim. Wading out by the side of the pier to push off I felt my courage deserting me. In every excuse I found a reason not to do it! The clouds would block out the heat of the sun; a force six wind would push me back; the coldness of the water would restrict my movement. I could not, though not, did not want to do this on this day and then right on cue up popped Dad and with one finger in the air, he said, 'come on Kenneth, let's just do one length' and I did – 1 length 10.5 miles.

Reading is to the mind, as exercise is to the body; is the old proverb, but switch them around and they come out the same. We seek solace in the gym, the water, on the field of play; lifting heavy weights demands concentrated effort, so does running a 10k, half marathon, or twenty six miles 365 yards; mind and body working hard leaves no space for worry, anxiety or boredom. It was the German philosopher Fredrick Nietzsche who said 'That which does not kill us makes us stronger' [accessed on 9.6.20 at https://www. brainyquote.com/quotes/friedrich_nietzsche_101616] and so it is. *Happiness is a by-product of commitment.*

With over seventy five years of exercise behind me I can look back and see the very things that bring contentment, a feeling of satisfaction, a job well done and an understanding of why!. If we have a why we have purpose; with purpose we have a future and with future we have happiness. In his book Man's Search for Meaning (1946) Victor Frankel talks of man's happiness not to be pursued, but as a side effect of a reason to be happy. Sheehan, Pearl, Joe Heathcote and his son all find happiness as a side effect of exercise. Frankel's description of happiness is interwoven with words used by Sheehan; tension, striving, struggle, all for a worthwhile cause; a goal, what one is and what one is to become. Finding that meaning brings happiness; happiness is the by-product of striving, running, lifting and swimming just that one length; the final mile in a 10k, half or full marathon; or the love of just being a bodybuilder. With all that we do, purpose, meaning and fulfilment inevitably means happiness, and to a greater degree a sense of balance to our lives. Living in the unimaginable confines of Auschwitz, Victor Frankel found a balance to his life by developing the power to find solace to hundreds of people who without hope would have died alone and goalless.

For all that we do there is a law; Criminal Law, Law of Attraction, the Seven Laws of the Universe, the Law of Cause and Effect, the Law of the Wild, the Unwritten Laws, Twenty thousand Laws just governing the use and ownership of guns and the twenty two inimitable Laws of Marketing. No one, in whatever life we live can escape the Laws of the Universe. It is said, there are only two sure things in life, death and taxes; except there is another and that is the Law of diminishing returns and that affects us all and every species. The law of growing old and how we manage it and the happiness it rings.

Finding the balance to these phenomena is the great challenge for the industrial world. Our Nations are becoming older along with our ageing limbs; the process of balance, movement, speed of thought, hearing, sight, taste and for many isolation, is the time we need to find happiness enjoying this twilight of our lives. We all come down to just one thing and that is, *'where do we find the inspiration, the inspiration to do what we have to do'* and that's all down to how we think. Everything we do begins with a thought; the thoughts become words, the words are then transferred into action, practice or movement; these become our habits and the habits become our destiny.

Think
Talk
Practice
Habit
Destiny

How we move, what we see, why we do it! No one can erase the memories of fulfilment, or the belly laughs of humour, but the quiet contemplation of me.

Edward Taub

Edward Taub is a behavioural neuroscientist on the faculty at the University of Alabama in Birmingham USA. He is best known for his involvement in the Silver Spring Monkeys case and for making major breakthroughs in the area of neuroplasticity and discovering/developing constraint induced movement therapy; a family of techniques which helps the rehabilitation of people who have developed learned non-use, as a result of suffering neurological injuries from a stroke or other cause.

Taub's techniques have helped survivors regain the use of paralysed limbs and have been hailed by the American Stroke Association as at the forefront of a revolution. The Society of Neuroscience cited Taub's work as one of the top 10 translational Neuroscience accomplishments of the 20th century and he was awarded the 2004 Distinguished Scientific Contribution Award from the American Psychological Association (2014).

Edward Taub is one of many Neuroscientists who believe that brain is not hard wired and can be manipulated to change to rewire after damage. Victims of stroke, brain tumours, traumas, can by exercise become rewired and carry on a near normal life and even recover fully in some cases.

Taub calls his method 'constraint exercise induced therapy.' In simple terms the patient is forced to work the affected limbs. Stroke victims with arm disability will work the arm and restrain the good arm accordingly (Wikipedia, 2020).

Norman Doidge

Taub is not alone. Another Neuroscientist, Norman Doidge, produced two books, *The Brain That Changes Itself* (2007) and *The Brains Way of Healing* (2015). Along with Professor Michael Merzenich's book *Soft Wired* (2013) they are just three of thousands exploring the possibilities of the New Age Therapies to address debilitating conditions of the brain.

Whatever the therapy, it is always satisfying to know that exercise will play a huge part in all kinds of recovery and successful recovery will culminate in people feeling better and happier than they would without exercise. We are now at the cusp of needing to discover new ways to treat not just the accidents of nature, but the ageing population and the onset of Dementia, Alzheimer's, Parkinson's and the many other diseases of our brains. Exercise will undoubtedly play a huge part in this new frontier of healing and hopefully a happier Nation or Nations.

Norman Doidge is a Psychoanalyst and is in the faculty of the University of Toronto's Department of Psychiatry. His book 'The Brain that Changes Itself' (2007) sold over a million copies and was chosen by The Dana Foundations Journal Cerebrum as the best general book in English ever written on the brain [accessed on 12.6.20 at https://www.dana.org/category/cerebrum]. At the research faculty of Columbia University's centre for Psychoanalytic Training and Research in New York, Doidge, like so many of his peers across the world believes in physical exercise in rehabilitation of the damaged brain; But, what of prevention? What about the problem of Obesity?

There seems little doubt that Dementia and Obesity are connected (Xu et al., 2011). In a large scale study by an international consortium of researchers obesity was declared a major public health threat (Ng et al., 2014). Whilst recent changes in the patterns of obesity in the population are certainly driven by environmental changes, the heritability of obesity is extremely strong. Researchers have found that genes can influence human bodyweight

(Maes et al., 1997). However, there is no doubt that physical exercise can have a positive effect on bodyweight and obesity (Chin et al., 2016).

In another study conducted at the University of Cambridge it showed that lack of exercise is responsible for twice as many deaths as obesity (Ekelund, 2015). Bringing this down to a simple method of calculation exercise saves lives, prolongs our existence and allows us to be happy and not dead. The more we read of these studies, the more we see the connection to exercise. However, exercise alone will not cure the world of all our ills, but it sure goes a long way to a happier life.

If you think you can

The year was 1967; I had a gym situated beneath a Typewriter shop in Bolton. In those day Gyms only opened in the evenings and maybe on a Sunday morning! My Gym under that shop was just 27 feet long and 14 feet across; it had whitewashed walls and a flag floor, 2 light bulbs, no running water, no changing room and significantly no women. The Gym of about 400 square feet was like most other Gyms across the Country and even the World. We were happy with that as there was little else. I called it The Chancery Lane Barbell Club, simply because it was in Chancery Lane. The only equipment in the room was Barbells and Dumbbells (Heathcote, 1988).

It was late December and I had not had one visitor all evening; just me and my thoughts and my thoughts then was that I should lock up and go home. I stood up from the bench I was sitting on and glanced at a poster, one of half a dozen I had put up on the whitewashed walls. This particular motivational poster simply said, *'If you think you can –you can.'* I remember subconsciously spreading my arms, a movement generated by some cells in some part of the creative brain and saying *'I need more space.'* But a little part of my brain was saying *'you can't even fill the space you already have!' I know* said the creative brain.'

It would take 4 years to find the space I wanted, 10,000 square feet, a massive leap from the 400 square feet in Chancery Lane. *'If you think you can, you can'*, said the poster, *and we did.*

Not only did we fill the space but we filled it with people; 2000 members in our first year of business and half of these were women! Not only did we have running water, we had changing rooms, showers, a spa and saunas; we also had a crèche, a beauty salon, squash courts and a restaurant with a salad bar. We had 2 gyms with machines made by the local Blacksmith – machines made in Bolton! There were no Suppliers in the 1960's.

Building the first multi-purpose Health Club would precede an industry now worth in the region of 40 billion dollars worldwide and all because of a poster that said, *'If you think you can – you can.'* We built a legacy out of an old school. People still come up to us after 5 decades to tell us how much they enjoyed the first club of its kind in the country. We knew even then that '*The Club*' we called '*Bolton Health Studio*' was not about facilities, equipment, showers, running water or squash courts, but about its people, friendship, comradery and sociability. Fifty years on people tell us they really enjoyed those days; in other words, *they were happy with what we provided.*

Happiness a geat legacy

Memories last longer than dreams.

I have a friend called Brian; like me Brian is 84 years of age. We both ran for our local running club where the competition was fierce and unrelenting, but fair. Brian would always have the edge in the shorter runs and I would have the edge in the longer runs. Unlike me, he is still running, these days more of a hobby with the ravages of time taking their toll. This friend has always lived close to the edge, a building worker, like me. The very nature of that industry is something like the old west; job done, move on, a building site completed, move on. Many don't, but Brian did. 'Benders' were not uncommon; brawls with some measure of unreliability never affected anyone other than him: a likeable loner. This friendship of ours was never close, but solid for what it was. We raced for our club, travelled, roomed together, and respected each other, our personalities never clashing, never losing that respect.

He still lives close to the edge; he is just as happy now as he was in the past. He is satisfied with a pint, a couple of bob on the horses or a wander around the town. Like me, he loves Western Movies and reminisces about the races we have done in Wigan, Leeds and Coventry or the overseas trips to the World Vets Championships in Berlin or Brugge. 'Ken he says, *Memories live longer than Dreams.*'

My friend finds happiness in small things and for him it is enough (Heathcote, 2017). I am always reminded of Victor Frankel's view that if we are no longer able to change a situation, we are challenged to change ourselves. (Frankel, 2004)

Brian still runs, I don't; his life brought him happiness and with his memories it still does. He shares the same philosophy that prevailed some fifty years ago! Another runner George Sheehan believed that success meant having the courage, determination and the will be become the person you were meant to be (Sheehan, 1975). Brian, like Dr Sheehan and Victor Frankel finds happiness in what he does and what he is.

Rob de Castella, better known as Deeks, was a man of rare talent; he was one of the best marathon runners of his time. His best period was in the 80's – World Champion – Commonwealth Champion – 4 times Olympia Champion – 1982 and 1986 Gold Medallist – Australian National Champion and World record holder for the Rotterdam Marathon in 1991 with a time of 2.09.42. Castella's record is second to none, a world class athlete in every sense of the word. It was in that year he would run a 10k in Moss Bank Park, my home town of Bolton. His host that week would be Steve Kenyon, a colleague of mine at Bolton United Harriers. Steve, like Deeks was a world class runner; his best time for the marathon being 2.11.00. One of Steve's greatest achievements was The Great North Run when he broke the British record which he held for a phenomenal 29 years until Mo Farah came along and broke it.

To have both of these two world class athletes in Bolton was a rare moment for me and to have both visit our Health Club was an equally rare moment. To be invited to train with them was even more rare and accepting their invitation was insane; not only was I totally outclassed but I was ten years older and to go out for a thirteen mile romp was just crazy, but it was extremely motivating, inspirational and adrenalin pumping that would last for several months. Both Steve and Deeks would be running at training pace; I on the other hand was all pumped up and running at racing pace – approximately one minute per mile slower. It was notable they were having a casual conversation for the thirteen mile journey; I was in oxygen debt on that run. At one point the 3 of us were reaching the peak of the highest point on the run and it was at the peak of my physical limit; my stomach ready to part company – the lungs fighting for survival and burning with the ferocity of a furnace, and the legs lactic acid and ready to part company with reality. Without any warning and with total acceptance Deeks turned his head and on seeing my distress that was cleverly hiding, he slowed, turned and said 'what a fantastic view.'

One of the best performance indicators for fitness is our ability to recover; that gesture from Deeks would give me sufficient time to normalise my output – no more than twenty seconds to recover and the final seven miles of our run downhill was an equal romp. There should have been no way for me to run with these guys, but I did, and that run would live in my memory; the feel good factor would last for months; even now thirty years later I still hold that memory in my mind. For them it was just another training run; for me, one of the happiest moments of my athletic career – an old Vet running with Stallions of their time.

Rewards

The brain has a dedicated reward system that motivates us to seek out things essential for our survival. In his book 'The Human Brain,' (2013) Moheb Constandi, describes how the human brain responds to things that give us pleasure i.e. eating, drinking, sex, bringing up children, listening to music and doing things for others. These and other things are rewarded by the release of substances from the brain. Dopamine, adrenaline and serotonin all provide us with a high, the feel good factor and the energy to sustain.

All of these are reflected in our approach to life; scoring a goal in soccer, finishing the 5k run, the sheer satisfaction of just doing and being or passing the finishing line. The anticipation of knowing you did it will release the substance called serotonin. It is the sheer pleasure of a walk in the country, a morning run, overcoming any barrier; My Dad's smile after swimming the length in that ice cold pool in 1945; the run with Deeks and Steve, the medal round your neck after completing a swim, bike ride or marathon, striving for consistency and achieving it – Dopamine – Adrenaline – Serotonin. Bill Pearl's enjoyment of just doing; Sheehan's pain and pleasure; the scientist's reward is to see the results of constraint induced movement therapy – Dopamine – Adrenaline – Serotonin – all bring us pride, pleasure and the feel good factor.

After the Second World War the young men of our nation were called upon to meet new challenges in a rapidly changing world. In 1947, National Service, a standardised form of peacetime conscription was introduced for all able bodied men between the ages of eighteen and thirty. I was just 19 years of age when I reported in to Fulwood Barracks in Preston and it was here I would do my basic army training. This consisted of learning to march to music; how to slope arms, present arms, shoulder arms and all other respects to kill people with guns. It has to be said I never wished to be a soldier and I certainly felt nothing for all these new skills I was set to learn at the tender age of 19. Knowing I had little choice I decided that this challenge needed something extra so I volunteered to join the elite parachute regiment. The implications meaning I was to train to a higher and more challenging level.

One of my first challenges was to jump out of an aeroplane and my very first experience of how the brain releases Adrenaline, Dopamine and Serotonin. Every single one of my exits tested my resolve; the adrenaline just before the jump was rampant, every nerve and sinew stretched to the limit. The euphoric release of Dopamine flooded the entire system when both feet met with terra firma. The Serotonin would appear later when normality was achieved, the reward for overcoming, controlling and mustering the fear, the forge, the fire and the flame; Sheehan's words now echoing in my mind sixty six years later. Adrenalin – Dopamine – Serotonin – The Brains Rewards. Only the mind and brain can understand our happiness, effort, fulfilment, achievement or simply just doing and being. All we need is life.

References

American Psychological Association (2014) *Psychology Science in Action*. Edward Taube, PhD. Behavioral Neuroscientist [Accessed 12th June 2020 at https://www.apa. org/action/careers/health/edward-taub]

Chin, S.H., Kahathuduwa, C.N. and Binks, M. (2016) Physical activity and obesity: what we know and what we need to know *Obesity Reviews*, 17, 12 [Accessed 17th June 2020 at https://onlinelibrary.wiley.com/doi/epdf/10.1111/obr.12460]

Constandi, M. (2013) *The Human Brain. 50 Ideas you really need to know*. London: Quercus

Doidge, N. (2007) *The Brain That Changes Itself*. New York: Viking Press

Doidge, N. (2015) *The Brain's Way of Healing*. London: Penguin Random House

Ekelund, U. (2015) Lack of exercise responsible for twice as many deaths as obesity. *University of Cambridge Research News*. [Accessed 15th June 2020 at https:// www.cam.ac.uk/research/news/lack-of-exercise-responsible-for-twice-as-many- deaths-as-obesity]

Frankel, V. (2004) *Mans Search for Meaning*. London: Edbury Press

Heathcote, K. (1988) The Gym Business. Newton Abbot: David & Charles

Heathcote, K. (2017) *We're Going To Live Forever: The secrets to eternal life*. Rothersthorpe, Northampton, UK: Paragon

Maes, H.H.M., Neale, M.C. and Eaves, L.J. (1997) Genetic and environmental factors in relative body weight and human adiposity. *Behavior Genetics*, 27, 4, 325-351 [Accessed 17th June 2020 at https://link.springer.com/article/10.1023/ A%3A1025635913927]

Merzenich, M. (2013) *Soft Wired: How the new science of brain plasticity can change your life*. San Francisco: Parnassus

Ng, M., Fleming, T., Robinson, M., Thomson, B., Graetz, N. and Margono, C. (2014) Global, regional, and national prevalence of overweight and obesity in children and adults during 1980-2013: a systematic analysis for the Global Burden of Disease Study 2013. *The Lancet*, 384, 9945, 766-781 [Accessed 17th June 2020 at https://www.thelancet.com/journals/lancet/article/PIIS0140-6736(14)60460-8/ fulltext]

Pearl, B. (1979) *Keys To The INNER Universe*. Phoenix, AZ: Bill Pearl Enterprises

Pearl, B. (1986) *Getting Stronger. Weight training for men and women. General conditioning, sports training, body building*. Bolinas, CA: Shelter Publications

Sandow, E. (2012) *Life is Movement: The physical reconstruction and regeneration of the people (a diseaseless world)*. California: CreateSpace Independent Publishing Platform [Accessed 12.6.20 at https://broscience.com/eugen-sandow/quote]

Sheehan, G. (1975) *Dr Sheehan on Running.* Emmaus, PA: Rodale

Sheehan, G. (1978) *Running and Being. The total experience.* London: Penquin Random House

Xu, W.L., Atti, A.R., Gatz, M., Pedersen, N.L., Johansson, B. and Fratiglioni, L. (2011) Midlife overweight and obesity increase late-life dementia risk. A population based twin study. *Neurology,* May 3 2011. [Accessed 17th June 2020 at https://n.neurology.org/content/76/18/1568]

Wikipedia (2020) https://en.wikipedia.org/wiki/Edward_Taub; [Accessed 12th June 2020 on https://en.m.wikipedia.org/wiki/Silver_Spring_monkeys]

Happiness and freedom from alcohol addiction

Jerome Carson and Paul Makin

In this chapter the authors share their own personal journeys of difficulties with alcohol addiction and how both overcame their problems. They then describe some research that they conducted looking at the role of flourishing in recovery from alcohol problems. They conclude by suggesting that just giving up alcohol is not necessarily going to lead to flourishing on its own. It may take many years before recovering alcoholics experience flourishing. They start by outlining something of the scale of the problem with alcohol in Britain today.

Alcohol use and abuse in Britain today

Many readers of this book may remember some of the older governmental television messages about alcohol abuse, such as, *'Everyone likes a drink. No one likes a drunk.'* Or some of the messages extolled by Alcoholics Anonymous, *'One drink, one drunk,'* *'One day at a time.'* (Alcoholics Anonymous, 2020). Alcohol forms an important part of all our lives. Virtually all of our major social occasions are marked by the presence of alcohol; meals, parties, weddings and even funerals. The person with a drink problem celebrates every success and when he or she encounters adversity, they 'drown their sorrows.' With drinking you always win. Yet, our use of alcohol comes at a great societal cost.

Information presented on the NHS and other websites reports numerous worrying statistics about our relationship with alcohol (Institute of Alcohol Studies, 2017). There were 358,000 admissions to hospital in 2018/19, where the main reason was alcohol. That is some 2.1% of all hospital admissions. In 2018 there were 5,698 alcohol specific deaths, and of these 79% were from alcoholic liver disease, with the highest rates being in the North East and North West of England. Some 76,000 people were treated for alcohol problems, with 133,000 prescriptions for acamprosate calcium, the main drug used to treat alcohol problems. In 2017, between 230 and 270 people were killed in accidents, where at least one driver was over the drink drive limit. Since 1987, alcohol has become 74% more affordable. Household expenditure on alcohol has doubled from £10.4 billion in 1987 to £20 billion in 2018. This excludes spending on alcohol in pubs and restaurants! This is not to mention the social and family problems caused by alcohol (NHS,

2020). Before going on to describe the research the authors have conducted into alcohol problems they start by giving a description of their own struggles with the 'demon drink.'

Jerome's story

My late father was an alcoholic. Sometimes it would be hard for him to walk past a pub without going in. I remember after the death of his mother, my Nan, that we went to a pub after the funeral. Someone asked him *'What he was doing over in Belfast?'* He replied, *'I've just buried my mother!'* That was I suppose as good a reason as any, to have a drinking binge. In the end and rather like another son of Belfast, George Best, the drink got to my father and he developed cirrhosis of the liver. While he had been able to give up a 40-cigarettes-a-day smoking habit and also managed to control his weight, alcohol proved one addiction too many and it ended up killing him. Yet, his own father had been a baker and a lifelong teetotal.

It was around the time of another bereavement, that of my mother when I was 16, that I had my first proper introduction to alcohol. As part of the grieving process, Dad and other friends and relatives would go to the pub. I was allowed to join them and would have a pint of lager and lime, to sweeten the bitter taste of the alcohol. Drinking became even more important when I entered the sixth form and I got completely 'plastered' on my 18th Birthday.

I went to Reading University to study Psychology. No subject could have been better chosen. I had a small group of male friends. Most of our social life was spent in halls of residence bars, the student's union or local pubs. 'Beer race day' represented a drinking zenith. We were only observers of this student event, when groups of five students with their legs tied together, had to drink a pint in six different pubs, around the town centre. The student union stayed open all day. We drank nine pints of beer that afternoon. I went for a sleep only to be wakened up by my friends hammering at my door and demanding I join them for another evening session, when we had a further seven pints. A total of two gallons of beer in one day. Your hard-earned taxes helped pay for all this, as these were the days when students not only had their tuition fees paid, but were also given grants to help pay for living expenses and halls of residence fees!

Somewhat unusually the year after I left University, I started monitoring my alcohol intake assiduously. I was hoping to train as a clinical psychologist and I had been reading about the importance of self-monitoring in the process of behaviour change. Accurately monitoring and recording your behaviour can help identify antecedents or triggers to your drinking, but can also help you control it. The problem was I never wanted to control it.

In 1983, I married and my wife was teetotal. Her own father had been an alcoholic. She, while never encouraging my drinking, was able to tolerate it, perhaps because of her own personal experiences. The pattern was that I would rarely drink, but when I did, it would often be to excess. I was never really satisfied by a single drink but could develop a 'taste' for it. We were friendly with a couple, where the husband liked to drink to excess, but his wife was virtually abstemious. On the birth of our fourth child, they came over to visit my wife in hospital and stayed the night with me. He said he had come to 'wet the baby's head.' This was a euphemism for getting drunk, which he proceeded to do. I of course kept him company. I was surprised the next day by my boss's wife turning up at my door early in the morning with a bouquet of flowers. I brought her into the kitchen to find a vase. She exclaimed, *'There's a man sleeping in your garden!'* It was of course the friend, who had decided to sleep off the alcohol in the fresh air. It would be fair to say that both wives were long-suffering. Such episodes of heavy drinking were never entirely harmless. Most people with a drink problem, even if they can remember the night before, will have got into numerous difficult situations, with consequences for those close to them? I must have been involved in scores of these before I gave up drinking finally, at the age of 59.

The question for this chapter is did recovery from addiction make me a happier person? The answer is probably not. I sometimes joke to friends that I have become more miserable since I gave up alcohol. I am however undoubtedly a better person. Most people who drink do not consider themselves to have a clinical drink problem, or to give it its proper term an alcohol use disorder. They all have a very powerful defence mechanism, called denial. There are several ways of assessing whether an individual really has a drinking problem. The Diagnostic and Statistical Manual of the American Psychiatric Association DSM V (APA, 2013), has a list of 13 criteria, eg. *'Alcohol is often taken in larger amounts or over a longer period than was intended,'* and another, *'A great deal of time is spent in activities necessary to obtain alcohol, use alcohol or recover from its effects.'* Six or more of these criteria indicate a severe alcohol problem. The World Health Organisation has an alcohol identification tool called AUDIT (Babor et al, 2001). This has questions like, *'How many alcohol drinks do you have on a typical day, when you are drinking?'* Increasing points are given for the more drinks that are consumed. Scores of 16 or more represent a high level of problems. In my prime I would have met both these sets of criteria.

For some people and I guess I am one of these, the only real solution to a drinking problem is abstinence. This approach was established in America in 1939 and led to the founding of Alcoholics Anonymous (AA). While I have never attended a single AA meeting in my life, or indeed sought their help, like them I have also learned that the only solution to a drinking problem is to stop drinking. Simple.

Paul's story

When I was asked to write this account, so many things came flooding into my head. Childhood memories, happy times, sad times, and past mistakes that led to dark places. The main thing was how far I have come in my ongoing recovery journey. I'm 35 years old and have been sober for five and a half years. To understand how I've got here I've done a massive amount of self-reflection on how I ended up an alcoholic, and the resulting consequences, and how I've battled back from it and improved my life.

I come from a typical background. Parents, one sister and one brother who are both older. We were and still are a close family. I also spent a lot of time with extended family, grandparents and cousins. We were a traditional working-class family. My childhood was unremarkable really. My parents were loving, but also instilled discipline and morals in me. We were all treated fairly and had life luxuries but were not spoiled. Every year we always had a holiday for a week in Cornwall. Christmas and birthdays were always special, and we had treats throughout the year. I was outgoing as a child and was quite popular at school, firmly in the middle of the pecking order, which I was happy with. School was a typical experience really. I worked hard and avoided trouble for the most part, occasionally pushing boundaries, which always preceded the inevitable and appropriate consequences. As is often the case, there was sibling rivalry between my brother and I. It was nothing major, the odd scuffle and mainly just irritations, but it did occasionally become extreme. That's about it for my childhood. As stated, unremarkable.

My life began to unravel when I was 16. Although I had had a good childhood, my parents separated when I was 16. With hindsight and conversations post separation, it was apparent they were not happy together for a long time. It is a credit to them that they managed to not let it impact on my childhood, but at the same time it came as a massive shock. Life was a bit confusing at that time with my parent's separation and starting college. My friends all went to a different college, so I was alone in a new environment. I met another group of lads and joined them which I thought was a good thing. How wrong you can be? I was bullied by them and made to feel worthless and became very isolated and introverted. In the space of a few months, my parents separated, I'd lost my core friendship group and was being bullied. I was so unhappy. I left college and began working with my uncle to earn some money, but I hated it. I was still introverted, and this was affecting my family life and friendships. I quit working with my uncle and drifted from job to job, which led to me moving out of my mum's house and in with my dad, again. Big mistake. When I was out with my friends, we had started drinking as we were that age, sneaking into some pubs being underage and going to mainly house parties. Because I was so introverted, I was the victim of 'friendly banter'. It was never malicious, but it influenced me. One night I had had enough. I drank heavily and came out of my shell. I was the life and soul of the party and everyone lapped it up, I felt great. In my head the drinking made me a better and more confident person. This was the first step on the wrong path.

I still drifted from job to job and ended up doing bar work in my local pub. I was now 18 and felt this should be my career. I worked hard doing as many hours as I could and even got some qualifications. I was still very unhappy in myself, but life wasn't bad. I had new friends that I'd made through the bar work and still had my core friendship group. I had a social life, was well thought of in my job, popular with regulars, but it wasn't enough and self-destructive behaviour was common. I lost jobs through oversleeping and making mistakes, and with hindsight I sub-consciously did not want this life. I was on a bad path. My family tried to advise me to get out of this cycle, but I knew best. This repeated for a few years until I ended up running a pub. Again, I thought I was happy. I wasn't. I further isolated myself in the pub. I drifted from my real friends and family which just made me unhappy. The answer, drinking. It was a 'lock in' every night with different people, my way of keeping it hidden. I worked to drink. When I did have a night off, I had the perfect excuse to get hammered, as it was my only time to let my hair down. I was now speeding down the wrong path.

One thing that had a real impact on me was a conversation in a pub with my dad. My brother had just announced his wife was expecting their third child, but it was an unexpected pregnancy and his wife was already 6 months pregnant. Everyone was shocked by this and I didn't think it was possible. That's when my dad told me. He just casually dropped in conversation that I was an 'unexpected' arrival and it was four months before they knew about me. Wow. In my screwed-up head, I went to the place that I was unwanted and had no reason to be here. That's clearly not the case as I have always been loved, so it was clearly irrational thinking. I've spoken about this with mum since and she explained what happened and it was because of a medical issue and was only ever seen as a positive thing, so my thinking was way off. It didn't stop me thinking this though.

I changed jobs and started working for a chain of pub restaurants. Life didn't change though. I still did as many hours as I could to be in the drinking environment and earn as much as I could to drink. I now lived 500 yards away from a 24-hour supermarket. They got a massive amount of business from me. I continued to drift from family and friends and started dating a woman from work. Looking back, it was never going to work, as I think it was me trying to force happiness and it backfired. It was volatile. I drank very heavily. We were on and off multiple times and we eventually split up and I moved away to Warrington. This is where things got bad and continued to plummet to rock bottom.

Warrington was awful. I had no support network at all, no reason not to drink. It was work, drink, work, drink. I didn't like the people I worked with. There were very few of the regulars in the pub that I liked. It was just me and my empty flat and my drinking. Debts were mounting up, my health was awful. I just felt pressure. On a few occasions I was sitting 'smashed out of my skull' in the early hours contemplating ending it all, as I was so unhappy and couldn't see a way out. Thank God I didn't. I turned 30 and had a small health scare that I managed to persuade my family was just exhaustion. I missed my niece's first birthday that summer because I chose to drink. This was the person I had become and I still feel immense guilt about it. I got fired from my job that summer because I made a mistake and rather than fixing it, I hid it because I was in such a rush to drink. I lost my job, home and career all because of my drinking. Granted it turned out to be the best thing that ever happened to me, but I'll move on to that.

I was now back home and so desperate for work to earn money, that I was doing door to door sales. This lasted a day each time. I was still drinking heavily, and my family were very worried. I eventually admitted one day to my mum and sister that I had been fired and hadn't resigned after all, to move back home. Obviously, that day I was half cut and carried on drinking after they left. My brother turned up a good few hours later to check on me and we argued. I was adamant I was going to keep drinking. It's a bit blurry still but I have vivid memories of sitting in the street clutching two bottles of wine. This was the week my family confronted me, and I admitted my problem and asked for help in stopping. As a family they formed a plan as I was not in a place to do this. I felt this amazing wave of relief that it was over, and I no longer had to feel the way I felt. I went to the GP and was prescribed detox medication over seven days. I moved in with my brother during this phase and I can safely say that was one of the worst weeks of my life. I felt awful. I got through it and I expected to feel amazing, but it was totally the opposite. I had no clue about life. I didn't know what to do. I had nothing. I remember thinking 'Is this it?' I wished I never stopped drinking, but knew it was the right thing to do. I am so glad I didn't cave in as life was finally beginning.

So, the start of my recovery wasn't brilliant. I didn't feel great and felt there was nothing in life for me. I started to go to a recovery centre. I had an assessment and was encouraged to go to the meetings and classes which I did. The day of the first meeting I stood outside for 20 minutes summoning up the courage to go in. I finally went in and there were about 30 people in this room, all at different points in their recovery. I didn't say a word, just listened. Hearing all these stories and listening to conversations made me realise I wasn't alone and that it was possible to recover. There were people from so many walks of life, nurses, lawyers, parents and builders. I was amazed. I decided to jump in headfirst to the recovery process. I went to all the classes and meetings I possibly could. I used the gym pretty much every day. I slowly began to open up to people and form relationships and started to enjoy life again. I reached out to old friends and told them about my issues. I spent more time with my family and relied on them for support. Life still wasn't great, but it was a massive improvement on what it was. I felt happier. My mental health was still very bad, so I was speaking to a counsellor about things. I made my life very structured and orderly. I had set routines and without that I would not be where I am today. The thing that really helped me was a course I did called 'Intuitive Recovery.' It was a course to teach you how to change your thinking processes. The tutor said one thing that really hit home and still does today. *'Make a fist, think about opening it.'* It obviously didn't open. *'Just because you think something, you don't have to do it.'* It was like a lightbulb came on in my head. I realised I was in control of my own life. I could control my thoughts and reject the bad thoughts. I did this and still do daily. It wasn't an instant fix but over time it became natural. My confidence soared.

I was now happier and had skills to control my thoughts. I wanted more in my life. I began to volunteer with an agency that some friends from recovery were involved with. They were setting up a dry bar. I thought this was great. We had a venue at a café in a park in Bury already. We built the bar from scratch, got supplies from my previous contacts and arranged entertainment for nights. It was a great feeling to be involved with something and feel like I was contributing something and had a purpose. I also helped volunteering with clients who had mental health disorders. It was such a great feeling to be helping other people. I was beginning to stand on my own in my own life. I got myself a flat and made it into a proper home, my first ever home. Everywhere else I previously lived was just a drinking den, so I took immense pride in my home. I decided I wanted to focus on my future, so I went to some University Open Days and decided I wanted to become a youth worker, but I needed some more qualifications. I began a college course studying social work, sociology and psychology. The psychology part really resonated with me and it clicked. I loved doing it. I was truly happy studying and just knew this was the path for me. My mental health was now a lot better. I was stronger. It felt like all parts of my life were coming together. I was back with my true friends and had found a social life. I started to go to gigs and plays at least once a month. I still used the gym. I still saw my friends from recovery. I had new college friends. Family life was so much better as I shared more and was just a better person. The happier I was in myself, the better life was becoming. By this time, I had also sorted my finances out. Debts were under control and being repaid. I was even able to have a holiday and went to Cuba. It was such an amazing holiday and I realised that I had found the life I wanted. I wanted to help people, to see friends and family, to have holidays, to have goals and targets and meet them. I also realised I was experiencing that exact life.

I completed my college course and started my degree at University. Because I enjoyed it so much, I decided to study Psychology. I needed to decide what pathway I wanted to specialise in, and I decided to study counselling. My life experiences up to this point, going through counselling myself, and my experiences at the recovery centre had led me to want to embark on a career of helping others, so this seemed a logical choice. It was the right choice. Studying Psychology has also massively helped me personally. I've learnt theories and skills that I've used in my life and it's improved my life so much. My confidence continued to grow. My self-awareness has grown. I've continued to develop as a person. I am now a positive person as I have learnt the importance of positivity and dealing with things and accepting them for what they are. I always find some form of positivity in all aspects of life or any situation, no matter how small. By doing this I control my thoughts and keep the dark side at bay.

Looking back on my recovery so far, I realise I wouldn't be where I am without everything I've put in place. I rely on my family and friendship group, both old and new. I have my independence with my driving. I have a balanced social life and go on holiday once a year. I take great pride in my home and have created a safe environment. Without the counselling and studying I don't think I would have my current mindset to deal with things allowing me to focus on what makes me happy. I've stumbled on a combination that works for me and enables me to thrive in my life and not drink and be happy.

If I was asked the question 'Do you think you'll ever be happy?' Just after I stopped drinking, I would have laughed and said not a chance, it's impossible. If I was asked the question 'Do you think you could still be happy and drink as well?' I can 100% say I don't want to or need to drink. I'm happy. Life is good and long may it continue.

Our research into flourishing in recovering alcoholics

Given both our histories we found common purpose in deciding to look at flourishing in recovering alcoholics. The concept of flourishing is a relatively recent one in Psychology and is said to be synonymous with the emergence of Positive Psychology. It is worth remembering that the main founder of Positive Psychology, Professor Martin Seligman originally believed that the concept of happiness could be achieved via three main routes. These were via the pleasurable life, the engaged life or the meaningful life (Seligman, 2002). The pleasurable life speaks for itself. Lots of money, nice car, big house, designer clothes, jewellery, holidays etc. Yet research shows this does not last. Better to go for the engaged life or the meaningful life. The engaged life is where you are able to exploit your talent to its maximum, e.g. the actress

Helen Mirren. The meaningful life, epitomised by Saint Theresa of Calcutta, is a life offered largely in the service of others. Yet, by 2011 Seligman had extended his theory to include relationships and accomplishments and the PERMA model was born (Seligman, 2011). PERMA standing for Positive Emotions, Engagement, Relationships, Meaning and Accomplishments. The main goal of Positive Psychology was to be flourishing and PERMA was the way to achieve flourishing. We wanted to see if people recovering from an alcohol addiction would be flourishing. We predicted that the longer people abstained from alcohol, the greater would be their level of flourishing.

To do this we collected data from 140 recovering alcoholics using an online survey. The survey required them to state how long it had been since they had had an alcoholic drink, which we converted into months. The survey also required them to complete the PERMA profiler questionnaire (Butler and Kern, 2016). This questionnaire is made up of twenty-three questions scored on a scale from 0 to 10. Each of the five PERMA domains has three questions that form a subscale total. The five domains are then added together and along with a single item on happiness, these 16 items give a total Flourishing score for that individual. Negative emotions and physical health domains are also represented by three questions each and there are two stand-alone questions, on loneliness and overall happiness. Like many questionnaires used by psychologists this one had been developed over a number of years and had been found to be both reliable (accurate) and also valid (it measured what it was supposed to). One of the advantages of using a questionnaire like PERMA, is that it has been used by researchers in many countries, so we have a lot of information on how various groups score on the scale.

Participants were separated into two groups. Group 1 consisted of the top 25 participants who reported the longest length of sobriety and Group 2 consisted of the bottom 25 participants who reported the shortest length of sobriety. Some participants failed to complete all the PERMA questions so an overall score could not be calculated for them. This meant Group 1 had 21 participants and Group 2 had 20 participants. Participants who have been abstinent for longer have significantly higher levels of flourishing (104.90) compared to participants with the lowest period of sobriety (83.10). These findings clearly demonstrate that being abstinent for longer allows individuals to flourish. These findings support previous studies that individuals who are abstinent in recovery for longer, display higher flourishing levels (McGaffin et al, 2015; Best et al, 2012). This shows that life can improve post addiction, but it requires a significant amount of time to do so. Although it is clear there is a relationship between flourishing levels and length of sobriety, it is not clear how flourishing improves over time.

Perhaps the most significant finding from this survey of flourishing in recovering alcoholics was that on average those who completed the PERMA

Scale scored 92.36. If we compare this to the 'normal' population from Peggy Kern's research, it is much lower than her average of 114.33. In fact, our sample of recovering alcoholics score lower than any group we have surveyed thus far, with the exception of the mentally ill. Therefore it would appear that recovering alcoholics are not flourishing as a group.

Alongside the PERMA profiler questionnaire, participants were required to complete 10 questions about their recovery process. The questions included motivations for and benefits of, stopping drinking, changes to relationships, if they had new goals and targets and the most damaging thing about their drinking. It was clear from the responses of both groups that participants had similar motivations for stopping drinking, with all participants experiencing some sense of loss, of health, job, relationships, money or homes. Participants with the highest flourishing levels and longest sobriety stated that the benefits of stopping drinking were that they had been able to either repair or replace what they had lost. Some did this by retraining in a new professional field, repairing or establishing new relationships or improving their physical or mental health.

'Health reasons, I had lost my job and home and pressure from family to admit I had a problem. I was also deeply unhappy with life. Life is now much better. New career on the way, better family life, healthier, happier and am a better person.'

'I feel better and that I have an end goal that I have a chance to work towards, basically a second chance. I will never get everything back, but I can do everything I can. I'm very driven to get back as much of my good life as I can and start new and replace all the bad I had in my life.'

The responses of the participants also revealed a common theme in having support throughout recovery. Participants who successfully managed to establish a support network, either through family or friends, counsellors or therapists or networking in rehab and support groups, had significantly higher flourishing levels, than those who did not have these in place. Responses demonstrated participants who had worked with counsellors or therapists had improved their mental health and had then managed to progress in other areas of their lives.

'I attended support groups and counselling and by talking to my friends. Talking has been so important to me and I continue to do so even though it's difficult.'

'Help from my counsellor, support groups that I went to and determination to stay clean. I also write diaries and share with people and also spending time with my son puts everything in perspective as I realise how lucky I am.'

Participants who reported the lowest flourishing levels reported that they did not have a support network in place. They either did not see their family or friends or had not seen a counsellor or joined a support group. Due to not doing this, they reported being in emotional pain or not having the skills or techniques to deal with their problems as they used alcohol as an escape. The pattern in these responses can be interpreted as unhappiness, and without the support network in place they are unable to progress in other areas of their lives so they will not flourish on as a higher level as participants who have a support network.

'To die, but hopefully quickly. I know it sounds grim but there is nothing I ever wanted to do that I can now achieve. The people I knew are all gone so I am left in pain, lonely, and unable to work and therefore poor.'

'No, I don't, quite the opposite. I've lost a social life, and I must face problems with no let up. My physical health problems are getting worse there is no cure. Alcohol used to be an escape.'

The responses concerning determination and positivity also differ for each group. Participants who reported the higher flourishing levels and were in the longest period of sobriety, reported increased levels of determination and positivity. They had the determination to either rebuild or develop new areas of their lives. This can possibly be linked back to developing a support network and going through counselling. The counselling may have strengthened their mental health creating the determination and increased positivity.

'I'm more determined and positive and now want to start a family whilst staying sober. Stopping drinking and the counselling has shown me how bad life was without me realising and I now am determined to enjoy life and never go back.'

'Achieving my goals and targets, starting a family and helping others through their recovery. I now feel I have a reason to be here and not just to be a sheep. I feel I make a difference and I'm embracing that.'

Again, significant differences in responses are present between the two groups. Participants with lower flourishing or a shorter period of sobriety, state that they just take each day as it comes, or they do not set targets or goals to achieve. They state they wish to stay as they are, saying they are happy now they have stopped drinking. The problem with doing this is they will not be moving on from what made them unhappy and led them to drink in the first place. Although they are currently sober, failing to move forward with life increases the risk of falling back into drinking.

'No hopes, just going day by day.' 'I never hope so I can't be disappointed.'

'To continue my life and put what happened to me firmly in the past. I just take each week as it comes.'

The participants' responses to the questions about recovery explain how flourishing increases, the longer time goes on. It does not happen naturally, and multiple areas of life need to be worked on. Paul's case study clearly demonstrates this as he openly says he felt worse immediately after stopping. Yet now he states he is very happy with life and flourishing in all areas. Although there is no magic formula for recovery, the common themes reported are motivation, benefits, and learning methods for coping. The results all show that taking these steps or similar steps will increase flourishing. That does not mean that if you do not do that, you are doomed to have a poor life or relapse, as it is possible to not work on any of these areas and still remain sober. It all comes down to individuals' perceptions. Some might be happy stopping drinking and ending their journey there, whilst others desire more in their lives. It is also not clear what these participants' flourishing level was whilst drinking. It is possible their flourishing level more than doubled from what it was, so they are experiencing a sensation of euphoria and happiness. What is clear is that it is possible to flourish in recovery and it depends on the individual and what their perception of happiness is.

Concluding comments.

The underlying message from AA of taking *'a day at a time,'* is essentially a pessimistic one. Today you are not an alcoholic. Tomorrow you might start drinking again? You can only truly say you are not an alcoholic today. The 'disease' is just about being controlled. In this chapter we presented two case studies from recovering alcoholics, Paul and Jerome. Others might say, 'Well these guys were never really alcoholics, they are different from many other alcoholics.' Yet, by whatever criterion you choose, Paul and Jerome met the criteria for alcohol use disorder. Are they happier now they no longer drink? Jerome said that he probably was not happier, but that he was a much better person. Paul's view was that he is much happier and if he was asked the question now 'Do you think you could still be happy and drink as well?' He can 100% say he doesn't want to or need to drink. Life is good, he has found happiness and long may it continue.

Jerome and Paul also reported on research they had carried out looking at flourishing in recovering alcoholics. In fact, they did not find much evidence of flourishing. People with alcohol problems scored lower than several other groups surveyed using the PERMA Scale. Statistics tell one story. Individual narratives tell another. People 'languishing in recovery,' to borrow a term from Corey Keyes (Keyes, 2002), have a different narrative. As one person remarked, '....*there is nothing I can now achieve...I am left in pain, lonely and unable to work and therefore poor.*' For individuals in this position, happiness is a distant dream.

References

Alcoholics Anonymous (2020) *Everyone Likes a Drink. One drink.* [Accessed 19th June 2020 at: https://www.bing.com/videos/search?q=%e2%80-%9cOne+drink%2c+one+drunk%2c%e2%80%9d+%e2%80%9cOne+day+at+a+time.%e2%80%9d+Alcohol+Anonymous&qpvt=%e2%80%9cOne+drink%2c+one+drunk%2c%e2%80%9d+%e2%80%9cOne+day+at+a+time.%e2%80%9d+Alcohol+Anonymous&FORM=VDRE]

Babor, T., Higgins-Biddle, J., Saunders, J. and Monteiro, M. (2001) *AUDIT: The Alcohol Use Disorders Identification Test.* Geneva: World Health Organisation.

Best, D., Gow, J., Knox, T., Taylor, A., Groshkova, T., and White, W. (2011) Mapping the recovery stories of drinkers and drug users in Glasgow: Quality of life and its associations with measures of recovery capital. *Drug and Alcohol Review,* 31, 3, 334-341.

Butler, J., and Kern, M.L. (2016) The PERMA-Profiler: A brief multidimensional measure of flourishing. *International Journal of Wellbeing,* 6, 3, 1-48. doi:10.5502/ijw.v6i3.526

Institute of Alcohol Studies (2017) Estimates of the cost of alcohol [Accessed on 8th July 2020 at http://www.ias.org.uk/Alcohol-knowledge-centre/Economic-impacts/Factsheets/Estimates-of-the cost-of-alcohol.aspx]

Keyes, C. (2002) The mental health continuum: From languishing to flourishing in life. *Journal of Health and Social Behaviour,* 43, 2, 207-222.

McGaffin, B. J., Deane, F. P., Kelly, P. J., and Ciarrochi, J. (2015) Flourishing, languishing and moderate mental health: Prevalence and change in mental health during recovery from drug and alcohol problems. *Addiction Research & Theory,* 23, 5, 351-360.

NHS (2020) [Accessed 7th July 2020 at https://digital.nhs.uk/search?query=Alcohol+statistics]

Seligman, M. (2002) *Authentic happiness.* New York: Free Press.

Seligman, M. (2011) *Flourish: A visionary new understanding of happiness and well-being.* New York: Free Press.

Faith and happiness

Mohammed Sadiq, Aishath Shahama, and Aashiya Patel

Introduction

This chapter explores faith, or in this context religiosity and its relationship with happiness. Aashiya begins by exploring faith in the context of religiosity and then discusses the concept of happiness through the lens of faith and religion. Shahama then discusses empirical literature which explores the relationship between religiosity and happiness highlighting its implications and possible uses. The chapter ends with Mohammed sharing a personal reflection on his relationship with faith and happiness and how the two have intertwined throughout his life.

Faith in modern society

The term faith can be described as having unwavering trust or confidence in a concept, person or thing. In the context of this chapter where we discuss religiosity, faith can be defined as trust and confidence in a God or the teachings of a religion. Thus, religiosity defines a person's involvement or interest in numerous facets of religious activity, commitment, and faith. This faith is based on conviction and belief in a higher power however those who subscribe as members of a religion can differ in the strength of their faith and devotion to the teachings of said religion.

Data published by the Office for National Statistics (ONS) (2020) outlining the results of the 2011 census survey show that 75.3% of the population of England are affiliated to a religion. Converging on survey statistics presented by ONS (2019) for our Northern town of Bolton, we are presented with data suggesting a decrease in religiosity between the years of 2011 and 2018. That data outlines 84% of the population of Bolton reported to be members of a religion in 2011 however this decreased to 70% in 2018. This then posits the question, what could have contributed to the decrease of religiosity in our Northern town over these seven years?

Fidrmuc and Tunali (2015) suggest that a decrease in religiosity could be due to the costs of being a member of a religion outweighing the tangible benefits. These benefits include access to social contacts, mental and material support in times of distress as well as spiritual benefits such as auspicious reincarnation or eternity in heaven. Costs however include restrictions posed by religious rules or guidelines which can go as far as dictating the activities that can be participated in as well as the food that can be eaten or the clothes that can be worn by its members. Therefore, due to the development of society into a functioning community which has systems in place for support with health care, legal and emotional counsel as well as easy accessibility to social contact with others through online networking, the benefits of subscribing to a religion no longer seem as enticing as these benefits can be gained through modern society without paying the costs that religion often requires. This leads us to our next point, if the benefits gained by following a religion are more easily attainable through our well-functioning modern day societies without having to burden the costs, we must also ask ourselves why then do over 70% of our population still identify as members of a religion? This could perhaps be because the benefits which are now readily accessible in our communities may satisfy our materialistic and social needs however do not provide us with the spiritual advantages which are gained through religiosity and faith.

Religiosity as a construct can be split into two dimensions as suggested by Allport and Ross (1967), intrinsic and extrinsic. An extrinsically religious person may use their faith for their own ends which can help them in obtaining security, sociability, distraction as well as status and self-justification. It can be argued that these are benefits which are now easily obtainable in a contemporary society. A person with this orientation of religiosity however may turn to God during times of need and utilise faith more when in distress, thus turning to God but without turning away from self. A person with an intrinsic religious orientation internalises their faith and molds their life around the teachings of the religion, simply put, religion becomes their motivation and faith is regarded as central to one's life. Empirical evidence posits that it is the intensity of religious attachment, or intensity of faith, which enhances well-being and happiness, not the previously discussed tangible benefits associated with religious membership (Fidrmuc & Tunali, 2015). This may offer an explanation as to why the majority of inhabitants of our Northern town still choose to follow a religion, as perhaps modern day society cannot account for the purpose and meaning in life provided by religion or how having a relationship with a higher power helps one to cope better with stressors (Hill et al., 2000).

Happiness is a subjective and multi-dimensional construct which consists of cognitive and emotional components (Veenhoven, 2011). As the field of positive psychology develops in leaps and bounds, so does the research into the concept of happiness. Seligman (2002) who is highly regarded as the pioneer of positive psychology, proposes that happiness consists of three separate components; positive emotion and pleasure, engagement and meaning. This theory supports the idea that happiness can be split into two distinct perspectives, hedonistic happiness which can be defined as pleasure seeking and avoiding pain, a perspective which aligns with the positive emotions and pleasure component of Seligman's (2002) theory. The second is eudemonic happiness, eudaimonia is a term which was coined by Aristotle to define a life which is lived in accordance with higher values, thus in this respect, eudemonic happiness results from having meaning in life, a sense of purpose, as such aligning with the meaning component of Seligman's (2002) theory (Ryan, Huta & Deci, 2008). This sense of purpose may be a contributor to the growing body of empirical literature which identifies positive links between religiosity and happiness, literature which is discussed in the following section of this chapter.

Relationship between religiosity and happiness

Over the past few decades, several research studies have been conducted endeavoring to explore the impact and relationship between religiosity, subjective well-being and happiness and it has been reported that to some extent greater life satisfaction and happiness is higher in people who are actively religious than their non-religious counterparts (Ciarrochi & Deneke, 2005; Francis & Katz, 2002; Hadaway, 1978; Pollner, 1989; Poloma & Pendleton, 1990; Willitis & Crider, 1988; Witter et al., 1985). Although studies have been conducted on different religions looking at the relationship between happiness and religion, Christianity and Islam are more studied than the others (Rizvi & Hossain, 2016). Hossain and Rizvi (2017) indicated that an increasing level of religiosity increases the happiness level of people, irrespective of their religious belief. Similarly, data from a European Social Survey conducted from 2000 to 2008 investigated the impact of religion on happiness. Results found that individuals who are religious are happier in general than non-religious individuals (Fidrmuc & Tunali, 2015). Likewise, in the Western context regarding religious identity, Ferriss (2002) found that people with a religious identity were happier than those who did not have a religious preference.

An area explored by researchers with respect to religiosity and well-being is cultural differences and differences among religions (Abdel–Khalek & Lester, 2017; Hossain & Rizvi, 2017; Ngamaba & Soni, 2017). A sample comprising 205 British (98 male and 107 female) and 220 Egyptian (105 male and 115 female) university undergraduate students were taken by Abdel-Khalek and Lester (2017) to explore the association between subjective well-being and religiosity. Results showed statistically and significantly higher scores on religiosity from Egyptian students and higher scores on happiness, mental health, and satisfaction with life from British students. Pearson correlations between the four scales (religiosity, happiness, satisfaction and mental health) showed statistically positive and significant correlations.

These results are consistent with a previous study (Abdel-Khalek & Thorson, 2006) conducted among Egyptian and American college students and a comparison done between American and Kuwaiti students (Abdel–Khalek & Lester, 2012, 2013). British students are seen as more secular, whereas more importance to religion may be devoted by Egyptian students as most Muslims engage in prayer and daily practice of their faith (Abdel-Khalek & Lester, 2017). Perhaps, there is less social pressure and social desirability in the United States of America (USA) or United Kingdom (UK) attached to being religious. In addition, this possibly illustrates cultural differences in political freedom (Thorson et al., 1997). Difference in subjective well-being between Egypt and the UK can be evident from World Happiness Report. Egypt is ranked in 138th whereas the UK is ranked in 13th place (Helliwell et al., 2020). Several literature reviews suggest implication of the relationship between religiosity and happiness (Koening et al., 2012; Tay et al., 2014; Vishkin et al., 2014). It was reported that religion contributes to happiness and emotional regulation (Vishkin et al., 2014). From surveying 1200 research studies Koening et al., (2012) found that the majority of the literature supported that religiosity has positive impact on mental peace, health and happiness. An international literature review carried out by Tay and colleagues (2014) concluded that religion was considered as a vital aspect of their daily lives by a majority of the people in order to find peace and happiness.

One might wonder then about the implications of the above research and what the reason may be for religious or spiritual believers being happier than non-religious individuals. Rizvi and Hossain (2016, p.1562) in a systematic review explain some reasons why the literatures on happiness shows that religious people are happier compared to those who are not. It is because religious belief gives people:

a sense of meaning of life
a sense of wellbeing or comfort
a genuine social network

Religious belief also makes people: *helpful; productive; hard-working; loyal; honest; accountable; truthful and sincere.* It also provides better health, physical shape and mental peace. Additionally, a social support network is provided that fulfils human desire. A practical implication, especially for religious people may be religious beliefs and practices potentially being integrated into psychotherapeutic procedures (Abdel-Khalek & Lester, 2017).

Triangles of religiosity and happiness.

Lyubomirsky et al., (2005) suggests to sustainably enhance well-being, the best route is engaging in intentional cognitive, volitional, and behavioral activities. Religious activities can be considered as intentional activities such as prayer, attending the mosque or church. It was found that fasting during the month of Ramadan can increase subjective wellbeing among Muslims (Campante & Yanagizawa-Drott, 2015). Among Hindus participation in mass gatherings and engaging in a pilgrimage event also impacted wellbeing (Tewari et al., 2012). It was also found that prayer fosters gratitude (Lambert et al., 2009) and amplifies its hedonic and eudaimonic well-being (Schnitker & Richardson, 2019). Gratitude has shown greater perceived mutual strengths (Lambert et al., 2010), strengthened friendships and social bonds (Emmons & Shelton, 2002; McCullough et al., 2001; McCullough et al., 2004). It has also been shown to lower depression (Wood et al., 2008), and predict more prosocial behavior (McCullough et al., 2001). Results showing evidence of praying and attending religious activities frequently were observed to be predictive of higher levels of happiness among several Western literatures (Ellison & George, 1994; Ellison & Levin, 1998; Ferriss, 2002; Greeley & Hout, 2006; Maselko & Kubzansky, 2006; Poloma & Pendleton, 1989; Soydemir et al., 2004; Stark & Maier, 2008; Witter et al., 1985).

Two studies used World Value Survey to examine religiousness and happiness. Ngamba and Soni (2017) compared different religions across the world and found development level of the country and individual religiosity played a significant role in participants' wellbeing. Snoep (2007) compared data from three countries, Denmark, Netherlands and USA. The result of the correlation showed a weak yet a positive relationship between religiousness and happiness. Correlation was most significant in the USA (average +0.13) whereas non-significant in the Netherlands and Denmark (average + 0.05). Howell and Howell (2008) found that an important role is played by a country's level of development in shaping people's subjective well-being. However, it was observed that religion is declining in more economically developed countries (Diener et al., 2011) and a decline in religiosity is associated with economic growth (Barro & Mitchell, 2004).

Dockery (2010) suggested that positive levels of happiness are associated with having a university degree. On the contrary, Kitayama and Markus (2000) found people with a low level of education often reported high levels of life satisfaction and levels of happiness. On the association between education and happiness Hartog and Oosterbeek (1998) reported:

'Education correlates strongly (and positively) with happiness scores in poor nations and weakly in rich nations. Happiness is generally found to be unrelated to intelligence as measured by concurrent tests'. (Hartog &

Oosterbeek, 1998, p. 247)

A total of 124 postgraduate students aged between 21 to 48 (74 female and 50 male) from three public universities in Malaysia volunteered to take part in Abu Rahim's (2013) study to examine the effect of life satisfaction and religiosity on happiness. The results showed that 67% of the participants reported being generally happy, of which females (61%) and Master Degree (53%) students were reported as being happier compared with male and Doctorate students. Among the three independent variables, life satisfaction (odds ratio 3.197) seemed to have the strongest impact on happiness compared with frequency of prayer and religiosity. Nevertheless, results suggest postgraduate students' happiness and the level of religiosity (odds ratio 1.862) were strongly related, as well as increases in the frequency of prayer (odds ratio 1.452) enhances happiness among postgraduate students.

Achour et al., (2017) examined correlations between subjective happiness and religious commitment among university students and the moderating effect of educational level on the relationship between religious commitment and subjective well-being. The study involved 230 volunteers, 47 postgraduate and 183 undergraduate Muslim students. The results showed that there is a strong positive and significant correlation between religious commitment and subjective happiness. Education level was positively associated with both subjective well-being and religious commitment.

'As religiosity increases, happiness increases—the increase is more evident for those with a high level of education which will lead to a better understanding and practice of religiosity which may lead to high levels of happiness.' (Achour et al., 2017, p. 1879)

Results may be influenced by better knowledge and understanding of religion with a higher level of education and achieve a high level in happiness and greater understating of religious practice (Achour et al., 2017). Another variable taken into account in religion and happiness studies is personality. Francis et al. (2016) tested religious affect and personal happiness with individual differences in personality in Turkey with 348 university students (122 male and 226 female). Tekke et al. (2018) replicated religious affect and personal happiness among 189 Sunni Muslim students (148 female and 41 male) in Malaysia. Both studies used the Oxford Happiness Inventory and the short-form of the Eysenck Personality Questionnaire Revised to measure happiness and personality respectively. However, Francis et al., (2016) used the OK Religious Attitude Scale (Islam) to measure religiosity whereas Tekke et al., (2018) used the Sahin-Francis

Scale of Attitudes toward Islam. Results from Turkish Muslim students (Francis et al., 2016) showed, with high extraversion and lower neuroticism there was an association with greater happiness. Additionally, positive religious attitude is associated among females and as well as individuals with low psychoticism. Furthermore, between happiness and religiosity, a small positive association was seen. Moreover, a multiple regression model demonstrated that religious people are happier. Similarly, in Sunni Muslim student samples (Tekke et al., 2018) results also showed positive religious attitude being associated with high extraversion and in females a small but positive association was seen between happiness and religiosity. In addition, a hierarchical regression model demonstrated similar results to the Francis et al. (2016) regression analysis, with religious attitude showing a small yet statistically significant predictor of happiness. These studies are vital in the development of empirical theology within an Islamic context.

Social norm theory suggests that people's subjective wellbeing tends to substantially boost when religion is considered socially desirable and normative in a society (Eichhorn, 2011) The higher levels of happiness and life satisfaction may perhaps be reported in a religious country by religious people due to the respect with which they are treated (Stavrova et al., 2013). Religious groups that promote good values such as gratitude, social connectedness, freedom of emotions, and freedom of choice may improve the subjective wellbeing of their members (Fischer et al., 2010; Jung, 2014; Kim-Prieto & Diener, 2009). When faced with life stressors, it was suggested that as a way of religious coping for Catholics and Protestants, turning to God might be beneficial for them as it may result in feeling happy but not for Jews (Cohen, 2002). Granqvist et al. (2012) suggested that the ability to love is increased with secure attachment to God and those who have secure attachment to God expect happiness and blessings in life as well as see the beauty in existence (Ghobari-Bonab et al., 2013). Having a religious identity, or religious belief not only makes you more content with your life, it also impacts your health, physical, social, mental, and emotional wellbeing as well. It is evident that an increase in the level of religiosity is associated with an increase in level of happiness, across all religions and nations. The relationship between happiness and religiosity is also influenced by education, personality, attachment, social/ economical level of a nation, intentional religious activity, attendance and group participation in religious groups.

To conclude, in this section we can see how modern practices are perhaps reflected through religion and mirrored in positive psychology. For example, charity which is encouraged in several religions promotes selflessness, fasting encourages gratitude, prayer shares qualities with mindfulness and lastly religion itself provides meaning to life. In the next and final section of this chapter, we share a case study exploring how faith and happiness have intertwined throughout the author's life and what he has learnt as a result.

A personal reflection: journey through faith and happiness by Mo Sadiq

My journey through life has been built on strong bedrock of faith, I was born into a Muslim family and from my very beginnings was introduced to Islam. It is a tradition and teaching In Islam that all Muslims should be recited the Adhan (Muslim call to prayer) by their fathers in their ear during the first few hours of birth. My father was no different and recited the call to prayer in my first few hours of breathing, a call to which I will follow for the rest of my life.

> 'Allah is the Greatest, Allah is the Greatest
> I testify, there is no God but Allah
> Muhammad is the messenger of Allah
> Come to prayer
> Come for success
> Allah is the Greatest, Allah is the Greatest
> There is no God but Allah'

I don't necessarily know if I was born happy neither can I prove that I was indeed born sad. However, I do know that from the very second I was born, I learnt and was taught to be sad. Sadness is a vital emotion that we learn as young babies, as we use it as a way, and sometimes our only way to express our emotions. It was God's gift to cry. Through this unique gift, I communicate with the outside world. The cry was a signal that I needed something, a signal that was open to interpretation by the recipients. It was society that coined the phrase – 'a cry of help'. Indeed, crying is a God given mechanism to protect us from harm. The more I cried, the more I was noticed and if it was not for my cry, I may have been overlooked. I fall, I cry, I get up. Frightened, I cry, hungry, I cry, and this singal, this 'cry for help' is what leads to the first fixed communication between my parents, siblings and I. Over the next weeks and months, I am vulnerable. Yet, God has created a natural bond of parenthood, alerting them when I am in times of need, in pain, sadness and even happiness. That bond allowed me to grow, knowing that I'd still have the support and love from my parents, no matter how far I went. Seasons come and go, I am growing strong and eventually, begin to explore the fascinating world before my eyes! Venturing into the unknown and without a thought, I take uncalculated risks. I learn to fly in the compounds of human behaviour, I learn to swim and hunt to laugh and to love as do all Gods lifeforms at the inception of life. I am protected by a power far beyond us, a power we, as humans, are unable to process, neither possess. My muscles are uniquely elastic, designed to flex to keep me safe. My bones are strong, strengthening me and supporting me with each step I take, further into this daunting world. As I walk into this world without instruction, I gain independence. My parents now seem far away, still, my cry brings them rushing to my side. I take my first step. I fall and I cry, yet the faces of my parents beam with happiness. How and why is this so? The answer to this question is the basis of what I seek 52 years later. From a young age, I was sent to Madrasah, a school to teach Muslim's about their faith and how they should use their faith in their everyday lives. I went there to learn what was wrong and what was right, what we should do and what we shouldn't. I spent the majority of my childhood in this place; learning things that I had no idea would be of great use to me in my later years. One of the greatest things It taught me was Salah, (prayer) and how to communicate with my Lord, a teaching that changed my perspective on life and my emotions. I didn't see the point of Madrashah at the time; but I understand and now know why my parents sent me to madrasah at a young age. Fifty two years later, I now know that the knowledge they taught me was priceless, perhaps I didn't know how important this knowledge would be to me at the time, as of course I was moody teenage boy, who wanted nothing more than to spend my time playing football with my friends and riding my bike across town instead of being cooped up inside of a classroom, filled with children and teenagers, just like me, learning about the history and teachings of Islam. Although at that time I may have not been grateful for the knowledge, I will forever cherish it. I, eventually, learnt that madrasah was to prepare me for life and help me understand that on days where I felt alone, isolated and sad, God would always be with me and how in times of difficulty I could turn towards Allah for help. It is with this thought, that led me, almost 40 years later to believe that faith and happiness are linked together.

As I grew older, I understood the true meaning to be sad, happy and every other emotion in between. I am a firm believer that as children, we are born naïve and innocent, unable to comprehend how the world works around us. It would not be till later in my life that I would realise that my childhood would be the natural, God given time I would learn and absorb information as though it was magically woven into my DNA. I had no choice in the matter, In order to survive, I was a magnet of seeking knowledge. I wanted to insert my finger into a plug socket, jump down the stairs, wander into the road and bathe in hot scalding water. No, No, No! I learnt that this word together with a waving finger from side to side meant that I should stop. Nevertheless, I do not understand, I want to paint the wall, run in the mud, splat food everywhere and then cry out loudly when I get the food in my eye. I don't know if and why I am making my parents unhappy, yet they continue to stop me again, again and again. I would later realise that these behaviours would continue through my youth and follow me into adulthood. The varying degrees of child and parent behaviour towards each other vary greatly, to the extent that they are beyond the scope of this chapter, yet contribute to the development of what I term 'Crying inside'.God taught me to cry externally, yet, here I was teaching myself to cry internally, in silence and solitude. I am now 52, and my wife says to me 'Don't be sad, be happy'!! However, I find this almost impossible, as over the past 40 years, I had learnt being in my head kept me safe. Here nobody would know or interfere with me. I could spend the majority of my time in this space and it felt comfortable and safe. I don't know at what point this turned into a human phenomenon of sadness and unhappiness. I do know however, that for the answer, I turned to God.

All my life, I have been taught and told to make 'Dua' (prayer) to the Almighty, in happiness, in sadness, in desperation, in thankfulness in life and in death. A plea to Allah to help his believers in the hardships in the world, but also an expression of gratefulness and gratitude, in times of Joy, where the support of Allah has led us to safety and comfort. To God, I'd ask him on occasions, ' Why am I unhappy and sad, I pray and ask for forgiveness. I have discovered the Quran – the fountain of all knowledge and even now, I am still in melancholy.' *'Everyone in heaven and earth entreats Him; every day He is at work'* (The Qur'an, 55:29) This scripture often reminds me, that there is a time and reason for everything that Allah throws upon us, whether it is a test or a reward, Muslims need to remember patience. We must remember the favours of Allah upon us and how they surround you from above and below – indeed, from every direction. We often need to remind ourselves, if you could count the graces of Allah, never would you be able to count them, as they were infinite *'He has given you some of everything you asked Him for. If you tried to count God's favours you could never calculate them: man is truly unjust and ungrateful.'* (The Qur'an, 14:34)

Throughout ages battles have been fought, great lands have been taken, the children of Egypt were freed from the wrath of Pharaoh. Humans have endured and stood the test of time. There however, exists a silent war, one that does not have a start and finish. These wars. are however not fought on the battlefield, but in, offices and homes of people. Internal conflict silently eats away at the very joy of life, sapping all our happiness and often, destroying our souls. Sometimes,I am no longer in control. Ultimately my thoughts trigger my emotional state. My thoughts originate in the past and with sheer vividness my brain has the ability to extrapolate thoughts in the future. I have now created three realities, the past, the present and future. It has taken me five decades to realize that happiness lies in the middle reality, whilst unhappiness thrives in the past and the future. The present reality is what I am grateful for. Through prayer, Allah brings you stillness. I kneel before God and repent, ask forgiveness and recite *Alhamdulillah* (praise be to Allah) numerous times at every prayer. *Alhamdulillah, Alhamdulillah, Alhamdulillah* – I reflect on the bounties of Allah and count my blessings.

Gratitude keeps you in the here and present, yet I am un- grateful!
I have learnt that life is made up of thoughts that if left untamed, will run wild like an animal. Each fall, leaves me battled and bruised emotionally. Each fall is a piece of happiness lost forever, however, I will fall and get back in the saddle many times during my life. I reflect, I pray, I gain strength, I ride, and I fall. With each experience, I am at peace with myself. Thoughts, emotions and our actions can stem from many sources. I take my hat off to fear. You rock! You have kept me safe on many occasions and truly thank the Lord for this trait. However, beyond its natural state, fear transcends into worry, anxiety, grief, sadness and keeps you in a state that shakes you at your very core. If thoughts can do so much damage, I question the very nature of the usefulness of this human trait. Thoughts create fear and fear creates thoughts. This vicious circle repeats itself like an endless record. How do I then break this cycle? The answer to this is the moment you realise that you don't want to endure its pain is the moment you let go. Simple, right? Yet, we keep hold of that which hurts us and makes us unhappy, perhaps because we are to unafraid to let go and suffer the consequences but In some way the brain gains an unconscious pleasure from our anguish and therefore keeps us in this steady unhappy state.

Allah is great, Allah is great. He is the fountain of all knowledge. Through prayer, we commit to Allah and recite Alhumdulillah, thirty-three times after each prayer. Through this affirmation, we practice gratitude. To be thankful, happy for Allah, for the pleasures that he has bestowed upon us. To be content with the present, to have faith in the unknown and to rest assured that Allah knows all that is in your heart and mind. The art of happiness is best crafted by having a calm and happy heart. A clear mind is a blessing and is best achieved by faith. The past is lost, hope is from the unseen, and rejoice the present hour.

I finish by quoting the Quran Surah 2,

'So remember Me; I will remember you. Be thankful to Me, and never ungrateful.'
(The Qur'an, 2:152)

Final thoughts

From the above case study of Mo Sadiq, it can be seen how religion has been embedded in his life and his faith has impacted his happiness. Prayer calling was whispered in to his ear when he was born while he was crying. Crying is portrayed as feeling of sadness therefore calling of prayer can be seen as a consolation and a reassurance. Does it mean the initial introduction of religion is to make you feel happy? He then describes about his childhood, maternal bond or attachment towards his parents. God can be seen as an attachment figure as well. Mo continues to explain about his education. It is concluded that education acts as a mediator of religiosity and happiness (Abu Rahim 2013; Achour 2017). The importance of knowledge can be seen among the first words revealed to Prophet Muhammad (PBUH), the first five verses of Surah Al-Alaq (The Clinging Form) *'Read! In the name of your Lord who created: He created man from a clinging form. Read! Your Lord is the Most Bountiful One who taught by [means of] the pen, who taught man what he did not know.'* (The Qur'an, 96:1-5). He then talks about forgiveness *'Oh God! Why am I unhappy and sad? I pray and I ask for forgiveness'*. Chapter 9 of this book focuses on forgiveness and happiness. Throughout the excerpt phrases describing of battles, resilience, gratitude and blessing can be observed. Previous studies have shown to support that intentional religious activity such as prayer, fasting or pilgrimage fosters gratitude and subjective wellbeing (Campante & Yanagizawa-Drott, 2015; Lambert et al., 2009). Would perseverance and resilience portrayed in Prophetic stories ultimately motivate you to be resilient? Therefore, happier? Finally, he concludes with *'The art of happiness is best crafted by having a calm and happy heart. A clear mind is a blessing and is best achieved by faith'*. Could this be implied as mindfulness? Praying could be considered as a mindfulness exercise. Mindfulness also contributes to mental well-being (Grossman et al., 2004).

References

Abdel-Khalek, A. M. and Lester, D. (2012) Constructions of religiosity, subjective well-being, anxiety and depression in two cultures: Kuwait and USA. *International Journal of Social Psychiatry, 58*, 138–145. doi:10.1177/0020764010387545

Abdel-Khalek, A. M. and Lester, D. (2013) Mental health, subjective well-being and religiosity: Significant associations in Kuwait and USA. *Journal of Muslim Mental Health*, 7, 2, 63–76. doi:10.3998/jmmh.10381607.0007.204

Abdel-Khalek, A. M. and Lester, D. (2017) Subjective well-being and religiosity: Significant associations among college students from Egypt and the United Kingdom. *International Journal of Culture and Mental Health*, 11, 3, 332-337. doi:10.1080/17542863.2017.1381132

Abdel-Khalek, A. M. and Thorson, J. A. (2006) Religiosity and death anxiety in American and Egyptian college students. In: M. V. Landow (Ed.) *College students: Mental health and coping strategies*. New York: Nova Science Publishers (pp 167–185)

Abu Rahim, M. A. (2013) The effect of life satisfaction and religiosity on happiness among post graduates in Malaysia. *IOSR Journal of Humanities and Social Science*, 11, 1, 34-38. doi:10.9790/0837-1113438

Achour, M., Mohd Nor, M. R., Amel, B., Bin Seman, H. M. and MohdYusoff, M. Y. (2017) Religious commitment and its relation to happiness among Muslim students: The educational level as moderator. *Journal of Religion and Health*, 56, 5, 1870-1889. doi:10.1007/s10943-017-0361-9

Allport, G. W. and Ross, J. M (1967) Personal religious orientation and prejudice. *Journal of Personality and Social Psychology*, 5, 432-443

Barro, R. and Mitchell, J. (2004) *Religious faith and economic growth: What matters most – Belief or belonging?* [Accessed 22nd June 2020 at https://www.heritage. org/civil-society/report/religious-faith-and-economic-growth-what-matters-most-belief-or-belonging]

Campante, F. and Yanagizawa-Drott, D., (2015) Does Religion Effect Economic Growth and Happiness? Evidence from Ramadan. *The Quarterly Journal of Economics*, 130, 2, 615–658 [Accessed 22nd June 2020 at https://doi.org/10.1093/ qje/qjv002]

Cohen, A. B. (2002) The importance of spirituality in well-being for Jews and Christians. *Journal of Happiness Studies*, 3, 3, 287–310. doi:10.1023/a:1020656823365

Ciarrochi, J. W. and Deneke, E. (2005) Happiness and the varieties of religious experience: Religious support, practices, and spirituality as predictors of well-being. *Research in the Social Scientific Study of Religion*, 15, 209-223 [Accessed on 22nd June 2020 at http://library.mibckerala.org/lms_frame/ eBook/%5BRalph_L._Piedmont,_David_O._Moberg%5D_Research_ in_t(BookFi.org).pdf#page=221]

Diener, E., Tay, L. and Myers, D. G. (2011) The religion paradox: If religion makes people happy, why are so many dropping out? *Journal of Personality and Social Psychology*, 101, 6, 1278-1290. doi:10.1037/a0024402

Dockery, A. M. (2010) Happiness, life satisfaction and the role of work: Evidence from two Australian surveys. *Working Paper. School of economics and finance* (pp 77). Perth: Curtin Business School

Eichhorn, J. (2011) Happiness for believers? Contextualizing the effects of religiosity on life-satisfaction. *European Sociological Review*, 28, 5, 583–593. doi:10.1093/ esr/jcr027

Ellison, C. G. and George, L. K. (1994) Religious involvement, social ties, and social support in a Southeastern community. *Journal for the Scientific Study of Religion*, 33, 1, 46. doi:10.2307/1386636

Ellison, C. G. and Levin, J. S. (1998) The religion-health connection: Evidence, theory, and future directions. *Health Education & Behavior*, 25, 6, 700-720. doi:10.1177/109019819802500603

Emmons, R. A. and Shelton, C. M. (2002). *Gratitude and the science of positive psychology in* C. R. Snyder and S. J. Lopez (Eds.) *Handbook of positive psychology*. Oxford: Oxford University Press (pp 459–471)

Ferriss, A. L. (2002) Religion and the quality of life. *Journal of Happiness Studies: An Interdisciplinary Forum on Subjective Well-Being*, 3, 3, 199-215. doi. org/10.1023/A:1020684404438

Fidrmuc, J. and Tunali, C. (2015) *Happiness and religion*, No 5437, CESifo Working Paper Series, CESifo Group Munich, [Accessed 22nd June 2020 at

https://EconPapers.repec.org/RePEc:ces:ceswps:_5437https://doi.org/http://
www.cesifogroup.de/portal/page/portal/DocBase_Content/WP/WP-C
ESifo_Working_Papers/wp-cesifo-2015/wp-cesifo-2015-07/cesifo1_wp5437.pdf]

Fischer, P., Ai, A. L., Aydin, N., Frey, D. and Haslam, S. A. (2010) The relationship between religious identity and preferred coping strategies: An examination of the relative importance of interpersonal and intrapersonal coping in Muslim and Christian faiths. *Review of General Psychology*, 14, 4, 365–381. doi:10.1037/A0021624

Francis, L. J. and Katz, Y. J. (2002) Religiosity and happiness: A study among Israeli female undergraduates. *Research in the Social Scientific Study of Religion*, 13, 75-86

Francis, L. J., Ok, Ü. and Robbins, M. (2016) Religion and happiness: A study among University students in Turkey. *Journal of Religion and Health*, 56, 4, 1335-1347. doi:10.1007/s10943-016-0189-8

Ghobary Bonab, B., Miner, M., and Proctor, M. (2013) Attachment to god in Islamic Spirituality. *Journal of Muslim Mental Health*, 7, 2. doi:10.3998/jmmh.10381607.0007.205

Granqvist, P., Mikulincer, M., Gewirtz, V., and Shaver, P. R. (2012) Experimental findings on God as an attachment figure: Normative processes and moderating effects of internal working models. *Journal of Personality and Social Psychology*, 103, 804–818. doi:10.1037/a0029344

Greeley, A., and Hout, M. (2006) Happiness and lifestyle among conservative Christians. *The Truth About Conservative Christians*. [Accessed 29th June 2020 at https://chicago.universitypressscholarship.com/view/10.7208/chicago/9780226306759.001.0001/upso-9780226306629-chapter-10]

Grossman, P., Niemann, L., Schmidt, S. and Walach, H. (2004) Mindfulness-based stress reduction and health benefits: A meta-analysis. *Journal of Psychosomatic Research*, 57, 35–43. doi:10.1016/S0022-3999(03)00573-7

Hadaway, C. K. (1978) Life satisfaction and religion: A reanalysis. *Social Forces*, 57, 2, 636. doi:10.2307/2577686

Hartog, J., and Oosterbeek, H. (1998) Health, wealth and happiness: Why pursue a higher education? *Economics of Education Review*, 17, 3, 245-256. doi:10.1016/s0272-7757(97)00064-2

Helliwell, J. F., Layard, R., Sachs, J. and De Neve, J. (2020). *World happiness report 2020*. New York: Sustainable Development Solutions Network

Hill, P. C., Pargament, K. I., Hood, J. R. E., McCullough, M. E., Swyers, J. P., Larson, D. B. and Zinbauer, B. J. (2000) Conceptualizing religion and spirituality: Points of commonality, points of departure. *Journal for Theory of Social Behaviour*, 30, 51-77

Hossain, M. Z. and Rizvi, M. A. K. (2017).Relationship between religious belief and happiness in Oman: a statistical analysis. *Mental Health, Religion & Culture*, 19, 7, 781–790. doi.org/10.1080/13674676.2017.1280009

Howell, R. T. and Howell, C. J. (2008) The relation of economic status to subjective well-being in developing countries: A meta-analysis. *Psychological Bulletin*, 134, 4, 536–560. doi:10.1037/0033-2909.134.4.536

Jung, J. H. (2014) Religious attendance, stress, and happiness in South Korea: Do gender and religious affiliation matter? *Social Indicators Research*, 118, 3, 1125–1145. doi:10.1007/s11205-013-0459-8

Koenig, H. G., King, D. E. and Carson, V. B. (2012). *Handbook of religion and health* (2nd edition). New York: Oxford University Press

Kim-Prieto, C. and Diener, E. (2009) Religion as a source of variation in the experience of positive and negative emotions. *Journal of Positive Psychology*, 4, 6, 447–460. doi:10.1080/17439760903271025

Kitayama, S. and Markus, H. R. (2000) The pursuit of happiness and the realization of sympathy: Cultural patterns of self, social relations, and wellbeing in E. Diener, E. M. Suh (Eds.) *Culture and subjective wellbeing*. Cambridge, Massachusetts: MIT Press (pp. 113-161)

Lambert, N. M., Clark, M. S., Durtschi, J., Fincham, F. D. and Graham, S. M. (2010) Benefits of expressing gratitude: Expressing Gratitude to a Partner Changes One's View of the Relationship. *Psychological Science*, 21, 4, 574-580. doi:10.1177/0956797610364003

Lambert, N. M., Fincham, F. D., Braithwaite, S. R., Graham, S. M. and Beach, S. R. (2009) Can prayer increase gratitude? *Psychology of Religion and Spirituality*, 1, 3, 139-149, doi:10.1037/a0016731

Lyubomirsky, S., Sheldon, K. M. and Schkade, D. (2005) Pursuing happiness: The architecture of sustainable change. *Review of General Psychology*, 9, 2, 111-131. doi:10.1037/1089-2680.9.2.111

Maselko, J., and Kubzansky, L. D. (2006) Gender differences in religious practices, spiritual experiences and health: Results from the US general social survey. *Social Science & Medicine*, 62, 11, 2848-2860. doi:10.1016/j.socscimed.2005.11.008

McCullough, M. E., Kilpatrick, S. D., Emmons, R. A. and Larson, D. B. (2001) Is gratitude a moral affect? *Psychological Bulletin*, 127, 2, 249-266. doi:10.1037/0033-2909.127.2.249

McCullough, M. E., Tsang, J. and Emmons, R. A. (2004). Gratitude in intermediate affective terrain: Links of grateful moods to individual differences and daily emotional experience. *Journal of Personality and Social Psychology*, 86, 2, 295-309. doi:10.1037/0022-3514.86.2.295

Ngamaba, K. H. and Soni, D. (2017) Are happiness and life satisfaction different across religious groups? Exploring determinants of happiness and life satisfaction. *Journal of Religion and Health*, 57, 6, 2118-2139. doi:10.1007/s10943-017-0481-2

Office for National Statistics. (2020). *Exploring religion in England and Wales: February 2020.* [Retrieved from https://www.ons.gov.uk/peoplepopulationandcommunity/culturalidentity/religion/articles/exploringreligioninenglandandwales/february2020]

Office for National Statistics. (2019). *Religion by Local Authority, Great Britain, 2011 to 2018*. [Retrieved from https://www.ons.gov. uk/peoplepopulationandcommunity/culturalidentity/religion/ adhocs/009830religionbylocalauthoritygreatbritain2011to2018]

Pollner, M. (1989) Divine relations, social relations, and well-being. *Journal of Health and Social Behavior*, 30, 1, 92. doi:10.2307/2136915

Poloma, M. M. and Pendleton, B. F. (1989) Exploring types of prayer and quality of life: A research note. *Review of Religious Research*, 31, 1, 46. doi:10.2307/3511023

Poloma, M. M. and Pendleton, B. F. (1990) Religious domains and general well-being. *Social Indicators Research*, 22, 3, 255-276. doi:10.1007/bf00301101

Rizvi, M. A. and Hossain, M. Z. (2016) Relationship between religious belief and happiness: A systematic literature review. *Journal of Religion and Health*, 56, 5, 1561-1582. doi:10.1007/s10943-016-0332-6

Ryan, R. M., Huta, V. and Deci, E. L. (2008) Living well: A self-determination theory perspectives on eudaimonia. *Journal of Happiness Studies*, 9, 139-170

Schnitker, S. A. and Richardson, K. L. (2019) Framing gratitude journaling as prayer amplifies its hedonic and eudaimonic well-being, but not health, benefits. *The Journal of Positive Psychology*, 14, 4, 427-439. doi:10.1080/17439760.2018.14 60690

Seligman, M. E. (2002) *Authentic happiness: Using the new positive psychology to realize your potential for lasting fulfilment*. New York: Free Press

Snoep, L. (2007) Religiousness and happiness in three nations: A research note. *Journal of Happiness Studies*, 9, 2, 207-211. doi:10.1007/s10902-007-9045-6

Soydemir, G. A., Bastida, E. and Gonzalez, G. (2004) The impact of religiosity on self-assessments of health and happiness: Evidence from the US Southwest. *Applied Economics*, 36, 7, 665-672. doi:10.1080/0003684042000222052

Stark, R. and Maier, J. (2008) Faith and happiness. *Review of Religious Research*, 50, 1, 120-125 [Accessed 22nd June 2020 at www.jstor.org/stable/20447531]

Stavrova, O., Fetchenhauer, D. and Schlösser, T. (2013) Why are religious people happy? The effect of the social norm of religiosity across countries. *Social Science Research*, 42, 1, 90-105. doi:10.1016/j.ssresearch.2012.07.002

Tay, L., Li, M., Myers, D., and Diener, E. (2014) Religiosity and subjective well-being: An international perspective. *Cross-Cultural Advancements in Positive Psychology*, 163-175. doi:10.1007/978-94-017-8950-9_

Tekke, M., Francis, L. J., & Robbins, M. (2017). Religious affect and personal happiness: A replication among Sunni students in Malaysia. *Journal of Muslim Mental Health*, 11(2). doi:10.3998/jmmh.10381607.0011.201

Tewari, S., Khan, S., Hopkins, N., Srinivasan, N. and Reicher, S. (2012) Participation in mass gatherings can benefit well-being: Longitudinal and control data from a North Indian Hindu pilgrimage event. *PLoS ONE*, 7, 10, e47291. doi:10.1371/ journal.pone.0047291

The Qur'an A new translation by M. A. S. Abdel Haleem (2004). Oxford: Oxford University Press. [Accessed 29th June 2020 at https://islamiclegacy.files.

wordpress.com/2018/07/translation-of-the-quran-by-m-a-s-abdul-haleem.pdf]

Thorson, J. A., Powell, F. C., Abdel-Khalek, A. M. and Beshai, J. A. (1997) Constructions of religiosity and death anxiety in two cultures: The United States and Kuwait. *Journal of Psychology and Theology*, 25, 3, 374-383. doi:10.1177/009164719702500306

Veenhoven, R. (2011) Greater happiness for a greater number: Is that possible? If so how? In K. Sheldon, T. Kashdan and M, Steger (Eds.) *Designing positive psychology; Taking stock and moving forward*. New York: Oxford University Press (pp.396-409)

Vishkin, A., Bigman, Y., and Tamir, M. (2014) Religion, emotion regulation, and well-being in C. Kim-Prieto (Ed.) *Cross-cultural advancements in positive psychology: Vol. 9. Religion and spirituality across cultures* (pp. 247–269). Springer Science + Business Media. Retrieved from: https://doi.org/10.1007/978-94-017-8950-9_13

Willits, F. K. and Crider, D. M. (1988) Religion and well-being: Men and women in the middle years. *Review of Religious Research*, 29, 3, 281. doi:10.2307/3511225

Witter, R. A., Stock, W. A., Okun, M. A. and Haring, M. J. (1985) Religion and subjective well-being in adulthood: A quantitative synthesis. *Review of Religious Research*, 26, 4, 332. doi:10.2307/3511048

Wood, A. M., Maltby, J., Gillett, R., Linley, P. A. and Joseph, S. (2008) The role of gratitude in the development of social support, stress, and depression: Two longitudinal studies. *Journal of Research in Personality*, 42, 4, 854-871. doi:10.1016/j.jrp.2007.11.003

Forgiveness and happiness

Reginald Amanze

'Forgiveness and letting go are steps on our road back to happiness.' Tian Dayton (1992)

Introduction

Traditionally, the concept of happiness was a philosophical topic debated and argued amongst philosophers and scholars down history but in recent years, psychology and indeed social sciences have shown much interest in it such that many research papers have been published and many still are on-going. This phenomenon is not unconnected with an increasing interest in the areas of mental health, general wellbeing and happiness amongst the general population thanks to positive psychology whose advent has greatly shifted focus from over emphasis on psychological pathologies and abnormalities to highlighting the enormous benefits in exploring and strengthening character amongst people and a conscious pursuit of happiness and life satisfaction by everyone. The general belief, that everyone wants to be happy and as such pursues things that ensure this, appears to justify the huge research interest being recorded in this construct. Similarly, happiness as the strongest predictor of health (Sabatini, 2014) could only inspire more works on how happiness itself can be increased. While previous works have established links between happiness and interpersonal relationship (Ji & Yoo, 2013), income levels (Stutzer, 2004), gratitude (Emmons & McCullough, 2003) amongst others, this work seeks to investigate the relationship between forgiveness and happiness. With reference to literature and on-going research, this chapter will attempt to answer questions such as; has forgiveness any link with happiness? Are forgiving people happier or are happier people more forgiving?

What forgiveness is not

One of the challenges in forgiveness research is the lack of consensus amongst scholars as to what essentially constitutes forgiveness and how it should be defined (Wade & Worthington, 2005). Ironically, there appears to be agreement on what forgiveness is not (McCullough et al., 2000). For Enright and Coyle (1998), related constructs that are often misplaced for or confused with forgiveness, should be separated and isolated. Scholars agree that forgiveness is different from reconciliation (Enright, 2011; Enright & Fitzgibbons, 2000; Fredericks, 2004; McCullough et al., 2000; Worthington, 1998), legal pardon (Enright & Human Development Study group, 1991), forgetting (Smedes, 1996) and condoning (Veenstra, 1992). It is not proffering excuses to explain away offender's freewill and responsibility, nor does it have to be religious or otherworldly, nor minimizing the hurt incurred (Luskin, 2002, p. 7-8). Forgiveness is not denying or suppressing anger (Stosny, 2013).

What forgiveness is

Agreeing what forgiveness is has proven over time to be challenging. A few definitions nevertheless, have been advanced by different authors. For McCullough et al. (1998), forgiveness is the reduction of negative affect toward the offender. It involves a reduction of negative feelings, behaviour and thoughts and an increase in positive thoughts, emotions and behaviour (Enright & the Human Development Study group, 1991). In other words, the process of forgiveness includes affective, motivational, cognitive and behavioural dimensions of human functioning (Miceli and Castelfranchi, 2011). Amanze and Carson (2019) define it as a process that involves developing and strengthening the capacity to give benefit of the doubt that enables the offended come to terms with, and let go of hurt with its negative affect, thereby giving way gradually to positive feelings towards the transgressor.

Why forgiveness?

Negative emotions caused by hurt and pain such as, resentment and anger harm the one who holds on to them and harbours them more than they harm the offender. To be able to live in the present and move on with life after getting hurt, one must wilfully opt for forgiveness, a process that sets one free from constantly reliving toxic anger, rage, bitterness and hate that keep one stranded in the past while missing out today's beauty. There are many benefits and outcomes accruing from forgiveness that impact on overall wellbeing. These include:

- decrease in negative emotions and depressive symptoms
- restoration of positive thinking
- better relationships
- reduction in anxiety
- increase spirituality

- increase self-esteem
- a greater sense of hope
- greater conflict management capacity
- improved coping ability with stress.
- Better physical health
- improve mental health
- better life satisfaction level.

(Harris and Thoresen, 2005; Enright and Fitzgibbons, 2000; Toussaint and Webb, 2005; Karremans, et al., 2003)

Forgiveness and happiness

The advent and further development of positive psychology that stresses the enormous gains in fostering human character strength and virtues such as, compassion, self-control, forgiveness amongst others (Toussaints and Friedman, 2008), has highlighted the benefits of harnessing the potentials of these character strengths individually, or as a group for the general good and flourishing of the human person. Forgiveness involves some positive processes that enable one not to deliberately avoid the offender but to positively re-assess and reconsider emotions surrounding the transgression (Pargament et al., 2000). Scholars in the recent time have expanded this consideration with the view that forgiveness can be adequately examined within the theoretical context provided by positive psychology (McCullough et al., 2000; Yamhure-Thompson and Snyder, 2003). The importance of forgiveness as a human strength was underscored by authors who identified promising research potentials in this area with regards to positive human functioning leading to positive outcomes necessary for resolving interpersonal situations in a positive healthier manner rather than mere preventing poorer mental health.

Empirical studies on mental health, wellbeing and forgiveness have disproportionately focused on negative outcomes. For instance, Brown (2003) and Maltby et al. (2001) found a link between unforgiveness and poor mental health such as anxiety and depression. However, in a study involving forgiveness and positive psychology, Karremans et al. (2003) reported a positive correlation between forgiveness and positive affect, self–esteem and expressed optimism. Consequently, an investigation into a possible link between forgiveness and happiness becomes a timely development.

Before proceeding further, a brief description of the concept of happiness will be undertaken. Lyubomirsky (2008) defined happiness as the experience of contentment, joy or positive wellbeing, and a feeling of a good, worthwhile and meaningful life. For researchers, happiness is life-experience marked by a preponderance of positive emotions (Myers, 2007). It is worthy to note that happiness as a psychological concept is used interchangeably with subjective wellbeing (SWB), a concept derived from three different theories of happiness in which each emphasizes different aspects of happiness. First, hedonistic theories focus on pleasant and non-pleasant experiences of life. Second, life satisfaction theories weigh on one's overall thoughts about one's life. Third, emotional state theories assess individual's overall experience of emotions (positive and negative affects) (Haybron, 2008).

Happiness considered only with regard to one or two of these theories is deficient of the wider content and purview of this construct. Previous attempts to define happiness under such perspectives have been corrected with the evolution of subjective well-being (SWB), a concept that captures the affective and cognitive evaluation of one's life (Haybron, 2008). To this effect, high scores in positive affect and life satisfaction and low scores in negative affect would lead to a high score in SWB happiness. Happiness could also be conceptualized under two categories; hedonic happiness and eudaimonic happiness. While the former is seen as the experience of more pleasure and less pain (affective dimension), the later involves the pursuit and achievement of personal growth, life purpose and meaning. In other words, happiness gained by attaining one's full potential and functioning at full capacity (AIPC, 2011).

If happiness can be described as the summit of human aspiration and contentment, and forgiveness in-turn involves human strength, engagement and positive thinking, a positive association is therefore expected between the two. While research on forgiveness has surged exponentially in the last decade particularly with regard to mental health and wellbeing, studies investigating forgiveness and happiness sadly are few. Available data on forgiveness and happiness or subjective wellbeing however, suggest a preponderance of association between them. One of the earliest works undertaken in this area was by Maltby et al. (2005) where forgiveness and happiness; the differing contexts of forgiveness using the distinction between hedonic and eudaimonic happiness, was investigated amongst 224 UK student sample. Enright Forgiveness Inventory, The Depression-Happiness Scale and the Oxford Happiness Questionnaire – short form was administered and the findings revealed a significant though low variance in both eudaimonic and hedonic happiness.

This relationship could vary depending on which aspect of happiness is under consideration. While for short-term hedonic happiness (state happiness), results suggest that non-engagement by the offended in negative cognitions about the transgression is very vital, it was also discovered that engaging in positive emotions and behaviours could lead to and or enhance long-term happiness (eudaimonic happiness). This study in effect, proposes a two-way relationship between forgiveness and happiness; a passive way and an active way. Either by consciously refraining from engagement in negative thought about the transgression or willfully practicing positive feelings or actions towards the offender, happiness is increased. In other words, practicing passive forgiveness ensures at least short-term happiness; it equally protects one from rehashing and engaging in negative anti-social behaviours resulting from rumination, revenge, anger amongst others. Long-term happiness-effect of forgiveness or rather active forgiveness supports and re-enforces the understanding of the dynamic interplay between forgiveness as a human strength and positive psychology leading to positive human functioning. This research also suggest that positive behaviour more than positive cognition (doing rather than thinking) leads to more enduring happiness and indeed flourishing.

Also, Shekhar et al. (2014) investigated the relationship between happiness and forgiveness amongst college students in India. The Oxford Happiness Questionnaire and Heartland Forgiveness Scale were administered on 100 students and the findings showed a significant difference in happiness and forgiveness levels across gender and a weak correlation between happiness and forgiveness.

Similarly, investigating whether gratitude and forgiveness contributed to subjective wellbeing more than the three orientations to happiness amongst 143 Hong Kong Chinese teachers, Chan (2013) found a substantial and significant correlation between gratitude and forgiveness on one hand and between forgiveness and subjective wellbeing on the other hand. Gratitude and forgiveness more than orientations to happiness predicted wellbeing and forgiveness was the strongest predictor of negative affect which is a sub dimension of happiness (life-satisfaction, negative affect & positive affect).

In another similar study, investigating the gender differences in the relationship between forgiveness and depression/happiness amongst 600 college students, 300 females and 300 males, with age range 19-28 and using the Transgression-Related Interpersonal Motivations (TRIM) Inventory to assess revenge and avoidance motivation as aspects of forgiveness, and short Depression-Happiness Scale measuring well-being. Results showed revenge and avoidance aspects of forgiveness predicting significantly depression for male while only revenge motivation predicted depression for females. Happiness however, was not predicted by both. This study then concluded that although revenge and avoidance motivation can lead to depression, however, decreases in them, would not necessarily lead to more happiness (Rijavec et al., 2010).

Again, Sapmaz et al. (2016) conducted a study to explore the relationship and predictive levels of gratitude, forgiveness, humility and happiness amongst 443 students in Turkey. The Heartland Forgiveness Scale, The Gratitude Questionnaire, The Humility Scale and The Oxford Happiness Questionnaire short form were used for forgiveness, gratitude, humility and happiness respectively. The results indicate that while forgiveness is positively correlated with happiness, only the forgiveness of situation (a sub dimension) of the 3-dimensions of forgiveness in the Heartland Forgiveness Scale was significantly predicting happiness.

Also, in another study investigating the forgiveness and subjective happiness of university students (N = 828) using the Forgiveness Scale and The Subjective Happiness Scale, Batik et al. (2017) found, a positive but low relationship between forgiveness and subjective happiness and forgiveness as a significant predictor of happiness. Similarly, a qualitative study was conducted by Rana & Gull (2013) to investigate forgiveness, subjective wellbeing and quality of life. Results from 20 semi-structured in-depth interviews indicated that most of the participants acknowledged and reported the importance of practicing forgiveness and its tremendous positive impacts on their personality and subjective wellbeing leading generally to an enhanced quality of life. Data obtained and analyzed highlighted certain categories of forgiveness beneficial effects such as; happiness, positive feelings, relaxation, positive social interaction amongst others.

Finally, Peterson (2015) conducted a study amongst university students (N=134) to examine the relationship between forgiveness and subjective wellbeing with religiousness and spirituality as moderating factors. Results indicated that relationship between forgiveness and happiness depends on the type of forgiveness as total forgiveness, forgiveness of self, and forgiveness of situation – sub dimensions of forgiveness in Heartland Forgiveness Scale HFS (Thompson et al., 2005), predicted subjective wellbeing while forgiveness of other only predicted positive affect. The author concluded thus, forgiveness correlates positively with subjective wellbeing. Certain types or dimensions of forgiveness predict SWB and that religiousness and spirituality moderates positively this interaction such that those high on forgiveness reported higher subjective wellbeing.

Implications

Happiness and forgiveness representing positive human feelings (Fordyce, 2005) and demonstrating human virtue as well as positive thinking (McCullough et al., 2000; Peterson and Seligman, 2004) respectively, are undoubtedly closely and positively related. Despite a dearth of studies in this area, available evidence from studies earlier reported here nevertheless, lends convincing support to this.

All the studies so far conducted on forgiveness and subjective wellbeing /happiness have supported a positive correlation between them such that high forgivers reported higher levels of happiness. Whether or not this positive association resulted from direct or indirect effects of forgiveness continues to generate debate and divergent views amongst scholars. A direct link in this sense may be positive or negative depending on whether or not all or some aspects of happiness is impacted by all or some aspects of forgiveness. Life satisfaction an aspect of happiness was found to have been predicted by forgiveness (Batik et al., 2017), and whereas some studies (Eldeleklioğlu, 2015; Munoz-Sastre et al., 2003) reported a weak link on one hand, another (Worthington et al., 2001) on the other hand, found a strong link. The discrepancy in the findings may have been caused by other variables that affect life satisfaction such as, loneliness, rumination about past mistakes and self-esteem (Munoz-Sastre et al., 2003). An individual's inability to let go of their past mistakes often fosters self-accusation, regret and rumination that lead to negative thoughts directed towards oneself such as, anger, a negativity impacting one's happiness level. On the contrary, however, if someone lets go and forgives oneself and past negative events, their subjective wellbeing is enhanced.

Similarly, by reducing negative affect, forgiveness has been found to be affecting happiness levels directly (Chan, 2013). This author found a strong inverse relation between forgiveness and negative affect and further reported forgiveness as the strongest predictor of negative affect. By willingly relinquishing the pursuit of revenge and ruminations occasioned by a transgression, forgiveness helps the offended to turn away from negativities and gradually replace them with more positive feelings towards the transgressor thereby increasing in-turn the overall happiness level. It is equally important to state that although forgiveness is linked with happiness, this relation is largely dependent on the forgiveness type under consideration (Peterson, 2015). While controlling for gender, age and year in school, Peterson (2015), found forgiveness predicting significantly happiness. Interestingly, on a closer scrutiny, it was discovered that all the dimensions of forgiveness (forgiveness; total, self and situation) aside the forgiveness of other (Thompson et al., 2005), predicted significantly happiness. This is not unexpected given the complex nature of this dimension of forgiveness that often requires someone to consciously consider one's relationship with the offender, a process involving or even capable of arousing variety of emotions on one hand and an attempt to grasp the motivation of the transgressor on the other hand. Forgiveness of other has been shown to lower negative emotions (Witvliet et al., 2004).

Exploring the robust positive relationship between forgiveness and happiness highlights the huge benefits of forgiveness interventions. In working with mental health patients particularly those dealing with unresolved hurt and transgression, sensitivity to the right intervention for the appropriate case is to be encouraged as different interventions are developed for different situations. For instance, an intervention developed for self-forgiveness may not apply appropriately for forgiveness of other.

Future directions and limitations

Although some of the previous research on forgiveness and happiness have been considered in the current work, more studies need to be encouraged notwithstanding. Review of the available literature indicates a robust and positive relationship between these two constructs, a relationship that varies depending on what type of forgiveness or happiness is being considered.

In the light of this finding, it is vital for future research to investigate happiness/subjective wellbeing in terms of other types and aspects of forgiveness as they emerge. The Bolton Forgiveness Scale BFS (Amanze and Carson, 2019) identified and conceptualized forgiveness under three dimensions; a. coming to terms and letting go, b. developing positive feelings, c. giving benefit of the doubt. Future research may examine possible interactions between these three aspects of forgiveness and happiness. Also, the mediating role of forgiveness may be explored with other variables that might affect people's happiness levels.

Happiness and forgiveness are important aspects of wellbeing in need of further research and exploration. Their relationship is robust and mutually beneficial. Research until now seems to have mostly focused on happiness in terms of forgiveness and not vice versa. Jiang et al. (2015) found that happiness rather than sadness brings greater forgiveness. In other words, happy people are more forgiving than unhappy people. In the light of this, there is need to investigate the effects of happiness levels on willingness to forgive. The impacts of large sample sizes and diversity on the credibility of findings can never be over emphasized. Hence, there is need for future research to consider this point in its investigations. This is important as almost all the previous studies in this area have been conducted only amongst students from only a particular university or college.

Finally, future research may consider incorporating qualitative measures in conjunction with other measures to minimize methodological concerns and limitations regarding the exclusive use of self-report measures (quantitative measures).

Conclusion

Research on forgiveness and happiness is on the rise not only as one is considered an end in itself and the other as means to an end, but equally as both represent important aspects of wellbeing and flourishing. Happiness involves a positive knowledge and feeling of fulfilment and satisfaction with oneself and one's life. Forgiveness entails letting go of hurts, pains and the negative emotions resulting thereupon and replacing them with positive feelings. Forgiveness and happiness are positively related and mutually beneficial to each other. While forgiveness generally correlates with happiness/subjective wellbeing, certain aspects of forgiveness predict happiness. On this note, one could argue that forgiving people are happier than less forgiving people. Evidence for this abounds in the studies so far conducted in this area some of which are discussed earlier in this work. There is also evidence that happy people are more forgiving than unhappy or sad people. Finally, the question would be, how far does letting go foster inner positivity and does positivity help people move on in life? Whatever your story in life is and whether you started happy or not, forgiving people of past offences or hurts can set you free, make you feel better and indeed happier.

How forgiving are you?

To find out how forgiving you are, kindly complete the Bolton Forgiveness Scale (BFS) (Amanze & Carson, 2019) at the end of this chapter and work out the score yourself.

References

AIPC. (2011). Happiness and positive psychology. *Australian Institute of Professional Counsellors Article Library*. [Accessed 17th June 2020 at https://www.aipc.net.au/articles/happiness-and-positive-psychology/]

Amanze, R. U. and Carson, J. (2019) Measuring forgiveness: psychometric properties of a new culturally sensitive questionnaire: the Bolton Forgiveness Scale (BFS). *Mental Health, Religion & Culture*, 22, 10, 994–1010. doi:10.1080/13674676.2020.1716211

Batik, M. V., Bingol, T. Y., Kodaz, A. F. and Hosoglu, R. (2017) Forgiveness and subjective happiness of University students. *International Journal of Higher Education*, 6, 6. Doi.org/10.5430/ijhe.v6n6p149

Brown, R. P. (2003) Measuring individual differences in the tendency to for- give: Construct validity and links with depression. *Personality and Social Psychology Bulletin* 29, 759–771

Chan, D. W. (2013) Subjective well-being of Hong Kong Chinese teachers: The contribution of gratitude, forgiveness, and the orientations to happiness. *Teaching and Teacher Education*. 32, 22-30. doi.org/10.1016/j.tate.2012.12.005

Dayton, T. (1992) *Daily affirmations for forgiving and moving on; powerful inspiration for personal change.* Deerfield Beach, Florida: Health Communications, Inc. [Quotation accessed 17th June 2020 at http://quotespictures.com/forgiveness-and-letting-go-are-steps-on-our-road-back-to-happiness-forgiveness-quote/]

Emmons, R. A. and McCullough, M. E. (2003) Counting blessings versus burdens: An experimental investigation of gratitude and subjective well-being in daily life. *Journal of Personality and Social Psychology*, 84(2), 377-389. DOI: 10.1037/0022-

3514.84.2.377

Eldeleklioğlu, J. (2015) Predictive effects of subjective happiness, forgiveness and rumination on life Satisfaction. *Social Behavior and Personality*, 43, 9, 1563-1574. https://doi.org/10.2224/sbp.2015.43.9.1563]

Enright, R.D. (2011) Psychological science of forgiveness: Implications for psychotherapy and education. Paper presented at the conference of Neuroscience and Moral Action Neurological conditions of Affectivity, Decisions and Virtue on 28.2.11 at Rome: Italy. [Accessed 17th June 2020 at https://truthandlove.com/wp-content/uploads/2017/06/Santa-Croce-paper-PDF-February-28-2011]

Enright, R. D. and Coyle, C. (1998) Researching the process model of forgiveness within psychological interventions in E. L. Worthington, Jr (Ed). *Dimensions of forgiveness: Psychological research and theological perspectives.* Philadelphia: Templeton Foundation Press (pp.139 – 161)

Enright, R.D. and Fitzgibbons, R.P. (2000) Helping clients forgive: An empirical guide for resolving anger and restoring hope. American Psychological Association. https://doi.org/10.1037/10381-000

Enright, R. D. and The Human Development Study Group (1991) The moral development of forgiveness in W. Kurtines and J. Gewirtz (Eds.). *Handbook of Moral Behavior and Development.* Hillsdale, New Jersey: Erlbaum (pp.123-152)

Fordyce, M. W. (2005) A review of research on the happiness measures: A sixty second index of happiness and mental health in A. C. Michalos (Ed.). *Citation classics from social indicators research.* Dordrecht: Springer (pp. 373–399)

Fredericks, L. (2004) A gathering on social and emotional learning, love, and forgiveness. Summary of proceedings at the conference of the Fetzer Institute. July, Kalamazoo, Michigan, USA

Harris, A. H. S. and Thoresen, C. E. (2005) Forgiveness, unforgiveness, health, and disease in E. L. Worthington (Ed.), *Handbook of forgiveness.* New York: Routledge (pp. 321-334)

Haybron, D. M. (2008) Philosophy and the science of subjective well-being in M. Eid, and R. J. Larsen (Eds.), *The science of subjective well-being.* New York: Guilford Press (pp. 17-43)

Jiang, F., Yue, X.., Lu, S., and Yu, G., (2015). Can you forgive? It depends on how happy you are. *Scandinavian Journal of Psychology*, 56, 182–188. https://doi.org/10.1111/sjop.12185]

Ji, K.J. and Yoo, J. Y. (2013) A study of Emotional Intelligence, Interpersonal relationship and Psychological happiness university student Division of Health. *Journal of Digital Convergence*, 11, 10, 653–660. https://doi.org/10.14400/JDPM.2013.11.10.653

Karremans, J. C., Van Lange, P. A. M., Ouwerkerk, J. W. and Kluwer, E. S. (2003) When forgiving enhances psychological well-being: The role of interpersonal commitment. *Journal of Personality and Social Psychology*, 84, 5, 1011–1026. https://doi.org/10.1037/0022-3514.84.5.1011

Luskin, F. (2002) *Forgive for Good: A Proven Prescription for Health & Happiness.* San Francisco, California: Harper

Lyubomirsky, S. (2008). *The How of Happiness: A scientific approach to getting the life you want*. New York: Penguin Press

Maltby, J., Macaskil, A. and Day, L. (2001) Failure to forgive self and others: A replication and extension of the relationship between forgiveness, personality, social desirability and general health. *Personality and Individual Differences* 29, 1–6

Maltby, J., Day, L. and Barber, L. (2005) Forgiveness and happiness. The differing contexts of forgiveness using the distinction between hedonic and eudaimonic happiness. *Journal of Happiness Studies*, 6, 1-13. Doi.org/10.1007/s10902-004-0924-9

McCullough, M. E., Rachal, K. C., Sandage, S. J., Worthington, E. L., Brown, S. W. and Hight, T. L. (1998) Interpersonal forgiving in close relationships: II. Theoretical elaboration and measurement. *Journal of Personality and Social Psychology*, 75, 1586-1603. doi.org/10.1037/0022-3514.75.6.1586

McCullough, M. E., Pargament, K. I. and Thoresen, C. E. (2000) The psychology of forgiveness: History, conceptual issues, and overview in M. E. McCullough, K. I. Pargament and C. E. Thoresen (Eds.), *Forgiveness: Theory, research and Practice*. New York: Guilford Press (pp. 1 -4)

Miceli, M. and Castelfranchi, C. (2011) Forgiveness: A cognitive-motivational anatomy. *Journal for the Theory of Social Behaviour 41*(3), 260-290. http://dx.doi.org/10.1111/j.1468-5914.2011.00465.x

Munoz-Sastre, T., Vinsonneau, G., Neto, F., Girard, M. and Mullet, E. (2003) Forgivingness and satisfaction with life. *Journal of Happiness Studies* 4, 323-335 https://doi.org/10.1023/A:1026251630478

Myers, D. (2007) Psychology of happiness. *Scholarpedia* 2(8), 3149. doi:10.4249/scholarpedia.3149

Pargament, K.I., McCullough, M. E. and Thoresen, C. E. (2000) The frontier of forgiveness: Seven directions for psychological study and practice, in M.E. McCullough, K.I. Pargament and C.E. Thoresen (Eds), *Forgiveness: Theory, Research and Practice*. London: Guildford Press (pp. 299– 319)

Peterson, C. and Seligman, M. (2004) *Character strengths and virtues*. A Handbook and Classification. American Psychological Association. Oxford University Press. New York

Peterson, J. (2015) Examining the relationship between forgiveness and subjective well-being as moderated by implicit religiousness and spirituality. *Clinical Psychology Dissertations* 3. https://digitalcommons.spu.edu/cpy_etd/3

Rana, S. A. and Gull, M. (2013) Manifestation of forgiveness, subjective wellbeing and quality of life. *Journal of Behavioural Sciences* Vol. 23, No. 2

Rijavec, M., Jurcec, L. and Mijocevic, I. (2010) Gender Differences in the Relationship between Forgiveness and Depression/Happiness. *Psihologijske teme* (Psy19, 1, 189-202. UDK – 159.947.5.072

Sabatini, F. (2014) The relationship between happiness and health: Evidence from Italy. *Social Science & Medicine*, 114, 178-187 https://doi.org/10.1016/j.socscimed.2014.05.024

Sapmaz, F., Yildirim, M., Topcuoglu, P., Nalbant, D. and Sizir, U., (2016). Gratitude, forgiveness and humility as predictors of subjective well-being among university students. *International Online Journal of Education Sciences*, 8, 1, 38-47. Doi:http://dx.doi.org/10.15345/iojes.2016.01.004

Shekhar, C., Jamwal, A. and Sharma, S. (2014) Happiness and forgiveness among college students. *Indian Journal of Psychological Science*, 7, 1, 088 – 093

Smedes, L. B. (1996) *The Art of Forgiving*. Nashville, Tennessee: Moorings

Stosny, S. (2013) *Living and Loving after Betrayal*. Oakland, California: New Harbinger Publications. ISBN 978-1608827527

Stutzer, A. (2004) The role of income aspirations in individual happiness. *Journal of Economic Behaviour and organization*, 54, 1, 89-109. https://doi.org/10.1016/j.jebo.2003.04.003

Thompson, L. E., Snyder, C. R., Hoffman, L., Michael, S. T., Rasmussen, H. N., Billings, L. S., Heinze, L., Neufeld, J. E., Shorey, H. S., Roberts, J. C. and Roberts, D. E. (2005) Dispositional forgiveness of self, others, and situations. *Journal of Personality*, 73, 313-360. doi: 10.1111/j.1467-6494.2005.00311.x

Toussaint, L. and Friedman, P. (2009). Forgiveness, gratitude, and well-being: The mediating role of affect and beliefs. *Journal of Happiness Studies: An Interdisciplinary Forum on Subjective Well-Being*, 10(6), 635–654. https://doi.org/10.1007/s10902-008-9111-8

Toussaint, L. and Webb, J. R. (2005) Theoretical and empirical connections between forgiveness, mental health, and well-being, in E. L. Worthington, Jr. (Ed.), *Handbook of forgiveness*. New York: Routledge (pp. 349–362)

Veenstra, G. (1992) Psychological concepts of forgiveness. *Journal of Psychology and Christianity*, 11, 160-169

Wade, N.G. and Worthington, E. L., Jr. (2005) In search of a common core: a content analysis of interventions to promote forgiveness. *Psychotherapy: Theory, Research, Practice, Training*, 42, 160-177. doi.org/10.1037/0033-3204.42.2.160

Witvliet, C. O., Phipps, K. A., Feldman, M. E. and Beckham, J. C. (2004) Posttraumatic mental and physical health correlates of forgiveness and religious coping in military veterans. *Journal of Traumatic Stress*, 17, 269- 273. doi:10.1023/B:JOTS.0000029270.47848.e5

Worthington, E. L. (1998). *"The pyramid model of forgiveness: Some interdisciplinary speculations about unforgiveness and the promotion of forgiveness."* In Dimensions of forgiveness: Psychological research & theological forgiveness, ed. Everett L. Worthington, Jr., 107-138. With a preface and an introduction by Everett L. Worthington, Jr. Philadelphia: Templeton Foundation Press

Worthington, E. L., Jr., Berry, J. W. and Parrott, L. III. (2001). *Unforgiveness, forgiveness, religion, and health*. In T. G. Plante and A. C. Sherman (Eds.), *Faith and health: Psychological perspectives*, 107–138. Hove, East Sussex: The Guilford Press

Yamhure -Thompson, L. and Snyder, C. R. (2003) Measuring forgiveness, in S.J. Lopez and C.R. Snyder (Eds), *Positive Psychological Assessment: A Handbook of Models and Measures*. Washington: American Psychological Association.

Bolton Forgiveness Scale (BFS)

Directions: *In life, negative things may occur causing pain and hurt to us. How are you most likely to react to them. Next to each of the following statements, kindly indicate on the scale of 1 - 6 how you would typically respond to the type of situation described. There are no right or wrong answers. Please be as open as possible in your answers.*

Statements	1 Always false of me	2 Almost always false of me	3 Some-times false of me	4 Some-times true of me	5 Almost always true of me	6 Always true of me
1. With time I can be understanding of bad things in my life.						
2. I have compassion for the person who wronged me.						
3. With time I let go of negative thoughts about bad things that are beyond anyone's control.						
4. If I encountered the person who wronged me I would feel at peace.						
5. I hold nothing against someone who hurt me as it could be that sometimes people don't really know what they are doing.						
6. I feel relief by forgiving someone who has hurt me.						
7. I wish for good things to happen to the person who wronged me.						
8. Generally I don't wait to be asked before forgiving someone who hurt me.						
9. With time I am understanding of myself for mistakes I've made.						
10. I hope the person who wronged me is treated fairly by others in the future.						
11. Although I feel bad at first when I mess up, over time I can give myself some slack.						
12. I believe there are no offences that cannot be forgiven under the right conditions.						
13. I eventually make peace with bad situations in my life.						
14. I pray for the person who wronged me.						
15. With time I can be understanding of bad circumstances in my life.						

BFS Scoring Instructions

Bolton Forgiveness Scale (BFS) has four scores to be calculated:

1. BFS-Coming to terms and letting go subscale BFS-ctlg = add up items 1,3,6,9,11,13 & 15 = 42 (highest score). 28 – 35 are high scores, 22 – 27 are good scores, less than 21 is low and poor

2. BFS-Developing positive feeling subscale BFS-dpf = add up items 2,4,7,10 & 14 = 30 (highest score) 18 – 23 are high scores, less than 13 are low and poor.

3. BFS-Giving benefit of doubt subscale BFS-gbd = add up items 5, 8 & 12 = 18 (highest scores) more than 12 is very good, less than 9 is low and poor.

4. Total BFS; add up all the 15 items = 90 (highest score). Score less than 45 is poor, 45 – 58 is good, 59 – 70 is very good and 70 and above is excellent (exceptionally forgiving)

(note that high & low scores in each case were worked out using the mean and standard deviation respectively)

Amanze, R. U., and Carson, J. (2019) Measuring forgiveness: psychometric properties of a new culturally sensitive questionnaire: the Bolton Forgiveness Scale (BFS). *Mental Health, Religion & Culture*, 22(10), 994–1010. doi:10.1080/13674676.2020.1716211

Happiness, music and the occasional creative

Chris Elliot and Kathryn Thomasson

Introduction and background by Kathryn Thomasson

A great many people might already be personally aware of the impact that listening to music has on our emotions and wellbeing. Music can remind us of different times in our life, both good and difficult. Music can lift our mood and energizes us, or can seem to express our sadness, so it may not be surprising to learn that music is good for our happiness. The power of music to support, heal and strengthen our lives has been part of our human history, with stories and myths beginning in ancient times and continuing through the centuries. In the biblical accounts from The First Book of Samuel (Ackroyd, 1971), King Saul summoned the then young David to rid him of his evil spirits through David's playing of his Lyre (16:23). The Greek hero Orpheus was able to use his music to charm all living things and even inanimate objects such as stones came alive when he played. In the famous epic poem by Homer, The Odyssey, (Homer., Fitzgerald, 1990), the power of the song of the sirens draws sailors to their deaths. Just as stories tell of the power of music, so do ancient philosophers propose that music is a powerful tool for wellbeing. Aristotle, in his seminal work Poetics (1961), proposes that art can create catharsis, a cleansing of emotions from the soul. Pythagoras used music to cleanse his thoughts in the evening, restore balance and harmony, and prepare for sleep, believing that music was a means of maintaining psychological balance in everyday life (West, 2000).

Just how important music is for our happiness has been the subject of recent scientific research which has shown that performing, creating and listening to music has significant health and wellbeing benefits. It has been suggested that it is a 'provider of vitality – that is, emotional stimulation and expression; tool for developing agency and empowerment; resource in building social networks; and a way of providing meaning and coherence in life' (Ruud, 2013: 10). Engaging in music can improve a personal sense of self, (Volgsten, 2012; Volgsten and Pripp, 2016). Even Ruud (2013) proposes that music is a form of '*cultural immunogen*,' (2, italics original), which is a type of protective behaviour that builds our emotional resilience in the same way that healthy behaviours strengthen our bodies. In health psychology there is a lot of evidence that shows how our attitudes and behaviours impact on our health and wellbeing. Ruud (2013) created the term because of what he sees to be the lack of interest in 'the interaction between the arts and health-related topics, such as stress, pain, and anxiety' (2). Engaging in music helps us recognise and center our own emotions, provides a sensory experience (Finnegan, 2012) and improves our social relationships and wellbeing (Robertson and Monaghan, 2012). Given its array of social and personal benefits, music has become a popular art form in participatory arts projects at community level and is frequently part of arts projects that bring people together.

The creative industries have been using cultural consumption, entertainment and participation in the arts as part of the growing activities that emphasize creative place making, and the economic development of urban areas (Chang and Wyszomirski, 2015). However the humanistic characteristics of these projects that support self-efficacy, self-actualization, empowerment, community collaboration and sense of community (Manjon and Guo, 2015) have been utilized in local group projects. These support individuals and wider communities to increase social inclusion and provide people with higher levels of wellbeing and social capital. Several studies have shown that using music in development activities working with community groups can have a powerful effect on group participants' individual health and have wider implications for community wellbeing (Dillon, 2006). From these case studies researchers have shown how making and performing music can express a community's individuality and provide opportunities for partnerships between local community groups and wider organizations such as the local council and businesses to form reciprocal, mutually beneficial relationships (Dillon, 2006).

Alongside music as a participatory art, like other creative endeavours, music has also gained rising traction as a creative and arts-based research method. Creative research is 'any social research or human inquiry that adapts the tenets of the creative arts as a part of the methodology [...] during data collection, analysis, interpretation and/or dissemination' (Jones and Leavy, 2004:1-2). Researchers choose to use arts practice as part of their research for many reasons, it can offer new perspectives on research, be more adept at answering questions that focus on aspects of human emotion and experience (Eisner, 2008). The arts are particularly appropriate for projects that give a voice to their participants, encourage equal participation and empower them through building confidence. The use of creative arts research is particularly useful where there is a variety of contexts, as it can bring people together from different cultures, generations, and socioeconomic backgrounds through creative participation (Brice and Fernandez, 2018; Taylor and Murphy, 2014).

When using creative research techniques in research studies, researchers often collaborate with artists across the different fields in creative practice. For our own research in happiness in Bolton the use of music and performance was an important part of the data collection techniques that were used in our Focus Groups. Professor Carson, Sandie McHugh and myself held these with various women's groups in the area. Our colleague and performance artist Chris Elliott made an important contribution to our groups through writing and performing songs. These would begin with reflections and conversations about happiness, considering how work, leisure, possessions and the world around us can influence our happiness. Using material from past life events and stories passed on through his family, Chris created songs that started our discussions with the groups on happiness. In the following paragraphs Chris recounts these stories and discusses how they influenced his own creativity.

Writing happiness by Chris Elliott

The occasional writer is not overburdened with offers of work. Likewise, his near relative, the occasional composer is similarly bereft of commissions. So, when I was offered the opportunity to contribute to the 'Happiness Project' I was delighted, believing that academic study and the creative arts are quite compatible bedfellows. As a song was required, it was easier for the occasional composer to start the project, all that was needed was a guitar, a piano, a notepad and the ability to recall the old maxim of 'keep it simple, keep it short and keep it repetitive'. The lyrics were a series of questions on whether possessions caused or contributed to happiness. I left it to the listener to provide the answer. The tune for the song was straightforward and the chord structure likewise. I find that excellent publication, Music Composition for Dummies (Jarrett and Day, 2008), to be an invaluable tool in composition. A recording of the song made on my 1970's cassette recorder (always analogue, never digital) completed the process.

The occasional writer did not start from scratch. He had already written a short play based on answers given by a fictional character to the questions posed by the original survey as his BA (Hons) Performing Arts 'final project' in 2015. He had presented this in the studio of the Octagon Theatre in the summer of that year. The performance went well, both he and his tutor pleased with the result. Returning to the answers given to the original survey provided enough material to begin to construct a series of short stories based on a single family and stretching from the 1920's to the present day. I should add the stories are based not in Bolton but in Lancaster. I am not a native of Bolton and was aware that any mistake in the text would be picked up by members of the audience who attended the 'Golden Oldies' group at the Meadowside Community Centre and would be (hopefully) listening to my storytelling. I thought that Lancaster was a safer bet. The Occasional writer carried out research on employment in the town and began to build up a picture of what trades and occupations would be open to members of the family and then considered how the different generations coped with changing circumstances and differing social trends as the twentieth century progressed. The stories were written to entertain but I hoped that they would stimulate the audience and perhaps make them recall and mention incidents that would be of use to the project.

The world of work

When Dad and Grandad came home from work, they always told the family what they had done and what they had seen. Grandad worked for Mitchells Brewery as a drayman. He and Vic Smith would deliver all over the town and in the surrounding countryside. Grandad liked his work. It gave him a chance to talk to people, to keep up with what was happening locally. 'Publicans know everything' he used to say. He loved his horses Silver and Diamond and was immensely proud of winning the 'Drayman of the Year' award three years in succession. On the wall, above the fireplace, was a big black and white picture in a solid oak frame. There was Grandad holding his trophy with the dray and the two horses in the background. 'Just remind me', Gran used to say, 'Which one of the two wi' the nosebags on are you?' Grandad used to tell us about his day, from beginning to end. He used to mention the pubs he had delivered to and the publicans and their wives. He talked about the weather and the things that had caught his eye, like a heron or a magpie, how the crops were doing when he was delivering in the country, how busy the town was and who he had met and what he had learnt as he went about his rounds. 'And I thought it were women who were supposed to know all the gossip' said Gran. 'This isn't gossip, woman' said Grandfather. 'This is a portrait of everyday life, as I see it.' 'Eat yer tea afore it gets cold' said Gran. She always had the last word.

My Dad worked as a marine engineer down at the Quay. When he was a young lad, he wanted to join the navy. Grandad was not keen on that and fixed him up an apprenticeship with a local firm of boat builders and repairers. In those days apprentices did what they were told, worked all the hours God gave them and were grateful for their wages at the end of the week. Dad used to tell us about payday, 'We'd all have to line up outside the office at the end of Saturday shift. I was always at the back. Eventually I'd find meself in front of the desk with the Gaffer and Mr. Allan the manager. 'Any breakages, Mr. Allan?' said the Gaffer. 'None this week' replied Mr. Allan. 'Give the lad his wages, then' said the Gaffer'. My Dad used to say that it was as if his wages came out of Mr. Allan's own pocket. He'd count out the money, look my Dad in the face and mutter 'I don't know, I really don't know....'

When the war broke out Dad was sent to Liverpool to repair damaged ships. Grandad had been right. Dad was on dry land and not serving in a convoy wondering if he was going to be torpedoed every minute of the day. After the war Dad went into partnership with a lad he had met at Camel Laird. 'You're going to run your own business?' said Grandad. 'By 'eck, things are looking up.' Dad used to tell us about his day. Who he had seen, how the repairs were going, what had come in and gone out and all the news from the quayside. Mum used to do the paperwork and they both sat down to complete the accounts books. 'Look at that' said Gran, 'Husband and wife working together in harmony'. 'We could work in harmony if you'd come on the dray wi' me', said Grandad. Both Dad and Grandad were proud of their work. The believed they were doing something useful. Nowadays they would be called part of the community, but they did not think like that. They were men who had a job to do and they did it to best of their ability because that was the sort of men they were. Work meant something more than money to men like my Dad and Grandad. It was part of you, what you were, and it was part of how others saw you. You could not be happy all the time. Grandad on his dray, no cover, being snowed on all day. Dad lying in cold water for hours at a time underneath a rusty hull. But it was something to be proud of.

Sports and pastimes

Grandad had an allotment. Every spare minute he had; he would be working on it. 'You're not hiding up there again, are you?' shouted my Gran. 'Just think of all the money I'm saving you, woman', he would reply. Grandad's allotment was a source of pride but was also a terrible worry to him. He just had to win first prize for his vegetables at the local produce show, it was a matter of honour. Beans, carrots, spuds, lettuce, tomatoes and every other type of vegetable you could think of, but it was his marrows that he was most proud of. I remember Gran saying, 'I'm surprised you don't bring the thing home and put it in bed to keep it warm'. 'Well', replied Grandad, 'I have thought of that, but you'd have had to sleep on the floor, and I didn't think that were right'. Everyone we knew had an allotment. It was not just the business of saving money and winning the odd prize, there was something calming about digging the plot and planting and seeing things grow. Grandad used to say that when he was at his allotment time seemed to stand still. Especially in those long summer evenings after work when the lads would get together for a smoke, chat about the day and how it had gone, whilst keeping an eye out for any birds who might fancy a quick snack. Satisfaction and a sense of achievement, for a job well done.

Dad used to love cycling. He was a member of a local club and as soon as his shift ended on a Saturday, he would get out of his overalls, have a wash and go out on his bike. There were hundreds of lads and lasses who did the same thing. You would see them everywhere at the weekends, whizzing along at high speed, a never ending stream of white tops and shorts. Passing through sleepy villages, up and down steep hills, accelerating on the flat, taking corners at high speed, everyone determined to give their best. There were competitions too. Dad was competitive by nature and if wanted something he was prepared to go all out to get it. Each year Waring and Gillow gave a cash prize and a cup for the winner of a thirty-mile road race that covered all types of terrain. It was, as Dad said, an endurance test. Dad was courting the girl who became my Mum, but she also had a soft spot for another lad, Terry Barnes, who worked at Warings as a Carpenter. 'Terry is bound to win' she said to my Dad, 'He's the best racer Waring's have got. He's been studying the route for weeks. You'll only get the route a week before the race and you'll not have time to study it like Terry has.' 'Keep the map in his locker, does he?' asked my Dad. 'He might' she said.

That Saturday after he had finished his shift, Dad changed into a clean pair of overalls and walked over to Warings. The factory was almost empty as everyone had left at lunchtime. Dad went up to the porter's lodge and told the porter that he was a cousin of Terry Barnes. Terry had left the map of the route in his locker and he would want it for this afternoon, so he had sent him over to pick it up. Could the porter show him Terry's locker and unlock it? The porter was a decent lad and said of course he would. As Dad was leaving, the Porter said 'No one's got an earthly apart from our Terry. That Cup won't be leaving the works, I can tell thee'. Dad was out every morning before work and back out as soon as he had finished. He did not come home until dark. Night after night and all weekend. No time for anything else. Grandad asked him if a pair of wings might not help, but Dad was determined. Eventually the day of the race arrived. Dad was in the leading group of riders because of his previous timings. He saw Terry Barnes speaking to one of Waring's directors. He thought Terry looked a bit apprehensive. Mum was there to see them off. She did not mention the map but gave my Dad an odd look. By now Dad knew every yard of the route, every pothole, every bump, every corner. Where you take a chance and where you had to be careful. Where you speed up and where you had to slow down. Dad used to tell me about the race. We used to follow the route together when I was older and had a bike of my own. He would point out where the riders got bunched up, overdid things going uphill, took the wrong turning or gave up and spent the afternoon in a wayside pub. 'I took the lead at the halfway stage' he said. 'There were only a dozen of us in wi' a chance by then'. Young Mr Gillow had an Avis and he drove in front with his chauffeur. He kept on shouting at Terry Barnes to overtake me, but Terry had left it too late'. Dad always stopped the story at this point to fill his pipe, light it and send out a long stream of smoke. 'I won by about three hundred yards in the end, most satisfactory'. Dad was awarded the cup by young Mr Gillow. As the young Director presented it to him, he whispered to Dad, 'So, you're the young villain that stole the route map are you? I'll make damn sure you don't enter next year'. Dad did not mind. He had won the cup and had won my Mum too. Who was the happiest man in Lancashire that afternoon? Well, it wasn't Terry Barnes, was it?

Possessions

'What on earth did people do before washing machines?' said my niece. 'When I was a boy we had something called Wash Day', I told her. You dare not go anywhere near the scullery in our house on wash day. You dare not go into the yard either. Wash Day was women's work and God help the man that interfered. Only my Gran could operate the Ascot without burning herself. My Grandfather said he would rather fire a trench mortar than get near 'that bloody thing'. My Dad told me he thought that Wash Days were a form of witchcraft that kept men out of their own homes and showed the superiority of women. Gran told Grandad that working with horses brought with it a certain aroma that needed a good deal of soaping, scrubbing and dollying to it get out. Mum told Dad that as he appeared to spend all day lying about in oil and grease he could hardly complain if his overalls lost their colouring after being washed. Neither man dared to complain.

I can remember the copper and the dolly tub and the mangle. But most of all I remember the steam. It got everywhere. In every nook and every cranny, it got on the walls, on the ceiling, on the furniture, even in the outside lavvy. It made the lavvy paper damp and steamed up the windows downstairs. This was not just our house. On Mondays it was everyone's house. The whole street was at it. You would have thought that each scullery had a steam engine in it. Gran and Mum used to wash whist listening to the wireless. They start early as soon as Dad and Grandad were off to work, and we knew that we were expected to leave for school as soon as we had our breakfast. No- one was to interfere; no-one was to offer help and certainly no-one was to offer advice. That came later when the washing was hanging proudly on the line and the women discussed the finer points of Wash Day. Mum and Gran used to stop to listen to 'Mrs Dales Diary' and have a cup of tea and then stop again for 'Workers Playtime'. Mum liked Arthur Askey but not Tommy Trinder. My Gran agreed. 'It's that cockney accent of his, it sounds like a wasp buzzing against a windowpane, I keep wanting to hit him with a rolled-up newspaper'. At last, the washing was done, and it was time for the mangle. This was operated with the sort of precise teamwork that you would usually find in a ballet troupe. Flatten the garment on the scullery table. Lift it off. Open the rollers and carefully place the front of the garment between them. Close the rollers and turn the handle and out it comes ready for the line, or perhaps not. Perhaps the garment got wrapped around the rollers or only part of the garment got through. Perhaps the rollers got stuck or opened at the wrong moment, spilling the garment on the yard floor. Perhaps you got your fingers caught in the rollers. It could be dangerous work. It was certainly frustrating, but it had to be done. You could not send Him to work in grubby clothes, what would people think? And it was a matter of pride to make sure that your wash was on the line before anyone else's in the street. After it was on the line you had time to have a chat. You also had time to examine the washing on the lines of your neighbours. My Gran never missed the opportunity to inspect their washing. And if it was not up to her standards, well, she never said anything of course, but they knew. You had to keep up standards and afterwards, however tired you were you knew you done a good day's work. 'The only pity is', said Gran, 'We're not paid for it.' 'Perfection has its own reward' said my Mum.

The same niece asked me how people kept in touch with their friends and family that were not local. I told her we used to write to each other. She looked at me as if I were about to describe something from the nineteenth century. We all wrote. Gran used to write to relatives every week. Passing on news of the family and what was occurring locally and all the gossip, of course. Mum wrote to her family, and friends who she had met during the war. Men wrote less. Dad told me he thought that women were better at that sort of thing. Nowadays we might say that they are more creative. Grandad would take ages over a letter. 'Let me write it, for you' said Gran. 'Don't be silly woman' he would say 'it's for the pigeon club, they'd know if I hadn't written it myself!' Eventually Dad got a telephone for the house. He had one at his workshop for years. Grandad and Gran were not keen on it and still wrote letters. As Grandad said, 'You can read a letter and get pleasure out of it as many times as you like, you can't do that on the telephone'. He was right there.

Dad ran a big BSA Gold Star motorcycle. He had a Morris van for work but had refused to buy a car. One day he turned up outside the house driving a brand-new Ford Prefect. He told me later that Mum had insisted. She told him that she was not going through another winter on the back of the bike. She also said that a lot of folks owned a car nowadays. It was not, she said, a luxury item anymore. 'It'll be a washing machine next, I suppose' said father. 'Funny you should say that' she replied. 'My Mum wants a word about that and all'. I suppose all this happened over about four or five years. I cannot remember us being pressurized into buying these things. No-one in the family took the adverts on television or in the papers seriously but almost without knowing it we gained all the things that a modern family should own. It was true that Dad was proud of his car and Mum and Gran swore by the washing machine. Grandad would not know what to do on Saturday afternoons without Grandstand on the television. Dad was making more money from his business and wages were rising in the factories and in the mills that remained. It was almost as though these possessions were yours by right. At a price of course, and if that price was a little too expensive, well the magic of hire purchase would do the trick. No need to be envious of next doors possessions, you could afford them too. Wash Day was not the same now folk had washing machines. Everyone was happy with these new possessions and that was all that mattered, was it not?

The world around us

Grandad always used to listen to the evening news on the wireless. I remember the chimes of Big Ben, a brief silence and then the voice of Alvar Lidell. We all used to listen to the wireless. I do not remember when people started calling it the radio. It was always the wireless to Gran and Grandad. There was news from home and abroad. News from the Commonwealth and from America and Russia and from Egypt and Israel and everywhere. 'You get more information listening to the nine 'o clock news than a weeks-worth of newspapers' said Grandad. 'That's because you read the Daily Sketch' said Dad. 'I don't have the time to read The Times on me round' said Grandad. 'Anyway, the horses like the Daily Sketch.'

About the time Dad decided we should have a telephone, Mum decided we should have a television. I remember Dad was not too keen as they were expensive and still considered rather vulgar. Grandad was all for it. 'By 'eck' he said. 'Wrestling and horse racing, rugby and cricket, I'm all for that.' 'You'll be putting your hand in your pocket, will you?' said Dad. 'After all it looks as if you'll be watching it the most.' Grandad gave him a wink, but not a contribution. It was not long before we all sat around watching the black and white screen. Mum and Gran would not miss Coronation Street and you could not get Grandad away from Grandstand. Grandad still listened to the nine 'o clock news on the wireless. 'It's not the same with pictures' he said. Dad agreed, 'You need to use your own imagination when you listen to what's going on, not have it served up on a plate before your eyes.' Mum used to shake her head at this. 'That's what it's for, pictures. It brings pictures from all over the world into our parlour.' 'I can do without pictures of that big jessie Bruce Forsythe' said Dad. 'Don't think you're watching the BBC when Sunday Night at the London Palladium is on' said Mum. 'I think he's marvellous' said Gran. As soon as the music for the show came on Grandad and Dad left for the pub. Television made you aware of what was happening in the world. Not that everybody wanted to know but if you watched the news, and what today they call current affairs programmes, you could not help but pick up something. Suddenly the world got smaller.

Gran and Grandad, Mum and us children all went to chapel. Dad went only rarely. It was part of life. Sundays were special. You got up a little later, had time for a decent breakfast, put on your Sunday best and off you went. I do not remember anyone questioning religious beliefs. The chapel had been there for a hundred years. My Grandads parents went and so did their parents. It was traditional. It was also the right thing to do. 'I feel better once I've been' said my Gran. Grandad once told me that if ever he fancied not going, he would remind himself of that day at Ypres firing his Lee Enfield at hundreds of Germans until the bolt was too hot to operate and then putting on his bayonet and climbing on the top of the trench. 'People can scoff all they like, but my guardian angel was with me that day.' Dad sometimes used to say that God was looking the other way when the convoys got bombed or torpedoed. Some of the ships used to come home with the dead still below decks and young engineers like him often had to help remove the bodies. Dad did go to chapel at Easter and Christmas. 'Well, you've got to visit sometimes' he would say, 'Otherwise the almighty will think you've forgotten about him.'

I remember going back to school one September after the summer holidays. The family had been to St Annes for our holiday. It was posher than Blackpool but only just down the coast from it. I think this must have been in 1967. One of the lads had changed colour. He was brown. We could not believe it. Neither could Mr. Raines the teacher. This lad, Jimmy Simmons, had been on holiday to Spain. The weather was so hot, he had changed colour. Soon, other lad's families went to Spain. The world was getting smaller. The old ways were changing everything seemed to be speeding up. My Grandad did not like it. He spent more time down his allotment with his vegetables and his old pals. 'I wonder sometimes if folk have time to listen to the birds or sit still and watch a sunset' he said. I was amused at this. I had my own life now and my own friends and pastimes. The old ways did not seem important anymore. I believed in progress. I could see the big picture. I knew exactly where I was going and where I wanted to be. It was not with Gran or Grandad or Mum or Dad. It was not stuck in some backwater with flat caps and football pools, gloomy pubs and even gloomier people. I wanted out. Dad's business got me through university and university got me a nice qualification in sociology and that got me a nice job with the civil service, in London, naturally.

The years passed, as they do. You do not notice it at first. Some well-deserved promotions and some small successes elsewhere. A house that is now worth what to my parents and grandparents would have seemed a fortune. Travelling back home less and less. Just the odd phone call and Christmas and Birthday presents. Grandparents die, aunts and uncles and then your parents. That makes you sit up. You start looking at things a bit more closely. A little doubt starts creeping in. You begin to think things over a bit more and start looking at yourself and your situation. You realize that however clichéd it might be, possessions and financial security are not everything. Things might be OK for you but there are goodness knows how many millions of people who have missed out on that bright future that you thought of as your birth right. And what about my immediate future? I never married. There were always things to do and see and visit and buy. Always another toy or pastime. Yes, I suppose I was selfish. Possessions rather than people, success rather than friendships. Hmm, a bit late for regrets now. It makes you think though. Perhaps if I moved back. I wonder if Grandad's allotment is still there. I wonder if my brother and sister and their families would welcome me. I wonder if there are any old mates still around. There is nothing like times winged chariot to get you looking backwards and get you to ask that question 'When were you last really happy?'

Afterthoughts

The Occasional Performer usually approaches a performance by running over past appearances, making notes on pro's and con's, going over the current material until he is (almost) word perfect and then spends time in prayer. You cannot be too careful in the entertainment business, so it always helps to have the original creator on side. After being announced by my colleagues I then explained to the audience the programme for the next thirty minutes or so. I opened with the song 'What makes you happy?' and was gratified to see that eye contact was still holding firm. I then asked the audience if they would 'Help me with a few old songs? I launched into the first verse and chorus of every song I could recall with the words 'Happy' or 'Happiness' included. The songs I chose were selected because I hoped that they would be known by the audience. Fortunately, I was proved right and the ladies joined in enthusiastically. With eye contact still holding I then announced that I would be telling a series of short stories which were based around several generations of the same family and how that family came to terms with changing times and attitudes. Did what made us happy then, make us happy now? Do todays conveniences and possessions make up for what some people say we have lost? I mentioned this as I hoped that during the question and answer session that would follow the completion of the survey these topics would be raised by the audience themselves. The stories being a precursor, albeit I hoped an entertaining one, to the survey itself. I have to say that the reception I received from the 'Golden Oldies' surpassed my expectations considerably. It was one of those small triumphs that leaves the Occasional Performer with a warm glow of satisfaction rather than the dreaded empty feeling of 'Thank goodness that's over with, how soon can I leave?' So, as a precursor it appeared to work. Creativity (albeit of the occasional kind) perhaps can partner certain academic research, and if it contributes to the general level of happiness of people, or helps us learn more about it, that is fine by me.

References

Ackroyd, P, R. (1971) *The First Book of Samuel*. Cambridge: Cambridge University Press

Aristotle (1961) *Aristotle's poetics*. New York: Hill and Wang

Brice, S. and Fernández A, S. (2018). Riding the tide. Socially engaged art and resilience in an uncertain future. in E, M Trell., B, Restemeyer., M, M. Bakema and B. van Hoven (Eds.) *Governing for resilience in vulnerable places*. Abingdon: Routledge (pp. 224-243)

Chang, W. J. and Wyszomirski, M. (2015) What is arts entrepreneurship? Tracking the development of its definition in scholarly journals. *Artivate: A Journal of Entrepreneurship in the Arts*, 4, 2

Dillon, S. (2006) Assessing the positive influence of music activities in community development programs. *Music Education Research*, 8, 2

Eisner, E. (2008) Art and knowledge in J. G. Knowles and A. L. Cole (Eds.) *Handbook of the arts in qualitative research*. London: Sage (pp. 3-12)

Finnegan, R. (2012) Music, experience and the anthropology of emotion In M. Clayton, T. Herbert, and R. Middleton (Eds.) *The cultural study of music: A critical introduction*. New York: Routledge (pp. 181–192)

Homer., Fitzgerald, R. (1990) *The Odyssey*. New York: Vintage Books

Jarrett, S. and Day, H. (2008) M*usic Composition for DUMMIES*. Hoboken: Wiley

Jones, K. and Leavy, P. (2014) A conversation between Kip Jones and Patricia Leavy: Arts-based research, performative social science and working on the margins. *The Qualitative Report*, 19, 38, 1-7

Manjon, S. B. and Guo, W. (2015) Think tank: A collaborative approach to student learning, organizational assessment, and community-based arts. Artivate: *A Journal of Entrepreneurship in the Arts*, 4, 2

Robertson, S. and Monaghan, L. F. (2012) Embodied heterosexual masculinities, part 2: Foregrounding men's health and emotions. *Sociology Compass*, 6, 2, 151–165

Ruud, E. (2013) Can music serve as a 'cultural immunogen'? An explorative study. *International Journal of Qualitative Studies on Health and Well-being*, 8, 1, 1–12

Taylor, P. and Murphy, C. (2014) *Catch the fire. An art-full guide to unleashing the creative power of youth, adults and communities*. Gabriola Island, British Columbia: New Society Publishers

Volgsten, U. (2012) The roots of music: Emotional expression, dialogue and affect attunement in the psychogenesis of music. *Musicae Scientiae*, 16, 2, 200–216

Volgsten, U. and Pripp, O. (2016) Music, memory and affect attunement: Connecting Kurdish diaspora in Stockholm. Culture Unbound. *Journal of Current Cultural*

Research, 8, 2, 144–164

West, M. (2000) Music therapy in antiquity in P. Horden (Ed.) *Music as medicine: The history of music therapy since antiquity.* Aldershot, England: Ashgate (pp. 51 - 68)

A bit of grim makes us great up North

Elisabeth Long

Introduction

Despite the prevailing stereotypical view of the grim North West of England with its dark satanic mills and rain 'that wets you through', there are many factors which suggest the local people are happy to be Northerners either by birth or mind set (Kay, 2003). These factors would undoubtedly include socio economic conditions such as the unexpected unspoilt countryside and the totally expected cheaper cost of living (Poulter, 2014). This study hopes to look beyond these material benefits and consider whether there is a legacy of values and beliefs inherited from previous generations, along with their flat vowels and shorter stature, that enables the 21st Century Northerner to be more resilient, and therefore, happier with his or her lot.

This brief exploration is focused on Bolton, the UK's largest town and would-be city, arguably based in either Lancashire or Greater Manchester depending on the age and regional loyalties of who you ask (The Bolton News, 2012). Its purpose is to look beyond the harsh facts and figures that so often portray and perpetuate the perception of life in Bolton today and consider if the town's history is a clue to why the current population manage adversity with humour and resilience. The content is based on 30 years' experience of working with local people who seek a happier existence for themselves and give their time to help others improve their mental wellbeing. The content is also overtly biased by the author being a Boltonian.

'Hey, Blakey, does your bus go by the dark satanic mills?' (song lyric Blackwell, 2005)

In the summer of 2017 an article by Andy Walton appeared in *The Guardian* quoting a line from a TS Eliot poem to summarise his feelings following a brief visit to his former home town (Walton, 2017). The line 'this is the way the world ends. Not with a bang but a whimper', contrasts the author's memory of being in a busy and seemingly prosperous Bolton during 1988, to the present town centre which appears to be losing its uniqueness, its people and its purpose.

There was more than a whimper throughout Bolton in response to this story. The article was reported in Bolton News and on the North West television news channels, and for two or three weeks after its publication online-interest groups scattered their arguments for and against Bolton described as a 'nothing of a town', throughout social media channels. Walton interviews a number of local people including the then Bolton North East MP David Crausby. Thanks to the common journalistic trait of adding respondents' ages, it is fair to assume the chosen few have been in Bolton long enough to witness a number of local and national changes, and found them wanting. Their comments mention former pride, sadness and loss of identity as the town they once knew seems to disappear around them.

A younger interviewee, Sam, 'a charity worker, 25', appears to initially agree with their negative stance and provides the phrase 'nothing of a town' quoted in the article's title; but balance is restored as both Bolton Council and Sam get further column inches to provide the now despondent reader with some optimism about the town's future. Sam adds: 'Bolton's got a real chance at making itself again. People are very generous, from a charitable perspective; people want to help each other. I would very happily have my family in Bolton and shop in Bolton and continue to invest in Bolton'. Walton ends the article by saying that 'the city [sic] will need many more like him' (Walton, 2017). Fortunately for Bolton there does seem to be many more like him. Despite the often unwanted changes to the town's external appearance, a brief review of its social history to the present day, would suggest that there has always been residents who share and practise Sam's views.

The news story's theme is to look at the physical impact on the town as it disentangles itself from its powerful industrial and manufacturing heritage. In the past civic buildings, ornately designed mills and an enormous choice of public places (including shops, public houses, theatres and cinemas), were tangible symbols of safety and prosperity for the local population, so it is not surprising that their gradual decline over the last 50 years or so leaves some feeling bereft and insecure.

Although nostalgia for the past is not a new phenomenon, previous visitors have been more impressed by the resilience of the inhabitants above the appearance of the town. The English author William Gerhardi visiting the town in the 1920s said: '[Bolton] looked like the bottom of a pond with the water drained off. In here, were the people who if they could endure this, could endure anything.' (Gerhardi, - quoted in Robinson, 2018 pp 7) Gerhardi's fleeting comment acknowledges the difficulties and stoicism of the people who lived and laboured within these disappearing edifices, but how they endured and thrived is not given consideration.

It is the social networks, community-led support and the friendships based on empathy and trust that existed in these buildings which resonate through the generations. Inherited social constructs are common to all cultures, but the Bolton way of being is built on centuries of interdependency and reliance on others to survive one of the bloodiest battles in the English civil war , the Industrial Revolution, the demotion of Bolton Wanderers to lowly football leagues and throughout it all the weather.

The town's motto, flashed under the Bolton Coat of Arms, like a subtitle, is 'Supera Moras' – meaning 'overcoming delays or difficulties'. There is not much Latin spoken here today, but this phrase is just as apt to the present generation as it was to our Victorian ancestors when it was unveiled in 1890 (Bolton Council, 2019). The values that held these communities together are still apparent in today's population. This continuing mind set may be less tangible than a Victorian mill, but the tacit understanding of how individuals and communities grow through difficult periods can be a real asset when facing the challenges of modern life.

> 'That's life, son. At your age it'll make you laugh but one day it'll make you bloody cry.' (Naughton, 1966 quote from Film script)

The importance of the psycho-social influence of the mills is identified by Ian Robinson in his book *The Town That Vanished* (2018). This work provides an insight into the famous 1930s Mass Observation studies in Bolton (or 'Worktown' as it was unimaginatively referred to). Robinson uses excerpts from the notes produced mainly by Southern-based academic students, and a smattering of local people with a bit of time on their hands, to discuss technological and cultural changes that have occurred in the town since its publication.

The Worktown records consist of hundreds of observations and conversations with Boltonians in both social and working situations. These studies provide plenty of evidence of interdependence between members of working communities, who offered both practical and emotional support to each other beyond the expected collegial responsibilities of their working relationships. Robinson states: 'Contrary to some of the benign sepia-tinged representations of working life common in popular culture, Britain's industrial towns were grubby and frankly downright ugly; however the sense of community that clearly existed amongst Worktown's mill workers is one aspect of life that is usually recalled with great affection by those who experienced it.' (Robinson, 2018).

Before the 1930s there are limited personal accounts which provide a glimpse into the relationships between families and workers. Alice Foley's (1891 - 1974) autobiographical book is a rare example and a definite contender for the 'Grim up North' award. Despite her having the 'advantage' of not going into the mill until she was 13, Foley had a life long struggle with male colleagues to become one of the UK's first female trade unionists. Yet her book *A Bolton Childhood* is full of kindness and humanity, summed up in the following statement: 'Life was ever meaningful, even if something of a battlefield, and we had abiding faith in the ultimate achievement of the human race' (Foley, 1973, p 43). As a millworker and trade unionist during the 1930s it is likely that Alice Foley may have crossed paths with a Worktown Mass Observer. For someone who lost her parents at an early age, if a conversation had happened between her and one of the researchers she would probably support Robinson's finding that:

'Bolton's mills and factories played an important socialising role, especially in the lives of young girls … this enduring female comradeship can be discerned in the shared moral values that governed the behaviour of the town's young women' (Robinson, 2018, pp 229)

In the 1960s the Mass Observation Movement was recognised as an attributing factor to the growth of social realism in literature, movies and television shows (Armstrong, 2014) This meant that lives of the Northern working classes were no longer just the subjects for dispassionate study by an elite few, but became entertainment for all (including an avidly cinema going Bolton audience). Although these films and programmes were fictionalised stories the screenwriters were often both Northern and from working class origins. This genre included the Bolton novelist Bill Naughton, whose plays *Spring and Port Wine* (1970) and *The Family Way* (1966) were adapted for the cinema and filmed throughout the town. Apart from providing a visual reference into this period of Bolton's past, both films deal with time honoured issues, such as lack of money, family discord and demands of work, which are as relevant today as they were 50 years ago. Although the viewer can expect a happy ending, the two Naughton films provide an early opportunity to see how 'ordinary people' develop social skills and resilience through trust and collaboration.

These are universal traits recognisable across history and geography, but the Naughton films in particular have a distinctive point of reference for Bolton audiences old and new. This special ingredient is what author Rosemarie Jarski describes as the 'humour of recognition', and is still evident in fictional representations of the North (Jarski, 2014). This would suggest that humour in reality plays an important part in human relationships and is a recognised way to cope with the certainty of the uncertainty of life.

The comedian Lucy Beaumont recognised that humour is many things, but believes in her article for The Daily Telegraph that 'mostly it's a coping mechanism. Having warmth in your comedy must be something to do with struggle.' Beaumont believes that the real differences in humour is not a south-north divide, but is actually about class. 'I think it's being working class that gives you the warmth. When it comes to the north and south, I don't believe that one is funnier than the other, but they [Northerners] do breed different comedians.' (Beaumont, 2014).

The concept of a supportive community network bound together by the use of humour to deconstruct shared adverse experiences may explain why local comic Peter Kay told Manchester Evening News he continued to live in Bolton because *'I can only write about what I know ... I'd be crap anywhere else.'* (Manchester Evening News, 1998). His subsequent career would suggest that this is not entirely true, but this self-depreciating statement recognises the origins of Kay's humour and the ongoing inspiration he gets remaining close to his roots.

Jarski emphasises the importance of humour as a sort of existential survival kit.

'The North of England's special kind of wit relies on self-depreciation, the desire to prick pomposity and the ability to find the comic in the tragedy of everyday life ... Laughter and tears are never far apart in Northern life ... with its rugged landscape and tough industrial heritage combining to create a people who find laughter in the darkest corners.' (Jarski, 2014).

Awareness of this coping strategy may explain why Bolton continues to home a fairly stable population to quarter of a million people. Some of today's population could probably trace their ancestry to those Boltonians in residence when the German philosopher Engels (1820 - 1895), visited town and described it as 'a dark unattractive hole' (Engels, 1845). This viewpoint has strangely echoed through the years with a current resident likening Bolton becoming 'a doughnut'! (Beaumont, 2014). Other Boltonians may not be as intentionally comedic as Peter Kay in describing the trials and tribulation of their modern day lives, but it is rare to have a conversation locally where humour is not used to create a connection or bond. Admittedly humour can be cruel, but delivered in a context where there is a tacit understanding of trust and respect between the giver and the receiver, the use of humour can lead to compassion. Lucy Beaumont sums this up the northern way of being simply by saying: 'If you can still laugh when things are tough, you've found the secret of happiness' (Beaumont, 2014).

'I'm sorry love. We're Northern and that's all there is to it.' (Cardmix, 2013)

Almost 30 years ago I was sat in a circle with about 12 other people in a large drawing room overlooking a beautiful garden in the centre of Rugby. It was the first day of my training to become a volunteer counsellor with the national charity Relate, and as is the general custom in these situations each member of the circle was asked to introduce themselves to the rest of the group.

I told the group that I was Elisabeth, with an 's' not a 'z', and following the birth of my first child I had decided to retrain as a teacher, following a career in the press and media. I mentioned my work as a volunteer receptionist for Relate in Bolton alongside other volunteer counsellors and a very well stocked library. I explained for a new mother the lure of intelligent conversation and the opportunity to read a few books in the relative peace and quiet of an office a couple of evenings a week, was a big attraction. All I knew about counselling at this stage I had gained from scanning text books on site, but I could not fail to see the positive impact it had on those who came weekly to our centre. To add a bit of gritty realism here - Bolton Relate's office at this time was three former bedrooms in a dilapidated terraced house on a cobbled street, next door to the Samaritans.

I soon became aware that this voluntary role complemented the learning I was gaining on my teaching programme. So, with trepidation I applied for a counselling training bursary to the Bolton Relate board, who with some worries about my former career as an itinerant journalist and writer, agreed to sponsor me. A few months later I was at Relate's National Training College in Rugby with other would-be voluntary counsellors from across the country.

There was a polite, but noticeable silence after I'd finished my introduction and I began to be slightly concerned that I may have said too much or even too little. There were expectant looks to the next member of the circle about to introduce herself, but rather than initially sharing her name, she exclaimed loudly to the group 'What a surprising story, and what a super accent!', and the group laughed.

Over the years I have often wondered why this comment left me feeling slightly uncomfortable and questioning why I was even thinking of becoming a counsellor. Yet I did become a counsellor, and for anyone else who describes themselves as such will know there are many opportunities to reflect on those niggly memories over the years. At the time I was not aware of the term 'Imposter Syndrome', a psychological phenomenon where someone's lack of confidence in certain situations makes them feel like a fraud (Clance and Imes, 1978). It would go some way in describing my reaction at the time. After all I was signing up to four years' unpaid work and training, which appeared to have no direct correlation with what I had experienced before. I was still amazed I had been selected by Relate, and beside this I was certainly taking my time adjusting to motherhood.

Looking through the lens of time I am surprised at how humorous I now find this incident and probably more importantly my reaction to it. Oh I laughed along with the group at the time, but internally my self-esteem was shrinking and I wanted to go home. Back in Bolton I could have shared my story, inwardly proud of my achievements but, making sure that I was self-depreciating enough not to come across as 'cocky'. (Cocky is a local expression for someone who appears overly confident, somewhat foolhardy and sometimes belligerent). If I was loud enough (so they could hear me at the back), mee-mawed if it was an older audience and injected an element of humour, I doubt anyone would have commented on how I sounded.

(Mee-mawing was a form of speech and mime with exaggerated movements to allow lip reading by workers in weaving sheds in the nineteenth and twentieth centuries).

The reason I now find this incidence amusing is that despite living and working in different parts of the UK, I had been aware of my northern-ness, but I had never considered it a hindrance to what I had wanted to achieve in life. This statement from a new colleague sparked a growing appreciation of the connection between my heritage and the direction my life was about to take. In retrospect I could not have possibly asked for a more fitting experience to launch my new career in helping people explore their feelings and adapt to change. At the time I felt I was being prejudged and raised doubts about whether I should become a counsellor or not. Three decades later I know this was an off-hand statement made by somebody who was probably equally nervous as I was. Unknown to the speaker she had tapped into my own misgivings, yet this awareness was my awakening. I began to realise I already had one key advantage before the formal training started and this was because I am a Boltonian!

I have been surrounded for most of my life by people who managed to 'get on wi' yit', (get on with it in local dialect) by using humour to express their compassion and care for their families and communities. By becoming a counsellor hopefully my native communication skills allow me to express warmth, interest and compassion. Yet it was the subsequent training and experience which made me consciously change my focus to working with people to help them lead more satisfying lives, as opposed to working at them to get their stories.

'You're going to have to start taking pleasure in the misfortune of others, Kenneth, or you're going to have a long and unhappy old age.'(Coronation Street, 2009)

Today 'trouble at t'mill' is more likely to be due to its conversion into apartments, and the inhabitants probably prefer eating pizza than pike caught in a mill pond, but life in 21st century Bolton can still be physically and mentally challenging. To review the town through local and national statistics, my unqualified conclusion would be to say in the local idiom that it is 'middling'. Government tables on a range of factors such as income, employment, health and education, place the town's results about mid-way in most studies when compared to similar sized towns in Greater Manchester (The Bolton News, 2015).

What is worth noting when considering the wellbeing and welfare of local people is the apparently growing disparity of health, wealth and employment outcomes within the Bolton boundaries. It is a truth universally acknowledged by economists and sociologists alike that once these factors are addressed people will be happier (Helliwell, 2013). National statistics state that over 40 per cent of Bolton's current population are living in parts of the town regarded as being within the top 20 per cent of the most deprived areas in England (Bolton Council, 2015). Unsurprisingly these deprived locations correlate with what were once the most heavily industrialised areas of the town, whose regeneration has been handicapped by recession and under investment. On the surface it seems like Bolton is a town of two halves, or 'haves' and 'have nots'. The discrepancy between household incomes, increasing levels of poverty and faltering life expectancy rates which regularly feature in both local and national press, would seem to suggest that we are drifting back to conditions that some of our predecessors would recognise. But if there was a way of time travelling between the 'sepia tinted past' and the present, could we identify inherited values and attitudes that help current communities face adversity and change?

The community-led organisation I co-founded in Bolton is based in a building built at a time when the industrial revolution was beginning to map out the future of our town. This former Regency mansion is a far cry from H G Wells' famous time machine, but I aim to use it as a vehicle to consider if there is a 'Bolton spirit' or communal way of being that is still detectable within my colleagues or those who use our services today. Silverwell House and its former grounds represent a microcosm of the history of Bolton, going back to the belief that its first local inhabitants were Bronze Age settlers (Bolton Council, 2008). Almost nothing is known about our oldest ancestors, but recent genetic research would claim they were migrants from Northern France who spread up the western part of Britain well before the Roman invasion (University of Oxford, 2008). As for what the Romans did for Bolton - practically nothing it seems, except build bypasses to avoid it.

Immigrants from Europe feature again in the town's medieval history when Flemish weavers in the 1330's settled in Bolton bringing their textile, clog making skills and surprisingly their dialect with them (Halliwell Local History Society 2020). Parts of the town at this time were under the demesne of a sheep farming family called Pilkington, who grew richer as Bolton's reputation for weaving fine fabric grew. Their descendants switched from wool to cotton manufacturing and one of them, Major John Pilkington (d. 1828) built Silverwell House in 1790. During his tenure he persuaded local inventor Samuel Crompton, often referred to as 'The Father of the Industrial Revolution', to share his Spinning Mule machine with other mill owners across the North (Daniels, 1920). The Mule may have heralded the start of mass production internationally and wealth locally, but the proud independent weavers who strutted up and down Bradshawgate with £5 notes stuck in the brim of their hats did not like it (Chapman, 1972). Pilkington had to employ a Georgian version of Group 4 security to prevent his mills from being destroyed.

A century before the land which Pilkington used to create his own personal park had witnessed an estimated 1,000 civilians massacred in 1644, as they defended Parliamentarian Bolton against the Royalist opposition in the English Civil War (Casserly, 2012). This bloody history did not stop another wave of weavers into the area, when refugee Huguenots fled religious persecution in France and literally set up shops in Bolton. Evidence of their three story houses and surnames are still scattered throughout the town, which during the latter part of the 17th century was known as the 'Geneva of the North' because of its strong non-conformist beliefs.

During the 1830s John Dean (1794 – 1851) lived in Silverwell. This was a time when workless people were rioting against the high cost of food, taxes and living conditions. Dean was both a Justice of the Peace and from a mill owning family, but he sympathised with the plight of the people. In 1838 he helped draw up a 'Charter of Incorporation' for Bolton, which a 20 year old Queen Victoria approved later that year. Dean may have empathised with his starving working class neighbours, but living at Silverwell House was becoming less 'des res' and potentially downright dangerous. In the same year he is working on an important part of Bolton's history he is also trying to rent out the property. It is not clear whether this is an economic or safety decision, as rioting was taking place close to his home and his place of work at the Magistrates' Court. The rental notice from 1838 provides a glimpse into the mindset of the early 19th century mill owning plutocracy (Bolton Chronicle, 1938). Alongside its numerous rooms, wine cellars and butler's pantry, it also lists an indoor 'water closet', which was probably as shocking to the average Victorian Boltonian as the hurricane that blew through Bolton one year later taking the roof off Silverwell House (*Liverpool Mercury*, 1839).

The WC could have been a strong selling point for the Malletts, a family of doctors from Nottingham who moved into the house in the late 1850s. George Mallett Senior (1803 – 1871) became a surgeon at the town's first Infirmary where he continued to work throughout his life, alongside managing to run a private clinic at home for the town's 'leading families … in the higher circles, as well as amongst his humbler neighbours'. The latter patients probably did not have much use for his book, *A brief history of bathing: with remarks on the necessity and directions for use of the bath*' (Bolton Chronicle, 1871). They may have had a share in a tin bath, which they probably regarded as sufficient rather than necessary. Like Mallett, who helped develop the town's museum and gallery in his spare time, other key members of the community had a sense of duty to provide for services that would enhance the health and wealth of the growing working population. From the middle of the 19th Century these new immigrants were the Scots and Irish fleeing from hardship in their own countries. An early female professional dedicated to improving the lives of women was Sarah Corbett, who became the headmistress of one of the country's first girls' schools founded at Silverwell House in 1879 (Millington 2008). The mathematically minded Mrs Corbett, was one of the first female graduates from Cambridge, which was probably why she valued the teaching of 'Arithmetic, Algebra, Geometry, French, German and Natural Science' to local girls (Bolton Evening News, 1880).

Six years after the school had moved to Chorley New Road and became Bolton School Girls Division, Silverwell House disappeared from view. Originally built in fields on the edge of the town centre, by 1887 it was now right in the middle of Bradshawgate Bolton's busiest thoroughfare. At the end of the 19th century it was unlikely that you would still find weavers with fivers in their hats, but this street with its impressive Victorian architecture was the thriving hub of Bolton's social life, hosting expensive shops, theatres with the latest acts, newly emerging cinemas and many many pubs.

No wonder that local architect Captain Marshall Robinson was allowed to cover the last of Pilkington's parkland with a huge Drill Hall attached to the East facing facade of the building. This structure provided a central event space for education, training entertainment and wellbeing for all, with the old house relegated to being one wall of the new building. Over the next century Silverwell House faded out of public memory and thousands of Boltonians prepared for the first World War, played Badminton and other sports, attended exhibitions of mill machinery and cars, paraded their dogs in shows and drank real ale in a big shed over its former gardens. The building was exposed when the Drill Hall was demolished in the 1990s. Its 21st Century life to date has been as an office block and from 2016 the place myself and my colleagues work from.

'Because this is the place in our hearts, in our homes
Because this is the place that's a part of our bones.'
(Walsh, quoted in *Manchester Evening News*, 22nd May 2018)

The history of Silverwell provides just a whisper of the events and people who have shared our space throughout the centuries. We can hope from their recorded achievements that these earlier inhabitants would have considered part of their lives happy or fulfilling. We do know their situations would have been materially different to us, but like present day Boltonians they faced significant personal and societal changes during the times they lived in and around Silverwell. From the limited information we have about these people we know they faced tragedy and despair, which adversely impacted on their sense of self and belonging. We can hope our predecessors have passed on their attitudes towards coping with adversity by developing resilience through having respect for themselves and others in their communities. The psychotherapist James Davies recognises that 'certain kinds of emotional discontent, far from being useless inconveniences, can be resources to be tapped in the service of greater wellbeing, not only for the individual at hand, but also for the community at large.' (Davies, 2011)

It is this positive attitude and way of being that my organisation, 1point, promotes to the 3,000 plus people per year who pass through our centre at Silverwell House. We are a not-for-profit community enterprise owned by a collaboration of local charities who offer counselling, psychotherapy and training to anyone in Bolton who is experiencing depression and anxiety, the 21st Century's versions of tragedy and despair. In the context of this study it is interesting to report that one of our popular professional workshops is 'The Use of Humour in Therapy'. We treat the house as a working partner because it provides tangible evidence that your function and purpose may change over time, but if you are supported, respected and valued you can survive and thrive. We know from the feedback collected over the past four years we have been in residence, more than 12,000 visitors find its calming presence emits a sense of safety and feeling of belonging.

The house's function at present is to provide a central hub for 1point's collaboration of members who support about 160 counselling practitioners in different locations across the borough. About 12 per cent of these workers are paid, the remaining provide their time freely to offer between two to six appointments each a week to the Bolton population. In an in-house survey we were able to determine that roughly 35 per cent were currently completing professional therapy qualifications and the remaining workforce were either in alternative paid work or recently retired. It could be argued that it is these unpaid therapists are an example of the ongoing positive community spirit evident in Bolton throughout the centuries. This is supported by the fact that more than 80 per cent of them live and/or work in the borough (Long, 2016).

The town has a surprisingly long history of trained voluntary counsellors providing 'Talking Therapies'. One of the country's first National Marriage Guidance services (the former name of Relate), began operating from the Victoria Halls in the 1940s. This agency has an unbroken 70 year plus record of service in Bolton and paved the way for more voluntary counselling and befriending activity in the following years. The popularity of these services promoted the development of training courses to meet the needs of those wanting to access services, and those wishing to enhance their therapeutic skills to help them.

It would be interesting to know how many thousands of Boltonians have undertaken some form of counsellor training in the town. I believe there are so many of them, that when Peter Kay speaks of being stopped on a street in Bolton and asked 'Now where am I going?', this could be equally an invitation to a theoretical existentialist debate, rather than someone asking for directions! (Kay, 2003). Alongside Relate, many similar styled national organisations have developed a presence in Bolton: well-known charities such as the Samaritans and Barnardo's work alongside small independent groups created to meet specific local needs. In 2017 a joint piece of research identified that the Voluntary, Community and Social Enterprise (VCSE) sector in Bolton was 'impressive in its size, diversity and scope of activities. It provides a significant contribution to Bolton's economy and to the health and wellbeing of local people needing help, support, information and guidance.' During this period the report estimates that Bolton's Third Sector provided 2.3 million positive interventions to the lives of Bolton citizens (Bolton Council, 2017).

The specific concept of the 'Big Society' defined by the Conservative Party in 2010 to link the VCSE sector with local government, seemed to have drifted into oblivion in these more politically challenging times (UK Government, 2010). However, the move towards a stronger working alliance between the statutory organisations and the communities they serve appears to be growing in the North West. Since the Government devolved health and social care responsibilities to the combined authorities of Greater Manchester in 2015, there has been a county-wide upsurge in new schemes and services 'co-designed' by statutory agencies and their partners from the VCSE sector (GMCA, 2013).

This is not the first time that the ten boroughs of Greater Manchester have presented a united front, but the formation of the metropolitan county founded in 1974 only lasted 12 years before being disbanded. This second coming appears more community and value driven than the old model and has increased opportunities for us to work alongside our neighbours who have the same history, the same humour and the same way of dealing with tragedy and success. These shared beliefs are perfectly summed up by the following words in Tony Walsh's rousing poem, 'This is the Place':

'Because this is a place that has been through some hard times: oppressions, recessions, depressions, and dark times.
But we keep fighting back with Greater Manchester spirit. Northern grit, Northern wit, and Greater Manchester's lyrics.
Because this is a place where we stand strong together, with a smile on our face, Greater Manchester forever.'
(Walsh quoted in *Manchester Evening News*, 22nd May 2018)

Postscript

It feels important to mention that whilst I was writing this chapter our closest neighbours experienced a major fire which made national and international news. The building accommodated over 200 students and thanks to the quick response of the local fire services everyone survived even though they lost their homes and belongings. Also quick to respond were the people of

Bolton who opened up their homes, provided clothing and food, not only to the students but other people that live close by. And this wave of kindness and compassion also spread to 1point as local organisations created room for us to keep services going whilst we had to vacate Silverwell House for seven weeks.

It was strange to see Britain's Prime Minister walking down Bradshawgate (hatless and fiver-less), and the Mayor of Greater Manchester standing on 'safe ground' outside our front door. I am pleased to say that apart from scorched window frames and a smell that feels like a few *Woodbine* smokers have taken residence; Silverwell House is still here in the centre of Bolton. Its solid presence providing a safe space for anyone to talk about how they felt about the fire or anything else that was making life difficult for them. Then life became difficult for us all as we faced Coronavirus spreading fear and anxiety across the world. Yet behind the closed doors and empty streets there are thousands of people cheerfully facing adversity, showing resilience, compassion and creatively reaching out to support their communities locally and elsewhere. This includes the 1point network staff and volunteers – with genuine appreciation I dedicate this chapter to them.

References

Armstrong, R. (2003) Essay on Social Realism. [Accessed 27th December 2019 at http://www.screenonline.org.uk/film/id/1037898/index.html]

Beaumont, L. (2014) The Secrets of Northern Comedy, *The Daily Telegraph*, 25 June

Blackwell, N. (lyricist) (2005) 'Depression Beyond Tablets' from the Half Man Half Biscuit album. Achtung Bono. Album, Label: Probe Plus Records

Bolton Community Volunteer Service (2017) *10gm – The State of the VCSE Sector Report.* Sheffield Hallam University: Sheffield

Bolton Council (2008) *Silverwell St & Wood St Conservation Area Appraisal.* [Accessed 27th December 2019 at https://www.bolton.gov.uk/conservation/conservation-areas]

Bolton Council (2015) *Indices of Multiple Deprivation: Briefing Report.* [Accessed 27th December 2019 at https://www.bolton.gov.uk/statistics-data/deprivation-statistics]

Bolton Council (2017) *Bolton Vision 2030 Report.* [Accessed 27th December 2019 at https://www.boltonvision.org.uk/conferences]

Bolton Council (2019) *Links in a Chain.* [Accessed 27th December 2019 at https://www.boltonmayors.org.uk]

Bolton Chronicle (1838) To Let Notice. 12th October 1838

Bolton Chronicle (1871) George Mallet, obituary. June 1871

Bolton Evening News (1880) Advertisement for A Girls' School. 20th August 1880

Cardmix (2013) *I'm Sorry Love. We're Northern and that's all there is to it'*, Greeting card

Casserly, D. (2012) *Massacre: The Storming of Bolton*. Stroud, Gloucestershire: Amberley Publishing

Chapman, S. (1972) *The Cotton Industry in the Industrial Revolution*. London: Palgrave Macmillan

Clance, P., and Imes, S. (1978) *The Reality of Imposter Syndrome*, cited on https://www.psychologytoday.com 2018. [Accessed 28th December 2018 at https://www.psychologytoday.com/gb/blog/real-women/201809/the-reality-imposter-syndrome#:~:text=Not%20an%20actual%20disorder%2C%20the,deserve%20the%20success%20they%20have]

Daniels, G. (1920) *The Early English Cotton Industry*. London: Longmans, Green & Company Ltd

Davies, J. (2011) *The Importance of Suffering*. London: Routledge

Engels, F. (1987) *The Condition of the Working Class in England*. London: Penguin Classics

Foley, A. (1973) *A Bolton Childhood*. Manchester: North West Workers Educational Association

Granada TV (2009) *Coronation Street)* (No further details available during lockdown 2020)

Greater Manchester Combined Authorities (2013) *Taking Charge of Our Health and Social Care in Greater Manchester Report*. [Accessed 27th December 2019 at https://www.gmhsc.org.uk/wp-content/uploads/2018/05/The-big-plan-Taking-Charge.pdf]

Halliwell Local History Society (2020) *Flemish Weavers and Clogs*. [Accessed 27th December 2019 at https://halliwell-lhs.co.uk/articles/flemish-weavers-and-clogs/]

Helliwell, J., Layard, R. and Sachs, J. 2013. *The World Happiness Report*. New York: UN Sustainable Development Solutions Network

Jarski, R. (2014) *The Wit and Wisdom of the North*. London: Ebury Press

Kay, P. (2003) *Live at the Albert Halls'*, Universal Pictures UK. Video distribution date 10th November 2003

Liverpool Mercury (1839) Hurricane. January

Long, E. (2016) *'1point Annual Report'* 1point. Bolton: north west Ltd

Manchester Evening News (1998) Northern Laughs. November

Millington, V. (2008) *A Thoroughly Modern Headmistress*. Carterton, Oxfordshire: Royd House

Naughton, B. (1966) (screenplay): *'The Family Way'*, British Lion Studios. Release date 18 December

Poulter, S. (2014) It really is cheaper to live in the north. *The Daily Mail*, 10th June

Robinson, I. (2018) *The Town That Vanished*. York: Worktown Publishing

The Bolton News (2012) Disappointment as Bolton Misses Out on City Status. 15th March

The Bolton News (2015) Bolton is Making Progress. 21st October

UK Government (2010) *Cabinet Policy Paper – Building the Big Society* [Accessed 27th December 2019 at https://www.gov.uk/government/publications/building-the-big-society]

University of Oxford (2018) *People of the British Isles Survey* [Accessed 27th December 2019 at https://peopleofthebritishisles.web.ox.ac.uk/home]

Walsh, T. (2018) This is the Place. *Manchester Evening News*, 22nd May

Walton, A. (2017) The North Remembers: How once-proud Bolton became a 'nothing of a town'. *The Guardian,* 22nd August

Acknowledgement

This is the Place, written by the poet, performer and author, Tony Walsh is reproduced here by kind permission of Forever Manchester.

Happiness and wellbeing in high schools: The Hummingbird Project

Ian Platt, Chathurika Kannangara, Michelle Tytherleigh, Sarah Banks and Jerome Carson

Introduction

Reductions in spending for specialist mental health care have taken place across the National Health Service (NHS) since 2008 (Docherty and Thornicroft, 2015). Local authorities have seen spending reductions of up to 32%. There has been a commensurate 48% decrease in the number of people with mental illnesses receiving appropriate care. Child and Adolescent Mental Health Services (CAMHS), have not been spared from this lack of appropriate treatment for mental health problems. Hindley (2014), conducted a survey involving members of the Faculty of Child and Adolescent Psychiatrists. Seventy seven per cent of respondents to this survey reported that they had experienced difficulties accessing admissions to inpatient beds; 79.1% stated that they had experienced concerns or incidents in terms of safeguarding whilst waiting for a bed; 76% reported that young people with unacceptably high-risk profiles had been managed in the community due to a lack of beds and 61.9% reported that they had experienced a young person being held in an inappropriate setting. Similar disinvestment as that discussed above, has taken place in education. Between 2010 and 2016, the Department for Education (DfE) budget was cut by 7.4% in real terms (Crawford and Keynes, 2015) and children are more likely to find mental health services through their school, than through any other referral system (Wolk et al, 2019). These issues all have the potential to have a negative effect on the mental health outcomes of children. The question then arises how one might intervene in these circumstances. The children's charity Medequip4Kids, in partnership with the University of Bolton and the University of Chester, have made small but significant steps in an attempt to intervene in these circumstances by launching the Hummingbird Project.

Scoping study

The Hummingbird Project began with a scoping study, in order to establish exactly what issues needed to be solved and what potential solutions might be most effective. The scoping study took place in two phases. Phase 1 aimed to discover the opinions of school leaders and Special Educational Needs Coordinators (SENCOs). Children in Europe spend more time doing school work than any other activity (Larson, 2001). It therefore stands to reason that educators are the professionals who have the greatest amount of contact time with school-aged children. They can therefore be reasonably expected to have insights and perspectives into child mental health that healthcare professionals and researchers do not. Mental health is often not covered in initial teacher training, and when it is, training is varied at best (Byrne et al, 2015). Therefore, educators tend not to have specialist mental health training and they may not necessarily have an extensive vocabulary relating to mental health. It therefore stands to reason that interviewing educators offers the opportunity to tease out information that other methods may not. Phase 1 used qualitative research methods, in the form of short, semi-structured interviews, over the telephone. These educators were asked what they believed to be the main causes of mental ill-health of school-aged children in the North West of England. They were also asked about the current state of mental health services for children, as well as the current state of mental health interventions in their schools. Once Phase 1 of the scoping study was completed, Phase 2 took place. Phase 2 involved in-depth, face-to-face, interviews. The hope here was that a more detailed interrogation of the needs of, and issues encountered by, educators in the North West might help to establish what might be done to intervene in the mental health of school students in the region. Results of Phases 1 and 2 of the scoping study are presented together.

Scoping study phase 1 method.

Phase 1 interviews were conducted over the telephone. The first point of contact was the Head Teacher at each school, followed by the SENCO or Head of Safeguarding. At the beginning of the telephone calls, consent was obtained verbally, and a script was read out to participants describing the steps taken to ensure anonymity. Contact details of the researchers was provided in case participants decided they wanted to withdraw from the study. One hundred and fifty one of the 3,499 total schools in the 23 Local Authorities in the North West of England were contacted for comment. Of these, 87 schools requested that questions be sent via email, though only 2 responded in this manner. A total of 23 schools provided responses to the interview questions, 15 of which were primary schools, and 8 secondary schools.

Scoping study phase 2 method

Thirty four schools were contacted to attempt to schedule an interview with the Head Teacher, SENCO, or Head of Safeguarding. Eleven such interviews took place, 4 of the interviews were with secondary school staff, and 7 with primary school staff. The smallest school was a rural primary school with a pupil cohort of 65 children. The largest school was a suburban secondary school with a pupil cohort of around 1,250 children. Interviews covered a variety of topics around mental health interventions in schools and varied between 15 and 45 minutes in length.

Scoping study results

Scoping study phase 1 themes

Theme: Deprivation
"Deprivation at home and not being ready to learn." School 1
Sub-theme: Family (N=15)
"Deprived area, lots of kids with parents who drink and take drugs." School 4
Sub-theme: Circumstances (N=16)
"Adverse home life and frustration at the lack of understanding." School 7
Theme: Variety of mental health problems
"Various problems including anxiety." School 3
Sub-theme: Attachment (N=12)
Parental issues such as splitting up causing attachment issues." School 4
Theme: Relationships
"We work closely with the school nurse to build relationships with parents and outside agencies." School 5
Sub-theme: Knowing the children (N=16)
"We know the children very well through relationship building." School 3
Sub-theme: Self-expression (N=18)
"We have many young people who express their personal distress in often what would be generally considered unacceptable behaviours." School 10
Theme: Signposting
"All we can do is signpost and counsel." School 4
Sub-theme: Service waiting times (N=20)

"Waiting list is a massive problem." School 15
Theme: Variety of interventions
"A wide range. We have a play-based counsellor visiting, talking therapy, sometimes just a change of environment." School 5
Theme: Lack of money
"Our policies are robust. Resources are the issue." School 21
Sub-theme: Staff (N=20)
"Mental health is an extra responsibility for schools. There are simply not enough people. People that deal with mental health have to have the time to do so." School 20
Sub-theme: Training (N=19)
"More funding is needed, particularly in order to train staff." School 13
Theme: Engagement
"It is difficult to get kids to engage if their problems are entrenched." School 4

Scoping study phase 2 themes

Theme: Deprivation (N=1-)
"The setting is one of the most deprived areas in the town. There are a whole host of economic and social issues in that area." Participant 2
Sub-theme: Parental issues
"Often it's the parents' problems you are picking up on as they're part of the school community." Participant 1
Sub-theme: Drugs
"Though there's not a lot of money in some of the households, there's a lot of use cocaine and heroin in this area, a lot of drug and alcohol abuse." Participant 7
Sub-theme: Domestic violence
"We get some developmental problems or PTSD linked with domestic violence." Participant 11
Theme: Variety of mental health problems (N=8)
"Wide and varied." Participant 8
Sub-theme: Getting worse
"Our concerns about emotional and mental well-being seem to grow by the day." Participant 9
Sub-theme: Girls vs boys
"Girls' mental health takes a different form to boys' mental health." Participant 6

Theme: Socialisation (N=10)
"We offer behaviour support to support a group of children who are isolated and lonely at playtime. Nobody wants to be their friend and as yet they haven't learned the friendly social norms." Participant 5
Sub-theme: Peer support
"We have a lot of peer-to-peer work where, particularly the younger children will be supported by older pupils who listen to them and read and chat with them once or twice a week." Participant 7
Sub-theme: Peer pressure
"I would say peer pressure, there's this self-image issue and not exclusively amongst the girls." Participant 7
Sub-theme: Social skills and self-expression
"We've got children lashing out physically and verbally because they don't know how to express themselves any other way." Participant 9
Theme: No written policy (N=8)
"Not the mental health. We've got a special needs policy. Mental health is in there. We don't have a separate mental health policy, no." Participant 3
Sub-theme: Informal processes
"Individual interventions tend to be less formal. There are staff who speak to children or children share experiences with." Participant 2
Sub-theme: Relationships and knowing children
"The teachers. They get to know, cos they see the children day in, day out." Participant 6
Sub-theme: Informal outcome measures
"There's been feedback given after the sessions that the coach has run with the classes with the year groups. I think that feedback's been given but other than that probably no." Participant 4
Sub-theme: Recent changes in approach
"Designated days throughout the year which are going to focus on mental health. We're also having whole staff training. We're having an inset day where for staff, completely around mental health of students with a small focus on mental health of staff but it is a big focus for the school this year." Participant 7
Sub-theme: Prevention vs intervention
"We try and do everything preventative rather than being reactive all the time." Participant 8
Sub-theme: Needs and opinions of child

"We also ask children to create their own person-centred paths so they kind of tell us on there if we're doing something that they don't want or if we're not doing something that they do want." Participant 7
Theme: Lack of resources (N=11)
"The funding that we're getting is increasingly struggling to pay for the teachers and teaching resources, not the specialists in the health arena." Participant 2
Sub-theme: Services
"Significant improvement in the CAMHS resource. Significant reduction in referral time. What does that person, that family do in the 12, 16, 20 weeks, the referral time?" Participant 7
Sub-theme: Support for children
"It's still very difficult to access the support you need if you've got children with serious mental health issues." Participant 5
Sub-theme: Money
"The funding gap is a huge thing. I think the government are not doing enough to support our young people." Participant 2
Sub-theme: Staff
"The counsellor. He was very good. He'd meet people but again he was only one person and he could only see one person at once. We've got a big need here." Participant 5
Sub-theme: Teacher mental health
"If you've got stressful and anxious teaching staff who are feeling looked upon by observations from senior management, from local authorities, from inspections who, in less than 50 minutes will kind of write off their career as inadequate then how are you going to produce healthy children?" Participant 3
Sub-theme: Training
"Would be great to look into for whole staff training but of course there's the cost implications for things like that." Participant 6
Sub-theme: Teacher understanding of mental health
"Staff to start understanding mental health because when you go to teacher training college you don't get that much help and advice on mental health." Participant 10

Scoping study discussion.

Educators in both phases of the scoping study believed that one of the main contributors to mental ill-health in school-aged children is deprivation, linked to adverse family backgrounds. These factors were mentioned by staff from 16 of the 23 schools who participated in Phase 1 of the study. Deprivation was also mentioned by 10 out of the 11 educators interviewed in Phase 2. This agrees with the literature, which shows a link between deprivation and many poor health outcomes, including mental illness (Marmot and Bell, 2012). The literature also links deprivation, family dissolution, and academic performance (Downey, 1994; Pong and Ju, 2000). It has also been shown that family history that included previous suicide attempts, depression, drug and alcohol abuse, and experience of assault, all increase childhood risk of suicide (Hickey and Carr, 2002). The same study also found an increased risk of suicide in children whose families are socially isolated and live in stressful, overcrowded conditions and in those whose families are not supportive of the child or deny the seriousness of their suicidal intentions. It has also been shown that domestic violence is associated with lower Intelligence Quotient (IQ) in children (Koenen et al, 2003). Family circumstances can also have an impact through father involvement (Flouri and Buchanan, 2003). Father involvement in the upbringing of a child from a non-intact family at the age of 7 is a protective factor against psychological maladjustment in adolescence. When a girl is aged 16, whether their father is involved in the family is a protective factor against psychological distress in adulthood. This is not the case for boys. This result relates to the findings of our scoping studies, that educators believe the factors that affect girls' and boys' mental health are different. In fact, research shows a number of differences. Girls tend to have lower self-esteem than boys, this difference can be related to appearance and athletic performance, and self-esteem has more of an influence on levels of depression in girls than in boys (Bolognini et al, 1996). Gender typicality is also a predictor of mental health, particularly amongst boys, and the relationship may be mediated by the social implications of not being gender typical (Jewell and Brown, 2014). Boys with mental health issues are more likely to turn to a family member and are less likely to seek out professional help, whereas girls tend to turn to friends before attempting to access mental health services (Chandra and Minkovitz, 2006).

The finding that mental health problems are getting worse agrees with research across many high-income countries, including England (Bor et al 2014; Achenbach et al, 2003). It is possible that this trend can in part be explained by improvements in diagnosis (Collishaw, 2015). Even so, according to the Department of Health (2015), around 5.8% (510,000) of children and adolescents in England have a conduct disorder, 3.3% (290,000) have an anxiety disorder, 0.9% (80,000) are seriously depressed, and 1.5% (132,000) has severe Attention Deficit Hyperactive Disorder (ADHD). There are some similarities between the genders, with bullying and low social support both contributing to poorer mental health in both boys and girls (Rigby, 2000). This, along with the finding in this scoping study that children's lack of social skills and inability to express themselves can contribute to poor outcomes, provides support for the relatively wide use of peer support schemes in the schools in question. However, one of the participants in the current study stated that their peer support system has only been used on one occasion since it began. This illustrates a point made by some participants that children's opinions must be considered. Kidger and colleagues (2009), showed that not doing this can lead to interventions targeting problems that do not match what young people say about their lives and needs. This can lead to the children viewing the support they receive negatively. If children believe an intervention is not confidential, available to all, or tailored to their needs, this negative view can get worse. Kidger and colleagues found that children's main concern is stigma. They feared being seen or treated differently to their peers. This fear can be a significant barrier, stopping children using a particular source of support. Therefore, it is important to ensure that pupils understand what a particular intervention provides. Kidger and colleagues recommend finding out pupils' opinions of services so that necessary alterations can be made. The intervention KidsMatter has been shown to be effective in improving mental health outcomes and is positively regarded by pupils (Littlefield et al 2017). KidsMatter attempts to improve social and emotional skills in order to intervene in mental health. This agrees with the findings in the scoping study that social skills and self-expression are important factors in children's mental health outcomes.

The finding that many schools do not have a formal, written mental health policy is consistent with previous literature (Palatay et al, 2016). It has been identified as a cause for concern by educators interviewed here, that many are already addressing. Some were concerned that the lack of specific guidance for teachers could negatively impact outcomes. However, rather than treating mental health provision as separate and distinct, embedding mental health provision into the school curriculum and wider culture could have some positives. Spratt and colleagues (2006), have stated that whole-school reviews of values, policies, and practices are better than treating mental well-being separately to teaching. They suggest that schools should build a whole-school culture that benefits all students using skills and knowledge from specialist mental health workers. This holistic approach has proven successful across age groups (White and Waters, 2015). Since teachers already intervene in children's mental health, focussing less on specialisation could help build relationships, making them better able to identify and intervene in student well-being. When children and adolescents were asked what qualities they considered most important in mental health professionals (Farnfield and Kaszap, 1998), their responses centred around four major themes; helpful qualities; counselling skills; the adults' ethical stance and helpful outcomes. What mattered to children was that adults possessed these qualities. The profession of the adult did not. In the words of one of the participants in this scoping study, 'It doesn't matter which style you have, as long as you've got a listening ear.' Although a holistic approach to mental health can be very beneficial, the lack of a specific mental health policy could be problematic. A whole-school approach should involve as many actors as possible (Feria et al, 2011). It is recommended that actions take effect on several levels (e.g. school, classroom, and pupils). There is also a need for initial assessment and final evaluation of any policies and practices affecting student mental health. One way of ensuring that schools adhere to these practices is an explicit written policy regarding child and adolescent mental health in schools. The finding here that many schools use informal processes for the identification of potential pupil mental health problems and for outcome measures is a concern. The lack of consensus on which mental health interventions are offered to pupils is another concern. One Head Teacher stated, 'I would go for it if somebody gave me a very strong personal recommendation of a company.' Participants here also tended to use their own, informal outcome measures. This agrees with the results of other investigations into school-based mental health provision. Head Teachers often find it difficult to know whether a service on offer is effective unless it comes recommended by a colleague (NAHT and Place2Be, 2017). Having said this, results from the scoping study suggest that school-based mental health provision in the region is improving. Some of the participants stated that their school had changed its approach to pupil mental health in recent months. Others hoped to in the near future. Changing from intervention in specific mental illnesses to the prevention of mental illness was mentioned by both groups. We should welcome a change like this as it agrees with research suggesting that school-based mental health identification and prevention programs are associated with improvement in academic and mental health functioning in children and adolescents (Levitt et al, 2007). We should also welcome the fact that participants in the scoping study spoke of the importance of putting the needs and opinions of children at the centre of mental health interventions. This has been stated to be an important factor that should inform policy in all areas of child and adolescent mental health (Fattore et al, 2009).

Participants in the scoping study mentioned a number of barriers that prevented them from properly intervening in their students' mental health. They believed that specialist mental health services do not meet the needs of their students. They also believed that waiting times to access these services are too long for the services to actually be useful to the children of the region. Both of these opinions are consistent with the existing literature (Frith, 2016; Anderson et al, 2017; York et al, 2004). However, if educators wish to intervene in children's mental health instead of relying on specialist services, embedding this intervention into schools comes with a unique resource burden (Fazel et al., 2014). The main barrier to intervening in student mental health cited in the scoping study was a lack of resources, which was mentioned as being a barrier in a number of different ways. One of these was that there is a lack of services available to refer children to. Participants believed that this led to many children not getting the support they need, leading to negative outcomes. However, Garralda (2009) has stated that comparing samples of referred and non-referred children has tended not to show differences in outcome. However, this could be at least partly be explained by the fact that there are large gaps in vulnerable children's health outcome data, making it difficult to assess whether current provision meets need (Evans, 2012). One resource that was mentioned as being in short supply by the vast majority of participants was money. Participants stated that there isn't enough money in school budgets for teaching, let alone for intervention in student mental health. This is perhaps predictable given the shrinking education budgets discussed above. Participants believed that lack of money effected schools in many different ways. Some said that there were not enough school staff to properly deal with student mental health. Lack of money and low staff numbers might play a role in teacher mental health, which was mentioned by some participants as impacting schools' ability to provide for the mental health of their students. Nagel and Brown (2003) showed that between 1/5 and 1/3 of teachers report that their job is very or extremely stressful. Skaalvik and Skaalvik (2015) showed that teachers in Norway had high job satisfaction but experienced severe stress and even exhaustion. This was true across age ranges and experience levels. However, different age groups used different coping methods. This might relate in some way with the finding of our scoping study that a change is taking place in the education sector regarding attitudes and approaches to mental health. Participants also believed that lack of money was leading to teachers not receiving appropriate mental health training. Some said that there has been very little mental health training in their school. Some said that a single member of staff might be sent to mental health training and then disseminate what they learned to other members of staff. Some participants said that initial teacher training did not include mental health. Whitley, Smith and Vaillancourt (2013), point out that teachers need the appropriate knowledge, skills, and attitudes to recognise mental health problems and be aware of the steps needed to involve affected pupils in classroom activities and make sure they receive the right care. Vieira and colleagues (2014), have shown that teachers struggle to identify the possibility of mental illness in pupils who internalise their problems, but that training can help them to identify problem cases and make an appropriate referral. Kutcher and colleagues (2013) highlight the importance of training in improving educators' knowledge and attitudes around mental health. They state that this might help schools provide effective mental ill-health prevention.

Pilot

Given that schools are a key site for mental health promotion, prevention, and intervention (Wolpert et al, 2017) and that school-based interventions can improve children's behaviour and outcomes at a benefit to cost ratio of 27:1 (Roberts et al, Marmot, 2016), we decided that it would be a good idea to attempt to intervene in the situation described above with a school-based intervention. Knapp, McDaid, and Parsonage (2011) have stated that there is a strong economic case for schools to employ mental health promotion programmes. This agrees with the findings of Lottman, Zawaly and Niemiec (2017), who stated that creating an early childhood environment for character strength development is an element of developmentally appropriate best practice. We therefore came to the conclusion that a Positive Psychology Intervention (PPI) that took on a psycho-educational model that focused on and improved strengths and abilities that students already possessed, would be the best way to improve outcomes for children in the region.

Pilot method

The pilot PPI was delivered to 90 students. It involved eight weekly 1-hour sessions, taking place in two schools during normal timetabled hours. The first session included pre-evaluation using the World Health Organisation-Five Well-Being Index (WHO-5) (WHO, 1998), the 12-Item Grit Scale (GRIT) (Duckworth et al, 2007), the Bolton Uni-Stride Scale (BUSS), developed at the University of Bolton (Kannangara et al., 2000), the Children's Hope Scale (CHS) (Snyder et al., 1997), and the bespoke Hummingbird Life Satisfaction Scale (HLSS). The HLSS was designed to gauge participants' understanding of the concepts covered during the PPI. The first session also included an introduction to the PPI for both students and teachers. Sessions two to seven covered concepts from Positive Psychology. These sessions took place with students, covering happiness and well-being, grit and resilience, growth mindsets and character strengths, mindfulness, mental health problems and stigma, and hope and gratitude, respectively. The final session included post-intervention evaluations using the same scales mentioned above and advice for students on how to build on the concepts introduced in previous sessions for the future.

Table 1
Pilot results

Scale	N	Start Mean	SD	End Mean	SD	t	p	Cohen's d
WHO-5	64	10.55	5.71	11.86	6.16	-2.71	0.01	0.34
Grit	29	37.07	6.98	37.14	7.18	-0.07	0.95	0.01
BUSS	32	33.50	6.38	34.50	7.25	-1.42	0.17	0.25
CHS	63	20.06	7.76	21.13	8.08	-1.71	0.09	0.22
HLSS	63	27.10	6.06	27.29	5.97	-0.36	0.72	0.05

Pilot discussion

There were statistically significant changes on participant scores on the WHO-5, with a small to medium effect size. Although changes in the other measures were not statistically significant, there were small positive improvements on all measures. This led to the conclusion that there was a basis for rolling out the Hummingbird Project to more secondary schools. However, we decided that the PPI should be revised so that it might prove more effective.

The decision was made to remove the session on mental illness and stigma as this is not part of Positive Psychology. Instead, it was decided to include a short discussion around stigma in session 1 to give students an opportunity to ask questions about mental illness. We also decided to shorten the PPI to six weeks as some half terms are shorter than eight weeks. The reasoning here was that having the PPI interrupted by a break of a week or more, might affect students' ability to follow the PPI as a whole. We also decided to remove the GRIT scale from the evaluation questionnaires. We removed the GRIT scale for three reasons. Firstly, the scores on this scale did not change much. Secondly, the GRIT scale measured a similar domain to the BUSS scale. Thirdly, we felt that the questionnaires were too long and this was cutting into session time that would be better used teaching students about the ideas in question.

Main study

Main study method

The main part of the Hummingbird Project involved six weekly one hour sessions, taking place during normal timetabled school hours. Session 1 involved pre-evaluation using the same scales as the pilot study, with the exception of the GRIT scale. It also included an introduction to the program for students and teachers and a discussion of stigma around mental illness. Sessions 2 to 5 covered concepts from Positive Psychology. These sessions took place with students, covering happiness, resilience and character strengths, hope, growth mindsets and gratitude, and mindfulness, respectively. The final session included post-intervention evaluations using the same scales mentioned above and advice for students on how to build on the concepts introduced in previous sessions for the future. There were 1,054 students from 14 secondary schools in Greater Manchester and Cheshire West and Chester who took part in the updated project. These students were aged 11 to 18 and 57% were female. The most represented group were year 7 students, with 40% of participants being from this age group.

Table 2
Main study results

Scale	N	Start Mean	SD	End Mean	SD	t	p	Cohen's d
WHO-5	657	12.47	5.43	12.94	5.95	-2.46	0.01	0.1
BUSS	584	36.63	7.03	37.23	6.44	-2.84	0.01	0.12
CHS	647	20.32	6.76	21.64	6.89	-6.11	<0.01	0.24
HLSS	633	28.26	5.46	29.13	5.74	-5.03	<0.01	0.2

Main study discussion

We can see from the above table that the Hummingbird Project resulted in a positive improvement in all four of the factors measured. This means that the average child taking part in the project sees improved well-being (WHO-5), improved level of resilience (BUSS), and increased level of hope for the future (CHS). Comparison of the scores on the HLSS shows that there were also positive improvements in the students' opinions about the topics covered in the project. The statistically significant improvements in student well-being, resilience, and hope were relatively small, as shown by the Cohen's d values being 0.24 or lower, representing a small effect size. It is reasonable to expect that the results found here might become more pronounced over time, as the students have more time to reflect on the project and practice the skills and techniques learned during the sessions. However, in order to test whether this is indeed the case, it would be necessary to perform follow-up testing. This has not been possible during year one of the main part of the Hummingbird Project due to budget and time constraints. However, some schools have expressed openness to this idea. Therefore, it may be possible to do this during later phases of the project.

One issue we experienced during delivery of the Hummingbird Project was schools selecting students to take part in the project, based on a perceived need for some kind of help. This connects with reasons we began the project. School and CAMHS budgets are both overstretched and there is a large gap between the need for mental health interventions and the provision of those interventions. Therefore, as soon as an intervention such as the Hummingbird Project comes along, school staff are likely to assign students who have a clear need for help with their mental health but are unable to access CAMHS services. The problem with this is two-fold. Firstly, the project was designed as a universal intervention and is not targeted at children with severe mental health problems. Secondly, when students are selected due to a perceived risk by school staff, they tend to be aware of this and do not respond well to being singled out, which can lead to behavioural issues. This agrees with the literature (Salerno, 2016), which shows that young people tend not to respond well to interventions for their mental health when they feel singled out or stigmatised. Almost half (509) of all students who took part in the project, were selected in such a way. At the beginning of the project we were very eager to ensure that we recruited schools and so were perhaps a little too easy going when it came to letting them decide how delivery took place. However, we are now able to show them that we know from experience that the project works best when it seems to the students to be a normal part of the school day using groups that they are used to being part of such as form groups, PSHE groups, or even class groups from whichever subject they would usually be studying at that time. We also have the data to back up this experience and show that students who are individually selected to take part in the project do not engage as well and do not benefit as much from the experience. The lack of time, space, and resources in schools across the country has the potential to negatively affect delivery of the project in a number of other ways. Therefore, it has been necessary to build tolerance into the project to make sessions longer or shorter and to have alternative activities for the students in case of some unexpected problem. Also, staff have had to think on their feet and to ensure that clear communication with schools is maintained, so that schools are always aware of what is needed from them and feel able to let us know, if and when an issue arises. We also have a policy document, signed by a representative at each school that lays out what is expected of schools to ensure the satisfactory delivery of the project. Therefore, if we have any concerns that they are not fulfilling these needs we can direct them to the document and offer any assistance that might help the school meet them. One problem that did arise around this kind of issue, was that leading up to the Christmas break, there were seasonal events, exams, and occasionally double-booked rooms. We understand of course that at times students will inevitably miss some sessions and this is sometimes unavoidable. However, we are more conscious of the need to try to highlight this issue to schools in the future, ensuring that we ask the question of whether there will be any activities that are likely to interrupt sessions. Another issue we encountered was the fact that, in school settings, students are used to questions having right and wrong answers. When asked to write and talk about their own experience and opinions they were reluctant to do so, in case they gave the wrong answer. This was overcome by highlighting anonymity and privacy, the subjective nature of happiness, and the fact that the project is a safe place to discuss thoughts and feelings.

It is our intention to improve the Hummingbird Project for the new academic year, in order to better meet the needs of high school students in the region. In future iterations of the project we will ensure that we are more insistent that the project is a universal intervention, intended for all students. When making arrangements with schools we will be sure to highlight the idea that making the project seem like a normal part of the school day is imperative for student engagement and outcomes. We will also make a number of changes to the content and delivery of the project. Firstly, the elements focusing on stigma will be either removed or adjusted to become part of more general discussions, as discussion of stigma around mental illness is not really an element of Positive Psychology and represents time spent talking about negatives which could be better utilised discussing the positives that the project is centred around. Another change that will be made will be to rewrite the character strengths section of the project. In the first iteration of the Hummingbird Project, the character strengths session involved students completing the online VIA character strengths survey (https://www.viacharacter.org/) in order to find out their five signature strengths. However, this was not only a long process, reducing the amount of time that could be spent discussing character strengths, but also involved the schools providing computers and internet access for all of the students taking part. This generally also involved a room change and there were a number of things that were liable to go wrong. In future, we propose doing tasks that involve worksheets and class discussions. We expect this will improve student understanding of character strengths (Durlak et al, 2011), and will remove the logistical problems involved in providing additional facilities for students for a single session. Other changes that will be made to the project include rearranging the order of the sessions, in order that students learn about mindfulness earlier in the process. The hope here is that this will allow students to better focus on their learning of some of the concepts that are completely new to them (Hyland, 2011). We also hope that rearranging the order of sessions, might lead to the project better linking concepts, so that students can better understand them. An attempt will also be made to make activities less reliant on students writing their answers, with more in-class discussions, more videos, and less time spent presenting to the students, to the same end.

One limitation of the Hummingbird Project is that it has been delivered by a single member of staff, with support from volunteers. If the project is to be sustainable, it will need to be scaled up for delivery by multiple trainers on multiple sites. Mackenzie and Williams (2018), have shown that fidelity to the original course materials and procedures is a significant factor in outcomes of universal school-based Positive Psychology interventions. Therefore, there may be issues if and when the project is expanded to include other delivery methods. If the project is adapted to become a train the trainer model, it may be very difficult to maintain fidelity to the original course materials. It will be important to ensure that those delivering the project in this way are closely monitored and supported. One possible way of overcoming issues regarding fidelity would be to offer an online version of the project. This would mean that all students who accessed the project would work from the same version of each resource. It might also be more appealing to current generations of children, since they are digital natives. However, if this approach is used, it would still be advisable to ensure that there is still a human aspect to the project so that children can ask questions and receive guidance from a skilled member of staff. This will help ensure children use the resources correctly and are given any support they might need to reassure them.

Another limitation of the Hummingbird Project is that it is an intervention designed for high school students. Prevalence of mental health problems in primary school students is 7.7% for all students, rising to 10.2% for boys (Green et al, 2005). Therefore, it would be advisable to attempt to re-design the project with the aim of working with this age group. The finding that the Hummingbird Project improves student flourishing is very promising. However, in future it would be advisable to show whether the project improves negative outcomes. It will be necessary in future to include some measure of depression and anxiety, as these have been shown to be the leading contributors to health burden in children and adolescents (Stockings et al, 2016). The results of these measures will be very interesting, as there is mixed evidence whether other PPIs reduce symptoms of these mental illnesses (Bastounis et al, 2016; Bolier et al, 2013).

Conclusion

The Hummingbird Project represents a significant step forwards in intervention into the mental health of secondary school students in the North West of England. The fact that positive changes have been made in the flourishing of over 1,000 students in the region's schools is cause for celebration. However, there are certainly many more steps needed in this journey, such as providing evidence that the Hummingbird Project not only improves flourishing in students but also reduces mental ill-health. Establishing sustainability of the project should also be a priority, whilst ensuring that the positives of the project are maintained in order to ensure that students' mental health is at the forefront of our thinking. The solution to this might involve a dual approach, involving a train-the-trainer model, paired with online resources for both teachers and students. It has also become clear that intervening in the mental health of younger students is an important next step. However, the project finds a happy medium in the dichotomy between prescriptive interventions delivered by professionals and those which encourage self-management using interactive elements that, according to Brown and colleagues (2019) are preferred by older adolescents. As mentioned by one of the students who took part in the project, the Hummingbird Project has the high honour of being 'The second best experience of my life'.

Acknowledgments

The authors are grateful to all the school staff and pupils who took part in the various stages of the project. We thank Ghazala Baig, Ghalib Hussain and Catherine North from the charity MedEquip4Kids. We are also grateful to the undergraduate and postgraduate students from the Universities of Bolton and Chester, who helped the first author facilitate the workshops in the schools.

References

Achenbach, T.M., Dumenci, L. and Rescorla, L.A. (2003) Are American Children's Problems Still Getting Worse? A 23-Year Comparison. *Journal of Abnormal Child Psychology*, 31, 1, 1-11

Anderson, J.K., Howarth, E., Vainre, M., Jones, P.B. and Humphrey, A. (2017) A scoping literature review of service-level barriers for access and engagement with mental health services for children and young people. *Children and Youth Services Review*, 77, 164-176

Bastounis, A., Callaghan, P., Banerjee, A. and Michail, M. (2016) The effectiveness of the Penn Resiliency Programme (PRP) and its adapted versions in reducing depression and anxiety and improving explanatory style: A systematic review and meta-analysis. *Journal of adolescence*, 52, 37-48

Bolier, L., Haverman, M., Westerhof, G.J., Riper, H., Smit, F. and Bohlmeijer, E. (2013) Positive psychology interventions: a meta-analysis of randomized controlled studies. *BMC Public Health*, 13, 1, 119

Bolognini, M., Plancherel, B., Bettschart, W. and Halfon, O. (1996) Self-esteem and mental health in early adolescence: development and gender differences. *Journal of Adolescence*, 19, 3, 233-245

Bor, W., Dean, A.J., Najman, J. and Hayatbakhsh, R. (2014) Are child and adolescent mental health problems increasing in the 21st century? A systematic review. *Australian & New Zealand Journal of Psychiatry*, 48, 7, 606-616

Brown, J.S.L., Blackshaw, E., Stahl, D., Fennelly, L., Mckeague, L., Sclare, I. and Michelson, D. (2019) School-based early intervention for anxiety and depression in older adolescents: A feasibility randomised controlled trial of a self-referral stress management workshop programme ('DISCOVER'). *Journal of Adolescence*, 71, 150-161

Byrne, J., Shepherd, J., Dewhirst, S., Pickett, K., Speller, V., Roderick, P., Grace, M. and Almond, P. (2015) Pre-service teacher training in health and well-being in England: the state of the nation. *European Journal of Teacher Education*, 38, 2, 217-233

Chandra, A. and Minkovitz, C.S. (2006) Stigma starts early: Gender differences in teen willingness to use mental health services. *Journal of Adolescent Health*, 38, 6, 754.e1 - 754.e8

Collishaw, S., 2015 Annual Research Review: Secular trends in child and adolescent mental health. *Journal of Child Psychology and Psychiatry*, 56, 3, 370-393

Crawford, R. and Keynes, S. (2015) Options for further departmental spending cuts. In C. Emmerson, P. Johnson and R. Joyce (Eds.) *The IFS Green Budget*. London: The Institute for Fiscal Studies (pp. 151-175)

Department of Health (2015) Future in mind: Promoting, protecting and improving our children and young people's mental health and wellbeing. *NHS England Publication Gateway Ref.No 02939*. [Accessed on 22nd June 2020 at https://assets.publishing.service.gov.uk/government/uploads/system/uploads/attachment_data/file/414024/Childrens_Mental_Health.pdf]

Docherty, M. and Thornicroft, G. (2015) Specialist mental health services in England in 2014: Overview of funding, access and levels of care. *International Journal of Mental Health Systems*, 9, 1, 34

Downey, D.B. (1994) The School Performance of Children from Single-Mother and Single-Father Families: Economic or Interpersonal Deprivation? *Journal of Family Issues*, 15, 1,129-147

Duckworth, A.L., Peterson, C., Matthews, M.D. and Kelly, D.R. (2007) Grit: Perseverance and Passion for Long-Term Goals. *Journal of Personality and Social Psychology*, 92, 6, 1087-1101

Durlak, J.A., Dymnicki, A.B., Taylor, R.D., Weissberg, R.P. and Schellinger, K.B. (2011) The impact of enhancing students' social and emotional learning: A meta-analysis of school-based universal interventions. *Child Development*, 82(1), 405-432

Evans, S. (2012) Assessing the health needs of vulnerable children, are the data fit for purpose? *Journal of Public Mental Health*, 11,3, 117-140

Farnfield, S. and Kaszap, M. (1998) What makes a helpful grown up? Children's views of professionals in the mental health services. *Health Informatics Journal*, 4, 1, 3-14

Fattore, T., Mason, J. and Watson, E. (2009) When Children Are Asked About Their Well-being: Towards a Framework for Guiding Policy. *Child Indicators Research*, 2, 57-77

Fazel, M., Hoagwood, K., Stephan, S. and Ford, T. (2014) Mental health interventions in schools in high-income countries. *The Lancet Psychiatry*, 1, 5, 377-387

Feria, I., Ortega, R. and Del Rey, R., 2011 Convivencia: An educational model of wellbeing in schools. In R.H. Shute, P.T. Slee, R. Murray-Harvey and K.L. Dix (Eds.) Mental *Health and Wellbeing: Educational perspectives*. Adelaide: Shannon Research Press (pp. 191-200)

Flouri, E. and Buchanan, A. (2003) The role of father involvement in children's later mental health. *Journal of Adolescence*, 26, 1, 63-78

Frith, E. (2016) Children and Young People's Mental Health: State of the Nation: April 2016. London: CentreForum

Garralda, E.M. (2009) Accountability of specialist child and adolescent mental health services. *The British Journal of Psychiatry*, 194, 5, 389-391

Green, H., McGinnity, Á, Meltzer, H., Ford, T. and Goodman, R. (2005) *Mental health of children and young people in Great Britain, 2004*. Basingstoke: Palgrave Macmillan

Hickey, D. and Carr, A. (2002) Prevention of suicide in adolescence. In A. Carr (Ed.) *Prevention: What Works with Children and Adolescents?: A Critical Review of Psychological Prevention Programmes for Children, Adolescents and their Families*. London: Routledge (pp. 336-358)

Hindley, P. (2014) *Written evidence for the House of Commons Select Committee Inquiry into Child and Adolescent Mental Health Services from the Faculty of Child and Adolescent Psychiatrists*. London: Royal College of Psychiatrists

Hyland, T. (2011) *Mindfulness and learning: Celebrating the affective dimension of education*. London: Springer Science & Business Media

Jewell, J.A. and Brown, C.S. (2014) Relations among gender typicality, peer relations, and mental health during early adolescence. *Social Development*, 23, 1, 137-156

Kannangara, C.S., Allen, R.E., Carson, J.F., Khan, S.Z.N., Waugh, G. and Kandadi, K.K. (In Press) Onwards and upwards: The development, piloting and validation of a new measure of academic tenacity- the Bolton Uni-Stride Scale (BUSS). PLoS ON, 15 (7): e0235157. Https://doi.org/10.1371/journal.pone.0235157

Kidger, J., Donovan, J.L., Biddle, L., Campbell, R. and Gunnell, D. (2009) Supporting adolescent emotional health in schools: A mixed methods study of student and staff views in England. *BMC Public Health*, 9, 1, 403

Knapp, M., McDaid, D. and Parsonage, M. (2011) *Mental health promotion and mental illness prevention: The economic case*. London: Department of Health

Koenen, K.C., Moffitt, T.E., Caspi, A., Taylor, A. and Purcell, S. (2003) Domestic violence is associated with environmental suppression of IQ in young children. *Development and Psychopathology*, 15, 2, 297-311

Kutcher, S., Wei, Y., McLuckie, A. and Bullock, L. (2013) Educator mental health literacy: A programme evaluation of the teacher training education on the mental health & high school curriculum guide. *Advances in School Mental Health Promotion*, 6, 2, 83-93

Larson, R.W. (2001) How U.S. Children and Adolescents Spend Time: What It Does (And Doesn't) Tell Us about Their Development. *Current Directions in Psychological Science*, 10, 5, 160-164

Levitt, J.M., Saka, N., Romanelli, L.H. and Hoagwood, K. (2007) Early identification of mental health problems in schools: The status of instrumentation. *Journal of School Psychology*, 45, 2, 163-191

Littlefield, L., Cavanagh, S., Knapp, R. and O'Grady, L. (2017). KidsMatter: Building the capacity of Australian primary schools and early childhood services to foster children's social and emotional skills and promote children's mental health. In E. Frydenberg, A. Martin and R. Collie (Eds.) *Social and emotional learning in Australia and the Asia-Pacific*. Singapore: Springer, (pp. 293-311)

Lottman, T.J., Zawaly, S. and Niemiec, R. (2017) Well-being and well-doing: Bringing mindfulness and character strengths to the early childhood classroom and home. In C. Proctor (Ed.) *Positive psychology interventions in practice*. Cham: Springer (pp. 83-105)

MACKenzie, K. and Williams, C. (2018) Universal, school-based interventions to promote mental and emotional well-being: what is being done in the UK and does it work? A systematic review. *BMJ Open*, 8, 9, e022560

Marmot, M. and Bell, R. (2012) Fair society, healthy lives. *Public Health*, 126, 1, S4-S10

Nagel, L. and Brown, S. (2003) The ABCs of Managing Teacher Stress: 1. *The Clearing House*, 76, 5, 255

NAHT/Place2be, (2017) Half of schools struggle to get mental health support for pupils. [Accessed 8th January 2020 at https://www.naht.org.uk/news-and-opinion/news/pupil-support-and-safeguarding-news/struggling-to-get-mental-health-support/]

Patalay, P., Giese, L., Stanković, M., Curtin, C., Moltrecht, B. and Gondek, D. (2016) Mental health provision in schools: priority, facilitators and barriers in 10 European countries. *Child and Adolescent Mental Health*, 21, 3, 139-147

Pong, S. and Ju, D. (2000) The Effects of Change in Family Structure and Income on Dropping Out of Middle and High School. *Journal of Family Issues*, 21, 2, 147-169

Rigby, K. (2000) Effects of peer victimization in schools and perceived social support on adolescent well-being. *Journal of Adolescence*, 23, 1, 57-68

Roberts, J., Donkin, A. and Marmot, M. (2016) Opportunities for reducing socioeconomic inequalities in the mental health of children and young people – reducing adversity and increasing resilience. *Journal of Public Mental Health*, 15, 1, 4-18

Salerno, J.P. (2016) Effectiveness of Universal School-Based Mental Health Awareness Programs Among Youth in the United States: A Systematic Review. *The Journal of school health*, 86, 12, 922

Skaalvik, E.M. and Skaalvik, S. (2015) Job satisfaction, stress and coping strategies in the teaching profession-what do teachers say? *International Education Studies*, 8, 3, 81-192

Snyder, C.R., Hoza, B., Pelham, W.E., Rapoff, M., Ware, L., Danovsky, M., HIghberger, L., Rubinstein, H. and Stahl, K.J. (1997) The development and validation of the Children's Hope Scale. *Journal of Paediatric Psychology*, 22, 3, 399-421

Spratt, J., Shucksmith, J., Philip, K. and Watson, C. (2006) 'Part of Who we are as a School Should Include Responsibility for Well-Being': Links between the School Environment, Mental Health and Behaviour. *Pastoral Care in Education*, 24, 3, 14-21

Stockings, E.A., Degenhardt, L., Dobbins, T., Lee, Y.Y., Erskine, H.E., Whiteford, H.A. and Patton, G. (2016) Preventing depression and anxiety in young people: a review of the joint efficacy of universal, selective and indicated prevention. *Psychological Medicine*, 46, 1, 11-26

Vieira, M.A., Gadelha, A.A., Moriyama, T.S., Bressan, R.A. and Bordin, I.A. (2014) Evaluating the effectiveness of a training program that builds teachers' capability to identify and appropriately refer middle and high school students with mental health problems in Brazil: An exploratory study. *BMC Public Health*, 14, 1, 210

White, M.A. and Waters, L.E. (2015) A case study of 'The Good School:' Examples of the use of Peterson's strengths-based approach with students. *The Journal of Positive Psychology*, 10, 1, 69-76

Whitley, J., Smith, J.D. and Vaillancourt, T. (2013) Promoting Mental Health Literacy Among Educators: Critical in School-Based Prevention and Intervention. *Canadian Journal of School Psychology*, 28, 1, 56-70

WHO, (1998) Wellbeing measures in primary health care/The Depcare Project. Copenhagen: WHO Regional Office for Europe

Wolk, C.B., Stewart, R.E., Eiraldi, R., Cronholm, P., Salas, E. and Mandell, D.S. (2019) The implementation of a team training intervention for school mental health: Lessons learned. *Psychotherapy*, 56, 1, 83-90

Wolpert, M., Vostanis, P., Martin, K., Munk, S., Norman, R., Fonagy, P. and Feltham, A. (2017) High integrity mental health services for children: focusing on the person, not the problem. *BMJ*, 357:j1500 [Accessed 8th February 2020 at https://www.bmj.com/content/357/bmj.j1500]

York, A., Anderson, Y. and Zwi, M. (2004) Eight Months to Eight Weeks: Reducing Waiting Times in a Child and Adolescent Mental Health Service. *Mental Health Review Journal*, 9, 2, 15-19

Happiness: Is there really a North-South divide?

Jerome Carson, Sandie McHugh,
Rosie Allen and Julie Prescott

Introduction

What Manchester does today, the rest of the world does tomorrow, a phrase from a confident Victorian city of Manchester, the world's first and greatest industrial city in Victorian times (Hall, 1998). Manchester still a great, but not pre-eminent city, sits in the North of England, yet is sometimes recognized as one of the less vibrant parts of England. This is not just a new phenomenon, this has historical roots. J.B. Priestly in 1934 identified four contrasting Englands. The Industrial North, described as still in the nineteenth century. England of the Dole, which was south Wales and parts of the North East England. Then there were two bustling Englands. The Southern Counties and Home Counties, where there were new industries, by-passes, housing estates with an increasing range of consumer goods, suburban villas with cocktail bars and motor cars. These two Englands had a rising standard of living, with the Southern and Home Counties ahead of the other two Englands which were experiencing decline and especially in the case of the England of the Dole, widespread poverty and deprivation. (Mowat, 1955)

How had this come about? In Victorian Britain, the North, Lancashire, Yorkshire, and cities like Newcastle-upon-Tyne, had developed heavy industry and there had been a large population expansion as people flocked to these areas for work. In the twentieth century they underwent a structural decline. The Great Depression of the 1930's was an indication of the weakness of a reliance on heavy industry and manufacturing to provide mass employment. Whereas the Victorians had enjoyed world dominance, other European countries developed their own industries and the United States became a world leader. After the Second World War, whole industries like coal mining gradually disappeared and others like textiles and engineering became miniscule compared to their past eminence as deindustrialisation continued. New industries and employment opportunities were created, but on a scale that was too small to replace the declining industries and to provide occupations for large numbers of people. New industries were often in different areas of the country. With a lack of regeneration, some areas became unattractive with derelict buildings, many towns and areas in the North of England became known as deprived areas. As Priestly had recognized over eighty years ago, the Home Counties and the South of England fared better, and the prosperity gap between the North and the South widened. It is argued that the disparity was hastened from the 1970s and rates of poverty increased. There is little sign of the divide narrowing and Dorling writing in 2010 could only see a widening gulf between the North and South (Dorling, 2010). Already behind the South, the North of England did not enjoy the same level of economic development as the London area in the 21ˢᵗ Century. Real economic output in the London region grew annually on average at a rate of 3.1% between 1998-2017, but in the rest of the UK, it was only 1.9% (Joyce and Xu, 2019). The Economic Recession of 2008-2010 had a part to play, with concerns that while the recession was finance led, the impact had been worst felt in the North and Midlands (Lee, 2014). In the decade since the economic crisis it is estimated that the squeeze on living standards has increased the inequality of the North of England where technological change and globalisation may have had most effect (Joyce and Xu, 2019).

What does this disparity mean for the northern areas, how does it translate into the experience of everyday lives? Transport and general infrastructure investment are lower in the North, not only further widening the gap, but also transport connections are important for economic activity and play a role in the quality of lives. In 2018-2019 capital investment spending per head for London was £1,456, the North West £954, Yorkshire and Humber £694, North East £706. Of these amounts, direct investment in transport per head was £654, £276, £139, £383 respectively (**Zarenko, 2020**). Examining the figures for public expenditure (central and local government and public corporations) per person in 2018-2019, London has the highest at £10,425, North West at £9,865, Yorkshire and Humber £9,123 with the North East faring better, with £10,183, and the South West of England £8,910. There may be less difference between the North and South here as all public expenditure includes social security benefits which involve more people in the North than the South (Brien, 2019).

Unemployment rates are higher in the North of England. For the period September – November 2019, the highest rate of unemployment was the North East of England at 6.2%, with the North West at 4.2% whereas the lowest were in the South West at 2.8% and the South East at 3% (Office for National Statistics, 2020, pp 16-17). The higher rates of unemployment in the North have not been eased by job creation. One in three new jobs (35%) were in London in the period 2007-2017. The North East of England had the lowest rate of new jobs at less than 5% (McCall, 2018). The Office of

National Statistics collects data on the percentage of workless households in the regions. This is where all adults aged 16-64 in a household are not in work. In 2018, the areas with the highest percentage of workless households were all outside the South of England (ONS, 2018). For children with this familial disadvantage, lack of confidence, uncertainty and low expectations can affect motivation and educational attainment (Children's Commissioner, 2018). The Centre for Social Justice reported that Blackpool, like some other deprived areas, experienced negative spirals with high levels of alcohol and drug usage. Local employers had difficulty finding local people with the skills or will to take up jobs, which had to be filled by economic migrants (Centre for Social Justice, 2013). Lower levels of job creation in northern areas of England may not be all due to a lack of investment. The talent pool may perhaps be a factor? How do the regions compare with education?

Education in the North in primary schools is recognized as generally good. However, the Children's Commissioner in 2018 reported that the North contained the highest proportion of secondary schools which were judged to be 'less than good.' Deprived communities and familial disadvantage were therefore added to by poor institutional performance. The proportion of children on free school meals is higher in the North and the attainment of these pupils is less than those in London. In London, pupils who had free school meals were twice as likely to go onto University, as those in the North. Children in the North and Midlands were less likely to attain good GCSE results in Maths and English, than those in other areas of England. A comparison of sixteen city regions for GCSE results showed that seven of the worst performing eight were in the North of England. High levels of poverty, historic low-levels of attainment, entrenched deprivation and high worklessness contributed to this disparity, but another factor was the higher levels of expenditure per pupil in London compared to northern secondary schools. In 2016 it was £1,300 less per pupil in the northern secondary schools, than in London (Children's Commissioner, 2018).

Universities take students not just from their own locality, but from the rest of the UK and abroad. The North has many fine universities, some with good international reputations and world leading research departments. However, the wealth of Oxford and Cambridge at an estimated £21 billion in 2018, is more than the combined investments of the other 20 ranked top universities. Many of these are in the North such as Leeds, Newcastle, Manchester, Sheffield, and Liverpool. The mega wealth of Oxbridge compared to the other universities provides a large advantage of power and prestige to attract new research funding (Adams and Greenwood, 2018). The relevance of the wealth of Oxford and Cambridge is not only in being able to use its wealth and prestige to be in the forefront of attracting research funds, but in the impact on the surrounding areas. There are large advantages to the regions where universities are situated, and they have a strong effect on the economic growth of the area. The richer the University, the greater the impact (Valero and Van Reenen, 2016). Both the cities and counties of Oxford and Cambridge are amongst the most prosperous in the country.

People in the North have on average between £4,000-£6,000 less in income per year. The South East as a region has the highest income, with the North East the lowest in England (Corlett et al, 2019). In 2018, in the town of Blackburn, the median gross weekly earnings of full time employees were £481 compared to £622 in Wycombe (Internet Geography, 2019). Debt levels are also higher relative to income in the North than the South. People in Warrington on average have three times the level of debt than those in Oxford. Debt can easily become a problem for people when there is an economic downturn or they experience a change in personal circumstances (Centre for Cities, 2020).

Areas where educational attainment is lower and that have a perception of being deprived may reinforce the comparative lower rates of job creation that the North experiences. Digital skills are lower in the North East and North West than in the South East. In the latter it is estimated that only 5% of the population had zero digital skills, whereas for the North East it is 12% and the North West 10% (ONS, 2019). Graduates from these areas often move away from their home town to the South East of England, or other regions where there are more job opportunities. The exodus is not what many young people want. They would prefer to have opportunities available in or near their home town. If the best educated or perhaps the most energetic and ambitious leave an area to move elsewhere, this alters the skill mix and the attraction of the area for job creation, thus worsening the labour market prospects for those left behind (Langella and Manning, 2019) .

The deprived areas of the North also experience health inequality with lower life expectancy. Using data from the Office of National Statistics for the period 2001 to 2016 it is estimated that in many deprived urban northern areas in Bradford, Leeds, Liverpool, Manchester and Newcastle life expectancy for a baby girl was 78 years for a boy 74 years. In affluent areas this would be 86 and 83 respectively (Bennett et al, 2018). This inequality has been widening since the 1980's with the largest contributors to life expectancy being higher levels of death from respiratory diseases, ischaemic heart disease and lung and digestive cancers in people of working age being higher in northern deprived areas.

Rates of suicide also display regional variation with the North East having the highest for men with London and the South East the lowest. For women the highest rates were in Yorkshire and Humberside again with the lowest in London (Marmot et al, 2020). Excessive alcohol consumption measured by alcohol related hospital admissions are higher in the North of England, some of the worst rates are in Blackpool. In a description of unhealthy towns six factors are identified; alcohol consumption, childhood obesity, lower male and female life expectancy, rates of lung cancer and self-harm. A geographic context was found with most of the healthy towns located in the South East and the least healthy towns in the North. (Goodair, 2020). The reasons for the health inequality have been considered as higher levels of unemployment, low wage employment, greater concentrations of poverty, less good provision of and access to health care (Bennett et al, 2020). Persistent poverty puts adults in greater risk of developing poor mental and physical health, for children it increases the risk of obesity and long term illness. It is estimated that it can mean 12 fewer years of life in good health (Goodair et al, 2020). Substandard housing i.e. that with inadequate insulation, internal space and poor kitchen and bathroom facilities can also impact on health of the inhabitants. In the Midlands, Yorkshire and Humber one in five houses were deemed to be non-decent (substandard) whilst in the South East this was 16%. Austerity policies following the 2008 Financial Market Collapse and the subsequent Great Recession have probably aggravated the inequalities as public expenditure in some sectors was reduced (Marmot et al, 2020). Environmental factors such as a lack of accessible open air spaces, a high density of fast food outlets have also been found to be more prevalent in deprived areas (Goodair et al, 2020). Smoking, alcohol use and poor nutrition are important causes of some of the diseases that contribute to life expectancy inequalities (Bennet et al, 2020). A link has been found between higher self-report of good health and the greater availability of green space, such as parks. Levels of reported general health correlate closely with the level of deprivation in a place. The higher the percentage of people reporting poor or not good health the greater the deprivation of the area (Goodair et al, 2020).

We have outlined above the health, education and wealth inequalities between the North and the South of England. Sandie and Jerome have been studying happiness in the Bolton area since 2013, see Sandie's book for a summary of this research (McHugh, 2017). On receiving a small grant from Research England, we wanted to compare happiness levels in Bolton and Luton. One a typical northern town, the other a similar sized town located just north of London. Our colleague Professor Patrick McGhee, suggested instead that we do a study using the Prolific website. This meant we could expand the scope of our study to cover the North of England and the South of England, and not just the two towns we originally proposed to study. Dr Julie Prescott and Rosie Allen joined our small research team and on March 18th 2020, we launched our survey on the Prolific website. Within two hours we had reached our target sample of 1600 participants. If we had not conducted an on-line survey, this research would never have been completed, as the following week the country went into 'lockdown' as a result of the Covid-19 pandemic. There is no doubt that the results have been affected by anxiety linked to the pandemic, and a number of our respondents commented on this. Our assumption is that people in the North of England will have been affected as much as people in the South of England, by the pandemic, and that the effects will be balanced out equally across the country.

Given the arguments presented earlier in this chapter about health, wealth and education, is seems reasonable to hypothesise that

People in the South of England will have significantly higher levels of happiness, than people from the North

To test this hypothesis, we administered a number of questionnaires to our participants. These were the measures we used.

Measures

1. PERMA Scale

This is quite a recently developed measure of flourishing. The American psychology professor Martin Seligman has argued that the main goal of Positive Psychology is to increase flourishing (Seligman, 2011). In a sense flourishing is the new 'happiness.' This 23-item scale measures the five key elements of flourishing. The term PERMA stands for positive emotions (P), engagement (E), relationships (R), meaning (M) and accomplishment (A), and as noted above is based on Martin Seligman's PERMA theory (Seligman, 2011). This scale has been developed by Margaret Kern and colleagues and has been extensively validated and tested cross-culturally, both by themselves (Kern et al, 2015; Butler & Kern, 2016) and by independent researchers (Ascenso et al, 2018; Ryan et al, 2019). In addition to measuring PERMA, is also has questions on physical health, negative emotions and a single question on loneliness and an overall happiness rating.

2. Office of National Statistics (ONS4) Wellbeing Questions. (Michaelson, Mahony & Schifferes, 2012).

These are four questions that are now used in household surveys by the Office for National Statistics, and sometimes referred to as ONS4. Each of the four items is rated on a 0 to 10 scale. One question asks the person 'How anxious were you yesterday?' Another 'How happy were you yesterday?' The two other questions are about life satisfaction and whether the individual feels they have a worthwhile life? Recent guidance has been provided for their use (ONS, 2018). These questions have been used by all government departments for a wide range of surveys and have been part of the Annual Population Survey since April

2011.

3. Clinical Outcomes in Routine Evaluation (CORE-10).
    This is a short 10-item measure of psychological distress taken from the larger CORE-OM (Connell and Barkham, 2007; Barkham et al, 2013). It is used in community services and in many Improving Access to Psychological Therapy (IAPT) services. Items are rated on a five-point frequency of occurrence basis, eg. *'I have felt tense or anxious,'* rated as 'not at all,' 'only occasionally,' 'sometimes,' 'often,' or 'most or all of the time.'

4. University of California Los Angeles (UCLA) Brief Loneliness Scale.
    We used the three-item version of this scale to measure loneliness (Campaign to End Loneliness, 2015). The short form was developed for use in large surveys (Hughes et al., 2004). The items are, *'How often do you feel you lack companionship?' 'How often do you feel left out?' 'How often do you feel isolated from others?'* Each item is rated on a three-point scale, 'hardly ever,' 'some of the time,' and 'often.' We decided to include this very short scale as there has been increasing concern about the effects of loneliness in modern societies.

5. Worktown happiness rankings.
    In the original Worktown study, the researchers asked Bolton residents to rank order 10 things that might contribute to their personal happiness. The items were economic security, knowledge, religion, humour, equality, beauty, action, leisure, leadership and politics. We used the exact same items in our present survey.

Remember **our prediction is that people from the South of England will have significantly higher levels of happiness than people from the North**.

Findings

In all 582 people from the North of England participated in the survey, and 992 people from the South. The average age of people from the North was 36.64 years (standard deviation = 12.95) and from the South is was 36.01 (sd = 13.04). We will present the scores for each group on the five main study measures.

PERMA Flourishing Scale

Table 1
Comparisons of scores on the PERMA Scale for people from the North and South of England.

	Northern sample n = 582	Southern sample n = 991	Significance
PERMA subscale			
Positive Emotions	18.08	18.40	ns
Engagement	19.82	20.16	ns
Relationships	19.67	19.21	ns
Meaning	18.11	18.43	ns
Personal Accomplishment	18.94	19.15	ns
Physical health	18.11	19.12	t = -3.010, df = 1574, p = .003
Negative emotions	14.37	14.48	ns
Overall happiness	6.29	6.31	ns
Total Flourishing	100.89	101.67	ns

What is striking from the above table is how similar the scores are for both groups. The only difference was in physical health. People from the South of England rated their physical health as better than people from the North of England.

Office of National Statistics Wellbeing Questions (ONS4)

Table 2
Descriptive statistics for the general population and the Northern and Southern samples on the Office of National Statistics (ONS4) Wellbeing Questions.

	ONS Annual Figures 2019-2020 c.150,000	Northern sample n = 584		Southern sample n = 992		Significance
		%	n	%	n	
Anxiety	Mean = 2.91	Mean = 5.35		Mean = 5.36		
High 6-10	20.39%	13%	78	14%	135	
Medium 4-5	16.20%	18%		18%	177	ns
Low 2-3	23.05%	102		16%	161	
Very low 0-1	40.36%	15%	88	52%	519	
		54%	316			
Happiness	Mean = 7.54	Mean = 5.37		Mean = 5.52		
Low 0-4	8.27%	36%	210	31%	305	
Medium 5-6	15.60%	26%	152	29%	293	ns
High 7-8	40.45%	29%	167	31%	304	
Very high 9-10	35.18%	9%	55	9%	90	
Life satisfaction	Mean = 7.69	Mean = 6.05		Mean = 6.13		
Low 0-4	8.27%	25%		24%	232	
Medium 5-6	15.60%	146		23%	231	ns
High 7-8	40.45%	21%	123	41%	411	
Very high 9-10	35.18%	44%	257	12%	118	
		10%	58			
Life worthwhile	Mean = 7.88	Mean = 6.45		Mean = 6.58		
Low 0-4	3.78%	20%	118	18%	178	
Medium 5-6	11.87%	22%	128	23%	231	ns
High 7-8	48.56%	37%	213	38%	375	
Very high 9-10	35.79%	21%	125	21%	208	

There are two things to note from the above table. Firstly, again there are few differences between the North and South samples. Second, the scores of the North and South samples are lower than the national averages, depicted in the ONS column.

Clinical outcomes in Routine Evaluation Scale (CORE-10)

This scale is really the antithesis of happiness as it measures psychological distress. If we follow the same reasoning as our main hypothesis, that people in the South will be happier than people in the North, then people in the North should show higher levels of psychological distress.

Table 3
Comparison of scores on the CORE-10 Scale for Northern and Southern samples.

Core-10 item	Northern sample N = 584	Southern sample N = 992	t test
Tense, anxious or nervous	2.21	2.27	ns
Support when needed	1.49	1.55	ns
Able to cope	1.41	1.40	ns
Talking is too much	1.20	1.19	ns
Panic or terror	1.13	1.12	ns
End my life	0.17	0.14	ns
Sleep problems	1.70	1.54	t = 2.252, df = 1574, p = .024
Despairing or hopeless	1.05	1.07	ns
Unhappy	1.62	1.57	ns
Unwanted thoughts	0.96	0.96	ns
Total Score	12.93	12.80	ns

The results are again striking in their similarity! People in the North did score higher on psychological distress, but it was only by 0.13 points. More people in the North reported sleeping problems, but this was not a large difference and by statistical probability we would expect to see at least one difference between two groups when we are making 11 comparisons.

UCLA Brief Loneliness Scale.

Table 4

Comparison of scores on the Brief UCLA Loneliness Scale for the Northern and Southern samples

item	Northern sample N = 582	Southern sample N = 992	significance
Lack companionship	1.81	1.85	ns
Feel left out	1.80	1.83	ns
Feel isolated	1.85	1.85	ns
Total score	5.46 (sd = 1.82)	5.53 (sd = 1.80)	ns

Again, there was only a very small negligible difference between the Northern and Southern samples.

Worktown Happiness rankings

Worktown Happiness Rankings for Northern and Southern samples, compared with original Worktown sample and another Northern sample, as shown in table 5.

Table 5
Comparison of Bolton sample in 1938, 2014 and North and South 2020

Rank	Worktown 1938	Northern sample 2014	Northern sample 2020	Southern sample 2020
1	Economic security	Humour	Humour	Humour
2	Knowledge	Economic security	Economic security	Economic security
3	Religion	Leisure	Leisure	Leisure
4	Humour	Knowledge	Knowledge	Knowledge
5	Equality	Equality	Equality	Equality
6	Beauty	Beauty	Action	Action
7	Action	Action	Beauty	Beauty
8	Leisure	Leadership	Leadership	Leadership
9	Leadership	Politics	Politics	Politics
10	Politics	Religion	Religion	Religion

Rankings of what contributes to happiness were identical between our Northern and Southern samples in 2020. They were very similar to those from a Greater Manchester sample in 2014. All three groups agreed exactly on the top five factors for happiness. The only differences are those that exist with the Worktown sample. Boltonians in 1938 were most concerned with economic security, then knowledge followed by religion. It would appear that religion greatly diminished in the twenty first century.

Discussion

Our prediction was that people in the South of England would be happier than people from the North, given the larger disparities in health, wealth and education between both groups. We looked at levels of flourishing, we used the four Office of National Statistics Wellbeing questions, we measured psychological distress and loneliness and we looked at how each group rank ordered 10 factors that are linked to happiness. We found no real differences between both groups. People in the South were not happier. But then again, neither were people from the North. It would appear that happiness in more likely to be affected by other variables that we failed to measure in our survey. Lest anyone think that the survey has proved poor value for money, we have found other things that may be more important.

Firstly, we have demonstrated that older people are coping better in the wake of Covid-19, than younger people (Carson et al, 2020).

Secondly, we have also shown that individuals who are lonelier are much more distressed than those who are not lonely (Allen et al, 2020). It is entirely possible that there are other factors, as yet to be discovered, that are more important in predicting happiness.

References

Adams, R. and Greenwood, X. (2018) Oxford and Cambridge hold £21bn in riches. The *Guardian*. [Accessed 27th July 2020 at 2018 https://www.theguardian.com/education/2018/may/28/oxford-and-cambridge-university-colleges-hold-21bn-in-riches]

Allen, R., Prescott, J., McHugh, S. and Carson J. (2020) *Only the lonely: Are the lonely more vulnerable to self-isolation during the Covid 19 pandemic?* Submitted for publication 2021

Ascenso, S., Perkins, R. and Williamon, A. (2018) Resounding meaning: A PERMA wellbeing profile of classical musicians. *Frontiers in Psychology*, doi.org/10.3389/fpsyg.2018.1895

Barkham, M., Bewick, B., Mullin, T., Gilbody, S., Connell, J., Cahill, J., Mellor-Clark, J., Richards, D., Unsworth, G. and Evans, C. (2013) The CORE-10: A short measure of psychological distress for routine use in the psychological therapies. *Counselling and Psychotherapy Research*, 13, 1 [Accessed 16th August 2020 at https://doi.org/10.1080/14733145.2012.729069]

Bennett, J.E., Pearson-Stuttard, J., Kontis, V., Capewell, S., Wolfe, I. and Ezatti, M. (2018) Contributions of diseases and injuries to widening life expectancy inequalities in England from 2001 to 2016: a population-based analysis of vital registration data. *Lancet Public Health*, 3, 586-97. [Accessed 30th April 2020 at http://dx.doi.org/10.1016/S2468-2667(18)30214-7]

Brien, P. (2019) Public Expenditure by country and region. *House of Commons Library Briefing Paper Number 04033*. [Accessed 22nd July 2020 at https://commonslibrary.parliament.uk/research-briefings/sn04033/]

Butler, J. and Kern, M. (2016) The PERMA-Profiler: A brief multidimensional measure of flourishing. *International Journal of Wellbeing*, 6, 3, 1-48

Campaign to End Loneliness (2015) *Measuring your impact on loneliness in later life*r. London: Author

Carson, J., Prescott, J., Allen, R. and McHugh, S. (2020) Winter is coming: age and early psychological concomitants of the Covid-19 pandemic in England. *Journal of Public Mental Health*. [June 2020 https://doi.org/10.1108/JPMH-06-2020-0062]

Centre for Cities (2020) *High Debt Levels in Northern England and Wales leave people badly prepared for economic downturn*. [Press Release accessed 4th May 2020 at https://www.centreforcities.org/press/high-debt-levels-in-northern-england-and-wales-leave-people-badly-prepared-for-economic-downturn/]

Centre for Social Justice (2013) *Turning the Tide. Social Justice in five seaside towns*. London: The Centre for Social Justice. Accessed on 30th April 2020 at https://www.centreforsocialjustice.org.uk/library/turning-tide-social-justice-five-seaside-towns

Children's Commissioner (2018) *Growing Up North. Look North: A generation of children await the powerhouse promise*. London: Children's Commissioner for England. [Accessed 26th March 2020 at https://www.childrenscommissioner.gov.uk/report/growing-up-north-a-generation-of-children-await-the-powerhouse-promise/]

Connell, J. and Barkham, M. (2007) *CORE-10 User Manual: Version 1.1*. CORE System Trust and CORE Information Systems Limited

Corlett, A., Clarke, S., McCurdy, C., Rahman, F. and Whittaker, M. (2019) *The Living Standards Audit 2019*. London: Resolution Foundation

Dorling, D. (2010) Persistent North South Divides in N. M. Coe and A. Jones (Eds) *The Economic Geography of the UK*. London: Sage (pp 12-28)

Goodair, B., Kenny, M. and Marteau, T. (2020) *Policy Report Series. Townscapes. England's Health Inequalities*. Cambridge: University of Cambridge Bennett Institute for Public Policy. [Accessed 3rd August 2020 at www.bennettinstitute.cam.ac.uk/publications]

Hall, P. (1998) The first industrial city: Manchester 1760–1830. *Cities in Civilisation*. London: Weidenfeld & Nicolson.

Hughes, M., Waite, L., Hawkley, L. and Cacioppo, J. (2004) A short scale for measuring loneliness in large surveys: Results from two population based studies. *Research on Ageing*, 26, 6, 655-672

Internet Geography (2019) [Accessed 26th May 2020 at https://www.internetgeography.net/topics/the-north-south-divide/]

Joyce, R. and Xu, X. (2019) *Inequalities in the twenty first century: introducing the IFS Deaton Report.* London: The Institute of Fiscal Studies. ISBN 978-1-912805-21-1

Kern, M., Waters, L., Adler, A. and White, M. (2015) A multidimensional approach to measuring wellbeing in students: Application of the PERMA framework. *Journal of Positive Psychology*, 10, 3, 262-271

Langella, M. and Manning, A. (2019) *Residential Mobility and Unemployment in the UK.* CEP Discussion Paper 1639. London: Centre for Economic Performance London School of Economics and Political Science

Lee, N. (2014) Grim down South? The Determinants of Unemployment Increases in British Cities in the 2008–2009 Recession. *Regional Studies*, 48, 11, 1761–1778

McCall, C. (2018) *London dominates UK jobs Growth in past decade.* BBC Shared Data Unit. [Accessed 23rd July 2020 at https://www.bbc.co.uk/news/uk-england-46288515]

McHugh, S. (Ed) (2017) *The Changing Nature of Happiness.* Cham, Switzerland: Palgrave MacMillan

Marmot, M., Allen, J., Boyce, T., Goldblatt, P. and Morrison, J. (2020) *Health equity in England: The Marmot Review 10 years on.* London: Institute of Health Equity. [Accessed 3rd August 2020 at https://www.health.org.uk/publications/reports/the-marmot-review-10-years-on]

Michaelson, J., Mahony, S. and Schifferes, J. (2012) *Measuring Well-being: A Guide for Practitioners.* London: New Economics Foundation

Mowat, C.L. (1955*) Britain between the Wars, 1918-1940.* (pp 480-490) London: Methuen & Co

Office for National Statistics (2018) Workless Households for regions across the UK. [Accessed 1st August 2019 at https://www.ons.gov.uk/employmentandlabourmarket/peoplenotinwork/unemployment/bulletins/worklesshouseholdsforregionsacrosstheuk/2018]

Office for National Statistics (2018) *Personal Wellbeing User Guidance.* [Accessed 7th April 2020 at Ons.gov.uk/peoplepopulationandcommunity/wellbeing/methodologies/personalwellbeingsurveyuserguide]

Office for National Statistics (2019) *Exploring the UK's Digital Divide.* [Accessed 5th March 2019 at https://www.ons.gov.uk/releases/exploringtheuksdigitaldivide]

Office for National Statistics (2020) *Regional Labour Market Statistics in the UK: January 2020* [Accessed 22nd July 2020 at https://www.ons.gov.uk/employmentandlabourmarket/peopleinwork/employmentandemployeetypes/bulletins/regionallabourmarket/previousReleases]

Ryan, J., Curtis, R., Olds, T., Edney, S., Vandelanotte, C., Plotnikoff, R. and Maher, C. (2019) Psychometric properties of the PERMA Profiler for measuring wellbeing in Australian adults. *PLoS ONE*, Dec 23 doi.org/10.1371/journalpone.0225932

Seligman, M. (2011) *Flourishing.* London: Nicholas Brealey

Valero, V. and Van Reenen, J. (2016) *The Economic Impact of Universities: Evidence*

from around the Globe. Cambridge, Massachusetts: National Bureau of
Economic Research

Zarenko, B. (2020) The Outlook for Public Expenditure. Presentation as part of *A
look ahead to the March 2020 Budget.* Institute of Fiscal Studies. [Accessed
27th May 2020 at https://www.ifs.org.uk/uploads/The-outlook-for-public-
spending-Ben-Zarenko.pdf]

Voices from the past: A qualitative investigation of letters on happiness from 1930's Bolton

Sandie McHugh, Julie Prescott and Jerome Carson

Introduction

In 2014 Sandie McHugh and Jerome Carson in collaboration with The Bolton News, replicated the Worktown Happiness Survey of 1938 (See Chapter 2). As far as they and the other members of the Centre for Worktown Studies were aware, this would make the town of Bolton unique with two comparative happiness studies, 76 years apart (The Bolton News 2014; McHugh and Carson 2016). The town's residents experienced very different socio-economic circumstances in 1938, compared to the second decade of the twenty-first century.

In 1938 the town was mono-cultural, with the population being engaged mainly in the textile, engineering, commercial or mining industries. The majority of children left state school at age 14. There was no National Health Service. Bolton Hospital was supported by voluntary contributions from wealthy cotton mill owners and other benefactors, with many of the employed giving one penny each payday. Workers paying National Insurance Stamps would be covered for medical care, and state benefits, but other members of the population were not. They had to pay for medical attention and did not receive any benefits. State assistance for sickness, unemployment or retirement was thus very limited, compared with today. Holidays abroad were only for the rich. Other fortunate Boltonians would get a day trip or a week's holiday at the Lancashire seaside resort, Blackpool. There were, however, 200 churches and chapels, 300 pubs, six dance halls and 47 cinemas, to visit in the town. Many homes would have 'wireless' sets to receive the BBC programmes. For other pursuits, there were several parks, bowling greens, an indoor wrestling stadium and the home of Bolton Wanderers football team, Burden Park. Today multi-cultural Boltonians have a much higher standard of living, with a comprehensive National Health Service (NHS), state benefits, and school to age 18, with the increasing option of university education. Employment is mainly in the service sector, high tech electronics and data processing. Travel beyond Bolton's borders is commonplace and holidays abroad are possible for the majority. Television and the Internet have largely replaced town venues for leisure and socializing.

Our aim in our study of the 1938 Worktown letters, was not only to enrich our picture of Bolton at a time as a representation of pre-war urban industrial society, but also to consider what we could learn for research into Happiness in our own times. The replication of the Mass Observation questionnaire in 2014, had shown that townsfolk were not happier at that time than in the pre-war period. Approximately a quarter of each sample reported they were happy every day, with more than half happy several times a week in 1938, and less than half in 2014. In the Bolton before the Welfare State, the NHS, State secondary and higher education and the 'modern consumer society,' the townspeople self-reported slightly higher levels of daily and weekly happiness in 1938. Whilst it could be argued this confirmed the theory proposed by Easterlin, that as countries became richer, they did not necessarily become happier, we wanted to utilize the knowledge of the essence of happiness in the 1930's to inform current research into general well-being (Easterlin, 1974; Easterlin et al, 2010). Greater understanding of happiness in an era with different economic and social characteristics, where people endured more hardship and fewer opportunities, could suggest possible strategies within the field of Positive Psychology to enhance the happiness and well-being for people today. This focus would be on enhancing a satisfactory normal life, improving well-being and developing practical interventions for individuals and organizations, where these are considered necessary (Seligman and Csikszentmihalyi, 2000).

Study background

'Happiness is one of the most elusive things in life. It cannot be bought, for money often brings the reverse of happiness. It cannot be commanded, for the more we plan for it, long for it, and dream about it, the further it seems to recede from us. In fact, it seems to come to us where we are not seeking it and have not made any elaborate preparations for it'.

The above is an extract from one of the 226 letters analysed from the 1930's Mass Observation Worktown Study that forms the basis of this chapter. The aim of this study was to explore perceptions of happiness from a group of Bolton residents responding to the invitation in April 1938 to, *'Write down what you think–Never mind about style or grammar'* in answer to the question *'What is Happiness?'* The Bolton Evening News promoted this competition with cash prizes of two and one guineas and a third prize of ten shillings and six pence. All competition letter writers, were then sent a Happiness questionnaire to complete and return. It was part of the investigation into the lives of ordinary working people living in the industrial northern town of Bolton, between 1937 and 1940. A project by the Mass Observation Movement, founded by anthropologist Tom Harrisson, poet and journalist Charles Madge, and artist Humphrey Jennings in London. The town, Worktown, was seen to represent the industrial north (Hinton 2013). The 1938 Happiness archive reported by Gazeley and Langhamer (2012), gave a first comprehensive overview of quantitative findings from the Happiness questionnaire and a preliminary coding of the letters using a binary system from Hadley Cantril (Gazeley and Langhamer, 2012, pp.166-167). This paper will explore in more detail the essence of happiness expressed by the letter writers so that their own voices illuminate the experience of their lives, to enrich our understanding.

The 226 freestyle letters varied in length, style and expression and from a population estimated to be 163,828 in 1939, are a small self-selected group (GB Historical, 2019). The context of the writing of letters and the purpose, for which they are written, should be considered with their use as primary historical data (Bodeker, 2004). The main motive of putting pen to paper was to win a monetary prize. In this competition there was no other medium, telephone, artwork, or personal representation they could use. The conditions encouraged their own free style, no 'finicky' concern about grammar. The competition structure meant these were not private correspondence between two individuals. The letters were to be read, and a judgement made on their worth for a cash prize. It is to be borne in mind when analysing the letters that they were meant to be read by strangers, not lovers, family members or associates within a business context. 'Professor John Hilton will judge them' the advertisement proclaimed. He may not have appeared as an unknown entity to many of the town's residents. A 'Lancashire lad,' Hilton was appointed the first Montague Burton Professor of Industrial Relations at Cambridge in 1931. He had early work experience in a cotton mill and engineering production, a spell in the Ministry of Labour, and in the 1930s gave radio talks on the BBC and penned contributions to a weekly column in the national daily *News Chronicle* (Gardiner, 2010: 704). He would have been known by reputation to many townsfolk as someone with an interest in ordinary people and with a sympathetic standpoint. He received many letters from members of the public from his work as a broadcaster and journalist and may have been regarded as a trusted public figure.

Methodology

A qualitative method involves a shift to examine discourse and communication and is research that gives people a voice. Qualitative data is seen as enabling the meanings of textual data to be explored, a 'turn to language' (Little, 2007). Using qualitative enquiry is said to encourage questioning and a fresh look at concepts often taken for granted (Shaw and Frost, 2015). Although it is not possible to work with the letter writers of 1938 as individuals, as it might be in contemporary action research, it does allow an appreciation of their experience through their own words that we can access in the Mass Observation archive. Therefore, the approach taken to analyze the data was an inductive thematic approach, considering the subject of Happiness not from our own perspective or survey results, but as a blank sheet to be filled with participants' voices.

All the happiness letters were typed verbatim, and analyzed with NVivo the qualitative analysis computer software package from QSR International. Two of the authors coded the data, which identified 26 nodes (and subnodes). These were subsequently reduced into five themes and twelve sub themes.

Findings

Qualitative analysis resulted in five general themes: Personal attributes/attitudes; Personal Relationships; Others, Money/Economic and Activities. The themes are represented in a hierarchical ordering. Each of these themes contained subthemes as shown in Table 1. Personal attributes/attitudes included expressions of contentment and peace of mind, references to religion, and to God. Under Personal attributes there were also comments on health. For Personal relationships this included writers' references to family, home, and to friends. The category Others meant giving and helping other people. Money/Economic encompassed having enough to live on, holiday pay, employment, economic security, and the importance of money to happiness. Finally, activities that brought happiness include numerous references to nature as well as references to general activities that brought about happiness such as music and going to the cinema.

Table 1
1938 letters five main themes and their sub themes.

Theme	Sub-theme	Example quote
Personal attributes attitudes	Contentment	*It is life's most treasured possession, for without it, life is a misery.*
	Peace of mind	*My opinion of happiness can be summed up in three small words, Peace of Mind.*
	Religion	*Happiness … an inward peace, hope and trust in God, which under no circumstances is shaken.*
	Health	*So, happiness is health and health is happiness, what more could one wish for.*
Personal Relationships	Family	*I already have the greatest things that count in a good comfortable home with a good wife.*
	Home	*To get some nice pieces of furniture and have a nice home.*
	Friends	*Friends contribute their share to my happiness…a tramp over the hills in company of friends…even if a breakdown in health came, the friends are still there, and that means peace of mind and happiness to me.*
Others	Giving to others	*What greater happiness is there than giving to others more unfortunate than yourself.*
	Helping others	*Happiness is the state of one's mind when you help others.*
Money Economic	Enough to live on	*One must have sufficient for one's needs, not too much to spare…buy everything, wanted and unwanted, nothing is ever appreciated.*
	Holiday pay	*To me and thousands more, holidays with pay would be a blessing'.* *'Yes, paid holidays would make me very happy*
	Employment And job security	*My idea of happiness is a nice steady job, with a wage that you could rely on every week.*
Activities		*I should be able to get all the necessary recreation for a man of 47, this consists mostly in a few hours in the bowling green in the summer and country walks with my wife, and in the winter.… a visit to a First Division football match at Burnden Park, and then spend the rest of the evening in peace and quiet listening to the various radio programmes. This then is my version of what happiness is.*

Personal attributes/attitudes

The overarching theme of personal attributes and attitudes encompasses contentment and peace of mind and the letters often reveal how these are linked with religion and good health. Money is mentioned within contentment, however money was mentioned so frequently as related to happiness, that it was coded as a separate theme and includes the subthemes of enough to live on, employment and job security and holiday pay mentioned in its own right Contentment/Peace of Mind.

The most frequent, contentment and peace of mind was mentioned by 35% of letters. One writer states; *'Happiness is, Peace of mind, body and soul. Happiness comes from within you. Contentment'*. Another said, *'Happy at home and work and contentment'*. There were many expressions of contentment as a description of happiness. 'In one simple English word *'Contentment'*. Another comment, *'Happiness ....and contentment with your lot, however humble it may be, I think a contented mind gives true happiness'*. In terms of peace of mind there may be an element of acceptance, for knowing one's place in the economic and social hierarchy, for some of the writers. *'Contentment with our lot and making the best of it'*. For some, reflections from religious teachings, *'And in the words of St. Paul, learn in whatsoever state therewith to be content'*. For others morality was important, *'To be perfectly happy you must first of all know Peace of Mind. If your conscience is always clear you have nothing to be afraid of'*.

Religion

Some of the statements appear to be part of a religious belief and relate to economic circumstance. *'The first one faith ...and when you have got that you have got peace within yourself'*. *'I would find happiness from enjoying a clear conscience, good health and steady employment'*. *'Enjoy my holidays knowing that I should have my wages when I came back and also, peace of Mind which in my Mind is what makes for Happiness'*. *'Happiness is having enough to pay your way which gives one that contented feeling...but if you are faced with the prospect of going into debt you could never be happy'*. The liberal references to love for some writers encompassed Christianity. *'My idea of happiness, is the love of God'*. *'Fully conscious of the love of God and his protecting care'*. *'God's greatest gifts, love is religion'*.

Health

References to health occurred in one fifth of the letters, not that many fewer, than references to economic security and money. *'If one had good health then they are well on the road to Happiness'*. *'Hundreds of people are afflicted with bad health...I thank God for good health'. 'Good health, I think in most cases this is required, as bad health leads to much unhappiness and despair'. 'My husband could attain a position, which would be secure as long as he is able to work, good health for us'. 'That given good health means an income to cover all reasonable dues and demands'.* Poor health increased the likelihood of being out of work bringing poverty and probable reliance on state welfare payments involving the Means Test (This was a way of judging, who most needed welfare). This was viewed as a degrading process, which could involve the sale of household items before relief payments were awarded (Gardiner, 2010: pp.35-51).

Personal relationships

Home life and family were as important to letter writers as giving and helping others, ranking equal second as the most frequent reference. The home conditions would be different to expectations in the twenty first century. David Vincent in his description of the growth of individualism after the Second World War, has drawn attention to the close living together in pre-war households and the later increase in couples having their own house and single occupancy housing (Vincent, 2018). Bolton Council began slum clearance after the First World War and by 1939, it had built 6500 new houses (Gent, 1995; pp.127).

Home

Most of the older housing stock in Bolton, as in many other towns, would not have had a bathroom, or indoor toilet. These deprivations by twenty first century standards were not commented on in the letters. Descriptions of a good home refer to the general environment and a valued spouse. Some of the comments reflect the gender roles in the home, with men as the breadwinners and women in the home. *'My version of an ordinary working man's happiness is having a little home he is proud of, with a good wife to look after it...sat in your castle'. 'Security in the home, with a dependable life partner'. 'Happiness in your home is to be always agreeable with your husband....a kind word for him on his return from daily toil, always to have his meals punctual for him...then you will both be happy'. 'A good home, a good wife and of course baby, and no interference from mother-in-law'. 'A wife who looks well after the home. When a man has done a hard day's work and he comes home to a good fire and a good meal, a pleasant wife and happiness. That is what I call Happiness'. 'Married life and a home of your own'.* Some of the references refer to hopes of their own house, *'A house to live in'. 'A home of one's own'. 'Happiness...with the peace of home and the love of parents'. 'I would like a home of my own'. 'I have a home of my own, a tiny one, but someday I hope to have it properly furnished'.* Private rented accommodation was in decline in the 1930's, with the rise of council housing (housing provided by local government) and owner-occupation, but three out of every five houses would be rented (Wilson, 2017).

Family

In the category of family, children could be described as causes of happiness. *'An arm fondly round his wife's shoulder, the young father gazes down at his newly born son and heir'. 'What more happy picture could you imagine than a mother with children who need and love her? A little child, something to love and cherish'. 'I am a married man with two young children perhaps they have something to do with my happy state of mind'. 'Mine depends entirely on a loving wife and family'. 'I think that no home is complete without a family, even if it is a small one'. 'To see my husband and son's smile, the sun bursting through my window, gives me all the happiness I need'.*

Friends

The many references to the words love and loving were extended outside the family and to friends. Friends are mentioned in some of the letters *'and my fellow workers are kind and friendly, and I have lots of friends'. 'A friend one can truly confide in'. 'Take pleasure in the company of friends'. 'Real true friends'. 'Genuine friends'.* The importance of home and family had the same frequency in the letters as others, giving to and helping. We argue this shows the concern many Worktowners had for their community, suggesting this was a less individualistic age than our own.

Others

The desire to assist others in need appears to have been prevalent in the town during the 1930's, as it would be in many other societies, where people lived and worked in close proximity, and where people would be aware of the hardship and privation of some of those around them. John Webster describes how there was a general atmosphere of mutual help in his street, *'especially in times of trouble or sickness. Neighbours would readily rally to help anyone in distress. It was in many ways a comfortable feeling knowing that each person had a helpmate should the need arise'* (Webster 1964: 64). Helping neighbours was the norm for some families as described by one of the letter writers, *'My neighbours are kind and clean my front flags (steps) when they do their own, and they put a tasty dinner on one side to give me a pleasant surprise sometimes'.* Helping others in the community was part of the wider scene in Worktown, and was reflected in the letters as the second most frequent reference, alongside that of family and home.

Giving to others

If people were in possession of a little wealth, or spare income, it was often seen to be used to help others, especially friends and those in the local community. *'Just a bit more money to be able to give a friend a little treat sometimes...neighbours, to be able to give them a few flowers, a magazine, or some fruit, or a little gift'.* 'Real happiness one must share the good things one has with one another'. 'Have a longing to help your poorer neighbours...charity...to give pleasure to someone else poorer than you'.

Helping others

Concern for other people and expressions of desire to give help are apparent in the conduct of the writers. *'My idea of finding happiness is simply this, to aim at being good...I mean doing all we can to help other people'.* The direct result of *'loving one's neighbour as thyself'.* *'Willingness to help others, cheerfulness and ready sympathy for others in trouble'.* Some of the letters reflected religious teachings as in this, *'JOY Jesus - First. Others- next and Yourself Last'.* *'Feeling at peace with God and having vast supply of love and sympathy for others'.*

Money/economic

The spectre of the possibility of having to go without essentials in life would sometimes qualify the happiness and wealth comments. *'Money itself can't buy Happiness, but it makes you happy and contented to know when you have enough for all your requirements and a little put by for a rainy day'.* This comment sums up the concern of many people for their economic security, there were limited welfare benefits available and Bolton's unemployment rate was seventeen per cent for men and thirteen per cent for women in 1936, high perhaps by present day figures, but lower than some other areas of the UK in the 1930's, notably the North East of England and South Wales (Denman and McDonald 1996). To be in work was a major concern for self-esteem and to have enough to live on. As one person said, *'individual happiness it is essential to have decent and constant work'.*

'Having enough to live on'. This theme of enough is related to contentment and to giving to and helping others. A view on the role of money in happiness mentioned above, a sufficiency of money would be used to help others as well as oneself. *'If you have enough money for food and clothing, and are able to pay your way, and put a little away for a rainy day, that should make you happy'.* Another letter stated, *'Just enough money to have a little bit of pleasure out of life'* and *'my idea of real happiness is to have an easy mind to be able to pay your way and have enough to eat and a little to spare'.* There appears to have been a general consensus that wealth would not create happiness. *'A million pounds*

cannot purchase happiness', 'Happiness is not bought'.

Holiday pay

Happiness was security to Worktowners, and with many of the cotton mills on short time, a regular weekly wage could be an aspiration. *'Not wealth', 'An assured income...paradise to us cotton workers who are never sure of two week's pay'.* In 1938, there was a campaign for holiday pay, and the letters reflect this. At the time of the Mass Observation advertisements for the Happiness competition, meetings were being held between the United Textile Factory Workers Association and Employers' Associations. When no agreement was reached, the Minister of Labour appointed a Committee to deal with question of holidays with pay and identified the future 1941-42 Parliamentary session for legislation. In June 1939, spinning, doubling and manufacturing sections of the textile trade, agreed one week's paid holiday per annum, on the basis of two per cent of gross earnings of the previous twelve months. This issue for the textile industry was not settled to everyone's satisfaction and went to national arbitration in 1950 (Hopwood, 1969). Comments made by the letter writers, *'regular wage with no deductions for holidays'. 'My husband to have a good steady job, good wage, so that we could have a holiday once a year'. 'My idea of happiness is a nice steady job with a wage that you could rely on every week, holidays included'.*

Employment and Job Security.

Many of the comments link health and employment together as the former affected the latter. Happiness is described as, *'being in regular employment and receiving a living wage'. 'If only my son was settled in a satisfactory job'. 'I would find happiness from good health and steady employment'. 'To enjoy good health and thus be able to keep to regular employment would bring me happiness'. 'I find happiness in having good health and hard work'.* The lack of this security is shown in the comment *'My husband's occupation is stripping and grinding in a cotton mill receiving a small wage...what a strain it is trying to balance budget with the bogey of unemployment always hovering around'. 'More employment would bring more happiness. Lack of occupation is not rest. A mind quite vacant is a mind distressed'.*

Activities

We can get a glimpse into what free time activities brought happiness to the letter writers. *'I can be happy with the simple things, a quick walk in the country'. 'To revel in country walks, beholding green fields, trees, sunsets and the wonders of animal life'.* Bolton situated in a valley, is surrounded by countryside and is also well served by public parks from wealthy benefactors such as Lord Leverhulme. The wonders of the natural world, and the temporary respite from the smog in the town, to the surrounding countryside or seaside, were obviously very attractive. *'Short walks in the country and sit under the hedgerows listening to the birds and bees, view the flowers in the grass, and the blossom on the hedges, and enjoy the blessed sunshine'. 'Occasional walks over the moors, and feeling the tinge of the fine healthy breeze in one's face'. 'My hobby a garden'. 'A little country place close by the sea where I could enjoy the breath of fresh air... the coming of spring heralded by the budding trees'. 'Happiness dwells in places of simple nature. In the song of a bird, the murmur of a stream'.* Work in the textile mills, engineering workshops and in the mining industry, would be arduous labour in a noisy and often dusty and dirty environment, so being outdoors on the moors or enjoying sea air would be especially welcome.

Blackpool an hour's rail journey away was the main day trip, and holiday destination for Boltonians, with special trains leaving Trinity Street Station in Bolton at regular intervals. These dance trains established around 1933, continued until the 1960's, and were 'accessible and popular amongst a wide range of age groups of Bolton's community...married couples, underage youths on their first trip to Blackpool, football fans to visit the dance halls after the match, single people, group outings' etc. (Clewlow 2010: 3). Letters sent in by school teacher Miss Hewner contained these comments from children, *'I would be happy if I went to Blackpool and had a ride on a donkey and stopped all day. I would play on the sand'. 'I would be happy if I went to Blackpool, and have all my meals there'.* The anticipation and planning for a Blackpool holiday was expressed by a housewife, being happy making rompers and holiday clothes for her children.

For indoor activities, music and reading were popular. *'To appreciate good music and good books'. 'Musical selections played on organs in churches and cathedrals and wireless. Sacred music, dance music, beautiful voices, operatic music can give us happiness'.* Radio expanded during the 1920's and 1930's bringing music into the home. Nine million households owned a wireless. By the outbreak of the Second World War, it is estimated that 98% of the population could listen on a cheap wireless set to one BBC service, as the Corporation broadcast opera, symphonies, chamber and modern music (Gardiner, 2010: pp.511-513). If the wireless was popular, the 1930's has been described as the age of the cinema, and there were 42 cinemas in the Bolton area. (In 2019, there are now only three cinemas, all multiplexes). Some of the letter writers saw these as important for their happiness. *'Films, to see good films can give an amount of happiness and upliftment. Wireless music and talks are a huge source of happiness to listeners'. 'A fine film, a good play'. 'I get happiness in so many different ways...listening to the Radio, going to Church'.* Many of the 200 churches in Bolton had social clubs and the town's public libraries and reading rooms provided facilities for Worktowners' spare time.

Conclusions

In the Introduction we stated an aim of using the knowledge from the Happiness letters to inform current research and contribute to Positive Psychology strategies of enhancing well-being. From our own Happiness surveys, we found that people do not consider that money or possessions brings happiness. (McHugh and Carson, 2017). However, for some there can be a general discontentment with contemporary life (Jackson, 2017). In 1938 peace of mind and contentment were highly prized. Worktown did not have a sophisticated consumer society, with constant persuasive advertising messages to purchase and acquire more 'stuff' (Jarrett, 2012; Williams, 2018). It had its own social comparisons between the posh streets and neighborhoods of the town, aptly described by Bill Naughton, (Naughton, 1988; 1995). Worktowners had lower incomes, very limited credit availability and fewer observations of more affluent lifestyles via the cinema, newspapers and magazines. It was television and the Internet that would later bring easier national and international comparisons of wealth and lifestyles, some of which are negative and can increase dissatisfaction with personal experience (James, 2007). The pools coupons could mean dreams of instant wealth for 1930's workers, but riches, status and fame were for the aristocracy and film stars, not for ordinary folk. Cultivation of a contented frame of mind and an appreciation of the advantages and opportunities of twenty first century living, is in our view, an important lesson from the letters.

Another lesson for our reflection is whether we should be spending more time caring about and helping others. Should we be making more connections in our local communities? The Global Internet offers a myriad of advantages for individuals and society, but should it complement rather than replace relationships that people experienced in the past? The Internet has been criticized as increasing solitude and interfering with personal relationships (Turkle, 2013). Giving to and helping those around us can increase the 'feel good' factor and be beneficial for our health. Stephen Frey argues that doing good raises personal happiness and caring for others is good for well-being (Frey, 2018). Volunteering has been associated with increasing general health and happiness, reducing anxiety and depression. It can also provide a way to actively participate in social and community life, also said to increase happiness and life satisfaction (Post and Niemark, 2007; Luks, 1988).

The letters give us a glimpse of life in Worktown, where personal peace of mind and contentment, the important place of others in the community, alongside home and family meant happiness. Security was having enough. Good health was valued as essential for not only earning a living, but also because health care was not affordable in the pre-National Health Service period. Leisure was often in the town and alongside co-workers and neighbours. For some this might only be an annual day trip to Blackpool. It suggests communal harmony. Simon Heffer describes society in the 1930's as more cohesive, simpler, as people knew each other and those in the street and did not lock their doors. They were unified within their own communities, compartmentalized in the locality, not unified nationally or globally through media and social media. Communities had local leaders, mill owners, professionals like clergymen and teachers (Heffer, 2018). If this was the case, the cinemas, newspapers and wireless would provide a window onto the wider world, from Worktown. After the Second World War, television, and later the Internet and social media, would create new communities more important than localities. The expressions in the happiness competition letters have shown the importance of others, and Christian values are evident of loving thy neighbour. The independent categories derived for the present data analysis do however overlap remarkably closely with those suggested by Lord Richard Layard. Layard identified seven factors that lead to happiness. These are family relationships, finances, work, community and friends, health, personal freedom and personal values (Layard, 2005: pp.63). These are very similar to our own categories and sub-categories, with the sole exception of personal freedom. While material circumstances between 1930's Bolton and contemporary society at the start of the twenty first century differ hugely, it would appear that happiness is still influenced by many of the same factors today, as it was then. Contemporary happiness researchers can learn a lot from the Bolton letter writers of 1938. If nothing else is should imbue us with humility when we think of the material wealth, good health and greater opportunities for travel and education, we all now enjoy compared to our grandparents' generation.

References

Bodeker, H.E. (2004) Letters as historical sources – some concluding reflections in Regina Schulte and Xenia Von Tippelskirch (Eds) *Reading, interpreting and Historicizing: Letters as Historical Sources EUI Working Paper HEC 2*. Florence, Italy: European University Institute Badia Fiesolana (pp199-202).

Clewlow, S.A. (2010) *From Bolton to Blackpool*. Manchester: available via saclewlow@yahoo.com.

Denman, J. and McDonald, P. (1996) Unemployment Statistics from 1881 to the present day. *Labour Market Trends*, 1, 5-18.

Easterlin, R.A. (1974) Does economic growth improve the human lot? Some empirical evidence. Nations and households in economic growth in *Essays in honor of Moses Abramovitz*, P.A. David and M.W. Reder (Eds.) Academic Press: New York and London (pp 89-126).

Easterlin, R.A., McVey, L.A., Switek, M., Sawangfa ,O. and Smith-Zweig, J. (2010) The Happiness-Income Paradox revisited. *Proceedings of the National Academy of Science in the United States of America*, 107: 52, 22463-22468.

Frey, B.S. (2018) *The Economics of Happiness*. Cham, Switzerland: Springer International Publishing.

Gardiner, J. (2010) *Britain's Forgotten Decade. The Thirties. An Intimate History*. London: Harper Press.

Gazeley, I. and Langhamer, C. (2012) The meanings of happiness in Mass Observation's Bolton. *History Workshop Journal*, 75, 1, 159-189.

GB Historical (2019) Bolton CB/MB through time | Population Statistics | Total Population, *A Vision of Britain through Time*. University of Portsmouth [Accessed 2nd January 2019 at http://www.visionofbritain.org.uk/unit/10003179/cube/ TOT_POP.]

Gent, L. (1995) *Bolton Past*. Chichester, West Sussex: Phillimore.

Heffer, S. (2018) *The Good Old Days: The Politics of Nostalgia*. BBC Radio 4. Producer Philippa Goodrich. Presented David Aaronovitch. Saturday 27th October. [Accessed 19th January 2019 at https://www.bbc.co.uk/programmes/m0000y2g]

Hinton, J. (2013) *The Mass Observers: A History 1937-1949*. Oxford: Oxford University Press.

Hopwood, E. (1969) A *History of the Lancashire cotton industry and the Amalgamated Weavers Association*. Manchester: Co-operative Press.

Jackson, T. (2017) Broken Promises – the engine of consumerism. *The New Internationalist website*. [Accessed 14th January 2019 at www.cusp.ac.uk/ consumerism disappointment]

James, O. (2007) *Affluenza*. Reading: Vermilion.

Jarrett, C. (2012) The psychology of stuff and things. *The Psychologist*, 26, 8, 560-564.

Layard, R. (2005) Happiness: *lessons from a new science*. London: Penguin.

Little, R. (2007) Methodological Pluralism and the History/Theory Link in the English School. *The Imperatives of Historical Praxis for IR Theory*: Part II, SGIR 6th Pan-European IR conference Torino, Italy.

Luks, L. (1988) Helper's high: Volunteering makes people feel good, physically and emotionally. And like 'runner's calm,' it's probably good for your health. *Psychology Today*, 22, 10, 34-42.

McHugh, S, and Carson, J. (2016) Happiness then and now. *The Psychologist*, 29, 5 406-407.

McHugh, S. and Carson, J. (2017) Happiness Perceptions a comparison of 1938 and 2014, in *The Changing Nature of Happiness An In-Depth Study of a Town in North West England 1938-2016*. (Ed. S. McHugh) Cham, Switzerland: Palgrave Macmillan (pp 69-85)

Naughton, B. (1988). *Saintly Billy. A Catholic Boyhood*. Oxford: Oxford University Press.

Naughton, B. (1995) *Neither Use Nor Ornament. A memoir of Bolton 1920's*. Newcastle upon Tyne: Bloodaxe Books Ltd.

Post, S.G. and Niemark, J. (2007) *Why good things happen to good people: How to live a longer, healthier, happier life by the simple act of giving.* New York: Broadway Books.

Seligman, M.E.P. and Csikszentmihalyi, M. (2000) Positive Psychology: An introduction. *American Psychologist,* 55, 1, 5-14.

Shaw, R. and Frost, N. (2015) Breaking out of the silo mentality. *The Psychologist,* 28, 8,638-640.

The Bolton News, (2014) Monday February 10th (pp 1, 6-7); Tuesday February 11th (pp 10-11);. Wednesday February 12th (pp 4); Thursday February 13th (pp 4); Friday February 14th (pp 11); Saturday February 15th (pp 4).

Turkle, S. (2013). *Alone together: We expect more from technology and less from each other.* New York: Basic Books.

Vincent, D. (2018) interviewed by Claudia Hammond, *The Anatomy of Loneliness,* Episode 3, BBC Radio 4, 16th October 2018. [Accessed 21st January 2019 at https://www.bbc.co.uk/programmes/m0000mj9/broadcasts/2018/10]

Webster, J. (1964) *A Tonge Moor Childhood.* Bolton: Novaprint

Williams, J. (2018) *Stand out of our Light: Freedom and Resistance in the Attention Economy.* Cambridge: Cambridge University Press.

Wilson, W. (2017) A Short History of Rent Control. *House of Commons Library Briefing Paper Number 6747.* London: Her Majesty's Government Office

Conclusions and the way forward

Sandie McHugh and Jerome Carson

If you have read this book obsessively, you will by now have arrived at this chapter having ploughed the previous fourteen. One of the strengths of an edited book is the variety of different literary styles, which is not always to the tastes of reviewers, who sometimes prefer consistency. When we set out to edit this book and to invite the varying contributors, Sandie and Jerome had no idea what the result might be? Some authors we knew well, such as our colleague Professor Bob Snape, others we had worked with, such as Chris Elliott, but we had never read work written by the majority of our contributors before. In a sense it was a gamble inviting such a diverse group of participants. We hope that you, the reader, will have been both impressed and stimulated by what you have read. It is our job in this final chapter to try and bring the themes expressed in the book together and also to look at the way forward for happiness research, which Sandie and Jerome have been engaged in since 2013.

Our own work in the field of happiness, which has been summarised in Chapter 2, was inspired by reading the letters on happiness written by the people of Bolton, as part of the Worktown research established in the town by Harrisson and Madge in 1937. The start of the Second World War brought this particular research to a premature end, but the researchers left behind a treasure trove of material for future researchers to pore over and develop (see Chapter 14). While Elisabeth, in Chapter 11, says that the term Worktown was an unimaginative choice, the same criticism, could be made of our choice of title, *Happiness in a Northern Town.* Why did we not call the book, *Happiness in Bolton?* That is a fair criticism, but perhaps with a subconscious view to marketing the book, we chose the former title. A book just about Bolton would of course mainly attract Boltonians, but what about folk from Bury, Blackburn, Burnley, Wigan, and Preston, and many other Northern towns and the great industrial cities of the North, Manchester, Liverpool, Sheffield, Leeds and Newcastle? We hope that this book will have wider appeal than just within the town of Bolton, though in fairness without the Worktown research, which has captivated many of us, we would not be writing this book. It was the great philosopher Soren Kierkegaard who stated, *'Life must be lived going forwards, but can only be understood by looking backwards.'* (Steve Jobs gives a similar message in his Stanford Commencement address, which can be viewed on YouTube). In this tradition we are now going to go back over what has been written in the book drawing out key themes, before looking forward. It would however be unfair for us as editors to start with our own work, so this summary will instead begin with the work of Professor Bob Snape in Chapter 3. While Bob is a highly valued colleague of the editors, he is also the Director for the Centre of Research in Worktown Studies at the University of Bolton. His academic specialism is the social history of leisure. In the more recent surveys, leisure is always rated in the top three or four of activities important to happiness. Bob draws a distinction between hedonistic pleasure and Aristotle's concept of eudaimonia. His quotation from Jeremy Bentham is another to treasure. Bentham stated, *'Happiness too is a slippery word.'* Indeed. In the days of the Worktown Study, just before the outbreak of the Second World War, Bob tells us that cinema and the wireless were sources of hedonistic leisure. Youth leaders on the other hand felt that more active forms of leisure were a source of character building.

Bob's discussion of the importance of the pub for both leisure and happiness finds contemporary resonance in the fictional Queen Vic pub in East Enders and the longer established Rover's Return in Coronation Street. He argues that the pub was, *'One of the basic institutions of working-class life.'* There were at the time of the Worktown Study 300 pubs in Bolton and indeed the pub so fascinated Harrisson and his colleagues, that this was one of the few books they produced from their study, *'The Pub and The People,'* (Mass Observation, 1987). Bob also draws our attention to holidays, something so many of us take for granted, yet these were *'...denied many Worktowners....'* because of poverty and even those who could afford one found it to be challenging financially. Bob quotes one Boltonian who stated, *'We've been away to Blackpool one day in fifteen years.'* Bob informs us that Blackpool was *'Lancashire's Mecca.'* Its *'raison d'etre was to guarantee the maximum opportunity for hedonic leisure.'* J.B. Priestley caustically remarked that Blackpool, *'....appealed to less intelligent and enterprising young people.'* This debate over class aside, Bob concludes, following Epicurus, that friendship is the single most important thing for happiness.' In the era of Covid-19, many of us have been re-discovering the delights of holidays in England.

Kathryn Thomasson in Chapter 4, describes the perceptions of happiness in three women's groups in Bolton. She stresses the crucial importance of relationships for happiness. She highlights the innovative work being carried out by the Percent for Arts Programme, delivered by Bolton at Home and its partners, the only programme of its kind in the UK. Along with the editors of this book, Kathryn took part in four Focus Groups including the three she had been working with closely in Bolton. The main themes that emerged from the groups were the importance of family and friends for happiness. All four groups agreed that having a lot of money would not necessarily bring happiness. It was also apparent that each group had different needs and aspirations. The Golden Oldies benefitted from the group camaraderie, which they felt made up for a perceived lack of social integration in their local neighbourhoods. The Young Women aspired to have an independent life and to fulfil their educational and work aspirations. For the Wonder Woman group, there were a lot of concerns around economic disadvantage, with many experiencing lives of financial hardship. On the other hand, the Sanctuary Story Tellers appreciated elements in our society that we have come to take for granted, such as education and health, to name but two. They could see huge benefits to living in our society. Likewise, the religious tolerance and sense of freedom we enjoy, was something that as asylum seekers and refugees, they were not always accustomed to. There is no doubt that for all the group participants, membership of these groups, brought its own happiness.

In Chapter 5, Julie Levy shares three stories from her career, two from working with children and adolescents with additional educational needs and the third a more contemporary tale of her involvement with Bolton Railway Station. For Julie a lot of her happiness has come from enabling others, and also through helping others find happiness from their achievements.

The first story she tells is of her four years as an art teacher in a 'Maladjusted' boarding school for teenage boys in Devon, most of whom came from either Inner-City London or Bristol. She described how she managed to engage them in creative tasks, based on her ability to come up with activities that they would join in with, from of all things, large weave tapestry to 'slip casting' to make ornaments mainly for their mothers or grandmothers. Some 30 years later one of her ex-pupils contacted her to let her know that he still had the clay house he made in her class.

Twelve years after this she applied to be the Special Educational Needs and Disability Co-ordinator at a comprehensive school in Wigan. The school was such a challenging one that one of the candidates for the post left before the end of her interview! As Julie notes, '*I however was made of sterner stuff.*' Indeed, she was. It was perhaps not surprising that most of these children led chaotic and deprived lives outside school. Julie established a 'Nurture Group' within the school, where a small group of pupils with additional needs could work in what I would say was a type of 'educational sanctuary.' This extended to staff and pupils eating together in their teaching room at lunchtimes. Absenteeism dropped, behaviour improved and Julie says the pupils even developed something of a celebrity status within the school.

The third case study concerned her work with the Bolton Station Community Partnership. They opened a gallery in one of the station platform buildings. They launched a national call out for Railway Workers Art. This led to only eight submissions, but as she points out, '*The quality and variety of the work was astounding.*' She goes on to comment, '*...these were men who had worked for years on their art in solitude...Most of them worked at home and although some of them had sold their work, it was not sales that motivated them. They were united by a common need to create.*'

What Julie describes in her Chapter, is in fact teaching of the highest order. Being able to engage groups whose previous experience of education and indeed life, had probably been very negative, at least in terms of the first two groups she talked about. She also has a unique gift which David Brandon has described as *'The trick of being ordinary,'* so that others are not intimidated by your own talents.

Ken Heathcote is a Bolton fitness legend. In July 2020, he was 85 years of age. His chapter draws the link between exercise and happiness or as the Latin saying goes, *'Mens sana in corpore sano,'* (A healthy mind in a healthy body). He modestly avoids telling the story of what he achieved on his fortieth and fiftieth birthdays. At the age of 82, he swam the length of Lake Windermere. In the chapter he introduces us to a small number of characters who had a profound influence in his life. Dr George Sheehan showed that running was really a battle against the self and not against others and that a life without risk or challenge, was unlikely to lead to joy or happiness. For Sheehan the greatest challenge was running. Bill Pearl was another person who had a major influence on Ken. Bill was the four times Mr Universe and the only man to beat Arnold Schwarzenegger in a body building competition. Ken managed to bring Bill to his health studio in Bolton.

One of Ken's greatest sources of inspiration was his own father. Just as World War Two was ending, his father had his back broken in three places in a colliery accident. Yet, his father would learn to walk again. Ken recounts the apocryphal tale of the day when his father and he arrived at the local swimming pool in the middle of December, only to find there had been no coal delivery. The water was close to freezing. Not realising that they were the only people who were going to swim, they entered the swimming pool to see all the members of the swimming club fully clothed in their winter gear. Ken's father told him, *'Let's just do one length.'* Ken has later recounted it was the fastest length he ever swam in his life! Over 20 years later, Ken sat in his small gym on another cold December evening, with the sobering thought that he had not had a single customer come to the gym that evening. Feeling sorry for himself he looked up at a motivational poster on the wall which stated, *'If you think you can, you can.'* Four years later he had moved from a gym of 400 square feet, to one that was 10,000 square feet and which included a spa, saunas, a crèche, beauty salon, squash courts and a restaurant. Bolton Health Studio was the first of its kind in the UK and led the way for the later massive growth in the fitness and wellbeing industry. Ken states, it was not just about facilities and equipment, but about *'...its people, friendship, camaraderie and sociability.'* Fitness and friendship. Together happiness.

Chapter 7 also partly used a case study model, the two main protagonists, Jerome and Paul Makin, were both recovering alcoholics. Paul asked later why his account of his own battle with alcohol was twice as long, as Jerome's, who was also twice the age of Paul. The probable answer is that Paul was probably more honest! Paul and Jerome connected their own stories to research they conducted for Paul's undergraduate thesis, which set out to look at flourishing in recovering alcoholics. While they found some evidence that people who had abstained for a longer period-of-time, had higher levels of flourishing, on average recovering alcoholics had much lower levels of flourishing than normative groups. This seems counter-intuitive. You might think that having given up alcohol after many years of problem drinking, that people would be bound to flourish, but the data suggest this is not the case. What is probably more important is the appraisal the individual makes about their situation. If someone sees themselves as in a situation of post-traumatic growth, they may be more likely to thrive. Sobriety also brings with it an awareness of the damage that the individual's alcohol problem has caused. Just as alcoholics are often in denial about the extent of their drinking problems, it may also be the case that they engage in a certain amount of denial when in recovery. Flourishing is not guaranteed in abstinence, but has to be worked at.

In Chapter 8, Mohammed Sadiq, Aishath Shahama and Aashiya Patel, consider the relationship between faith and happiness. They start by providing data which shows a decline in the number of people in Bolton claiming to be members of a religious group, from 84% in 2011 to 70% in 2018. They suggest that while most of us have access to adequate material and social needs, we may be lacking in the spiritual dimension. They review the literature which links happiness with religion. They present research findings that show that religion gives people a sense of meaning, wellbeing and comfort, as well as membership of a dependable social network. They end the chapter with a Case Study by Mohammed, which highlights the importance of his faith. He has learned that happiness resides in the present and unhappiness in the past and future. He is thankful and happy that he has been able to count on his faith throughout his life.

Reginald Amanze addresses the issues of forgiveness and happiness in Chapter 9. The importance of the link between happiness and forgiveness can be seen in the negative emotions aroused by those who feel they have been 'wronged.' These emotions are more likely to harm the person who holds them, than the actual offender. Reginald points out that the development of Positive Psychology has led to an increasing interest in the two topics. He reviews a number of studies that have examined the relationship between forgiveness and happiness. He suggests that happy people are more likely to forgive others. Yet, it may also be the case that forgiving people are happier than non-forgiving people. He ends his chapter by offering readers the challenge of seeing how forgiving they are on a new scale he has developed, called the Bolton Forgiveness Scale. Following a complex statistical process called factor analysis, Reginald suggest that forgiveness comprises three components. First, Coming to Terms and Letting Go, eg. *'I feel relief by forgiving someone who has hurt me.'* His second factor is Developing Positive Feelings, eg. *'I have compassion for the person who wronged me.'* The third element in his model is Giving Benefit of the Doubt, eg. *'I hold nothing against someone who hurt me, as it could be that sometimes people don't really know what they are doing.'* How did you perform on his Forgiveness Scale? Are you by nature a forgiving person? If you are, the chances are you will also be a happier person.

Chapter 10 presents the material crafted by 'The occasional creative, Chris Elliott', contextualised by Kathryn Thomasson. Kath reminds us at the start of the chapter about the power of music and story-telling, perhaps partly exemplified by the Radio Four programme, 'Desert Island Discs.' Music and storytelling have long preceded the more recent attempts by social scientists and arts researchers' attempts to 'quantify their benefits.' The longevity of both genres suggests that they tap into something deep in the human psyche. Chris played and sang his own compositions and told the following stories, described below in precis form, at a number of 'happiness sessions' delivered to four women's groups in Bolton and described in more detail by Kathryn Thomasson in Chapter 4. When it comes to writing, the performer is at a huge disadvantage, as their skill naturally lies in performing. Even the late great Clive James, though he may have felt himself to be both a writer and a performer, was a much better writer than he ever was a performer (James, 2009). Chris composed a special song for the groups he attended and also wrote a number of monologues, which he read out to the different groups. In his chapter he presents the material that he delivered to a group of Bolton women named 'The Golden Oldies.' The material was so well constructed I mistakenly assumed he was from the North, but it turns out he was a Southerner in 'sheep's clothing.' He started with his song, *'What makes you happy?'* It merits repeating in part here;

'What makes you happy, what makes you glad,
What makes the bad times good?
What makes you smile, what makes you laugh,
What makes you feel like you should?'

Chris went from singing to acting. His chapter presented four narratives; 'Edward and Jessie,' 'The world of work,' 'Sports and pastimes,' and finally 'Possessions.' The stories talk of a simpler, but perhaps happier past, no doubt 'sepia tinted,' as Elisabeth Long suggests in her chapter. *'Both Dad and Grandad were proud of their work…You couldn't be happy all the time…But it (work) was something to be proud of.'* In 'Possessions' the writer laments, *'… we used to write to each other,'* and how *'Eventually Dad got a telephone for the house.'* In the final story, 'The world around us,' the narrator recalls how, *'…*

we all used to listen to the wireless,' and *'Mum decided we should have a television.'* Anticipating how Boltonians would swap Blackpool for warmer climes with the advent of the package holiday, he commented, *'This lad Jimmy Simmons had been on holiday to Spain. The weather was so hot, he'd changed colour...The world was getting smaller. The old ways were changing.'* Later the narrator reflects, *'I wonder sometimes if folk have the time to listen to the birds or sit still and watch a sunset.'* Further evidence of the ability of fiction to connect, comes in the statements, *'Grandparents die, aunts and uncles and then your parents. That makes you sit up.'* He ends his final piece with the statement, *'There's nothing like Time's winged chariot to get you looking backwards and get you to ask that question, 'When were you last really happy?''*

Somewhat modestly Chris concludes his chapter with the statement, *'Creativity (albeit of the occasional kind) perhaps can partner certain academic research, and if it contributes to the general levels of happiness that's fine by me.'* We rather suspect sadly, that the contributions of the actor and performer, will outlast those of the researcher.

In Chapter 11, Elizabeth Long has written a wonderful chapter about her own history, the story of Bolton itself and the narrative surrounding Silverwell House, where she is based. Elisabeth and her charity 1point, have been located in this historic building since 2016. Her chapter introduces the reader to many of the colourful characters, who have featured in the history of the town, from Alice Foley, Bill Naughton to Peter Kay, to name but a few. Elisabeth told us of her own journey from working in the press and media, to volunteer receptionist for Relate, to training as a counsellor herself. There is so much wisdom and 'food for thought' in her account. She commented at one point, *'...made me change my focus to working with people to help them lead more satisfying lives, as opposed to working at them to get their stories.'* She quotes the psychotherapist James Davies, *'...certain kinds of emotional discontent far from being useless inconveniences, can be resources to be tapped in the service of greater wellbeing, not only for the individual at hand, but also for the community at large.'*

The postscript to Elizabeth's chapter tells of the suffering brought about by one local and one global event. The Cube Fire on Friday evening of November 15th. 2019, led to over 200 students losing their accommodation. Yet the next day and for many days after, the ordinary people of Bolton responded in their hundreds bringing in toiletries, clothes and food for the students, many of whom had lost all their possessions. Most recently, the town, like the rest of the country and indeed the world, is having to cope with the Covid-19 pandemic. Yet as Elisabeth pointed out, *'...behind the closed doors and empty streets there are thousands of people cheerfully facing adversity, showing resilience, compassion and creatively reaching out to support their communities locally and elsewhere.'*

Embedded in Elisabeth's account is a quotation from the comedian Lucy

Beaumont who stated, *'If you can still laugh when things are tough, you've found the secret of happiness.'* This quotation captures the essence of the town of Bolton.

In Chapter 12, Ian Platt, Chathurika Kannangara, Michelle Tytherleigh, Sarah Banks and Jerome described the Hummingbird Project run in partnership with the children's charity, MedEquip4Kids and the Universities of Bolton and Chester. This project is trying to address the happiness of future generations. In its first year the project was delivered to over 1000 students in 14 high schools in Greater Manchester and Cheshire. This six-week psychoeducational intervention started by considering the issue of stigma and mental illness. Over the course of the programme students learned about happiness, resilience, character strengths, hope, growth mind-sets, gratitude and mindfulness. The authors presented results in the chapter that showed how the project had led to improvements in wellbeing, resilience and hope. A second year of the intervention led the authors to see if in addition to boosting wellbeing, they could also reduce the symptoms of mental illness, which the project has done. Year 2 of the project had to be terminated earlier as schools were forced to close because of the Covid-19 pandemic. At the same time, Claudine McFaul has developed Hummingbird Primary, and has delivered this intervention aimed at primary school children, to a school in Liverpool and one in Greater Manchester. It is hoped that Hummingbird Primary can be delivered to schools in the next academic year.

Hummingbird 1 and 2, have been delivered by Ian Platt, assisted by student volunteers from the two Universities involved. The authors point out themselves that this model of delivery is not sustainable in the long run. It would have to be scaled up for delivery by several trainers in a range of schools, probably by staff from the schools themselves. The authors are currently considering how to deliver such an intervention, which might also involve an on-line element. They caution that it might be difficult to obtain fidelity with the original course materials and there might well be 'mission creep,' as some teachers might seek to incorporate their own material into the programme. Given that the vast majority of mental health problems start in childhood and adolescence, this intervention might have a preventative effect. The quotation with which the authors end the chapter, with one participant stating that, the Hummingbird Project was the second-best experience of his life, leaves us all wondering, now, what was the best?

Chapter 13 tried to answer the question, 'Happiness is there a North/South divide?' Jerome, Sandie, Julie Prescott and Rosie Allen conducted an online survey of over 1600 people from the North and the South of England. The survey used a range of well-established measures to compare levels of flourishing, mental distress, loneliness and wellbeing. It also used the rank ordering task of the 10 items related to happiness that the

Worktown 1938 survey used. The authors expected to find North-South differences in happiness, given the well-known disparities in health and wealth between the affluent South and the poorer North. To their surprise there were no differences of note. People in the South did not have higher levels of flourishing, lower levels of mental distress, less loneliness and better wellbeing. Their rank ordering of the 10 items linked to happiness was identical, though different to the 1938 rankings. Other factors are therefore more likely to be important, rather than location in the North or South of England. Statistical analysis showed that women had higher levels of flourishing, but also higher levels of psychological distress. It was an omission not to have looked at the relationship between income and happiness. That might also have shown differences.

In Chapter 14, 'Voices from the past,' Sandie McHugh, Julie Prescott and Jerome Carson, describe how they looked at the happiness letters written by Bolton citizens in 1938 in response to a competition, *'What does happiness mean to you and yours?'* These letters are a unique set of data. Worktowners wrote over 200 of these letters. They provide us with a unique glimpse of what made people happy in 1938. Many of the contributors struck Jerome as being like philosophers. People in those days had so much less (see Chapter 2). It seems hard to believe that very few of them had any holiday pay. Sandie and Julie devised a code to categorise the themes from the letters. Remarkably the things that made people happy in 1938, were very similar to the categories devised by Professor Lord Layard in the early 21st century. A trip to Blackpool was the most that many people could hope for as their holiday. Today, the advent of Covid-19 and government travel restrictions, have stopped many people from their annual trips overseas, but it is doubtful that Boltonians will revert to trips to Blackpool. Life was simpler in 1938, but undoubtedly much harder. Any comparison between the two time periods shows the huge advances in education, medicine, technology, travel and leisure opportunities, to name but a few. Yet are we any happier today in Bolton than folk were in 1938? I'm not sure that we can say they are?

In the introductory chapter we briefly discussed definitions of happiness, now we can consider what can be added from the chapters of this book. When is a happy experience not likely? The basic physiological needs of air, water and food, Maslow's hierarchy, followed by safety from the elements , i.e. clothing and shelter without these then experience is miserable (Maslow, 1943). Our knowledge of war and conflict zones illustrate that although there can be glimmers of humour or happiness this cannot be sustained. Domestic abuse and natural disasters are also not conducive to happiness. The news reporting from present day conflicts in Africa and Syria clearly show the misery etched on the faces of the population and in the recounting of their traumatic experiences. Comparisons of happiness levels throughout the world indicate that safety and stability of political systems impact directly on the population, with life expectancy and freedom to make life choices being important. Within the top ranked five happy countries in 2014-2016 are Scandinavian countries of Norway, Denmark and Finland whereas in the bottom five are Rwanda, Syria and Central African Republic, (Helliwell et al, 2017). Julie Levy in the Devon Boarding School taught art to young men many of whom had not had the chance to feel safe and cherished, some had been abused as children or abandoned by their parents. Some had drifted into crime. Their basic needs of safety and security had not been met and consequently flourishing was not an experience they had been able to enjoy. The school provided some stability and Julie facilitated her students to create their own pottery pieces, providing them with freedom of choice and the feelings of accomplishment.

Happiness then becomes possible when basic human needs are met. Far from 'want' many people today in Western economies have an excess of goods and possessions. The more people have does not necessarily correspond with a happier life. Our research has shown that Bolton people in the twenty first century enjoy a much higher absolute standard of living, access to facilities of the welfare state, NHS and educational opportunities, which could not have been imagined in the 1930's. Yet their reported levels of happiness are not higher than in the 1938 study. Findings from both databases indicate that increased wealth by itself does not increase happiness. The Worktowners in 1930's Bolton, as reported in our Chapter 2 valued having 'enough' and to being free from the worry of debt. Many of their letters state that being rich would not make them happy, some even believing that greater riches would bring dissatisfaction. Contentment with what they had was prized and with 'Peace of Mind' was the most frequent explanation of happiness. Respondents in our 21st century questionnaires as well overwhelmingly rejected the notion that material goods and wealth would bring happiness. Two groups bucked this trend, Refugees and Asylum seekers, and the Wonder Women (women from disadvantaged backgrounds and with possible histories of abuse), their experiences of 'need' had encouraged a view that the amount of money you had to live on directly affected happiness. However, along with all the other groups they did reject the notion that wealth and possessions would enhance happiness. In the same vein it is probable that we did not find any significance difference in happiness levels between the North and the South of England (Chapter 13) because the higher general standards of living experienced in the South has not lead to higher levels of happiness.

Once basic needs are met, humans can then engage in belonging and love, self-esteem and perhaps self-actualization, the top of Maslow's pyramid of human motivation. Motivation at self-actualization level is by intrinsic values such as truth, goodness, perfection, beauty, excellence (Guest, 2014). These additional levels of the pyramid are likely to require more than just having sufficient resources to meet basic needs. Belonging and love need personal space, perhaps a home with artefacts that have personal meaning. Indeed our possessions become extensions of the self, a sense of identity, indicating who we want to be and where we want to belong. Increased income is sometimes spent on collection of specific brands, fashions objects on which attachments can be formed (Jarrett, 2013).

Self-esteem can involve participation in the community, which often requires resources of time and money. It might involve membership of religious, charity or leisure organizations. The pursuit of educational, sport or other goals can be part of the process of self-esteem and self-actualization. Paul Makin in Chapter 7 describes the importance of finding goals and targets as he recovered from his addiction. They helped him to build a new life, a career in helping others and studying psychology increased his confidence and self-awareness. Julie in Chapter 5 describes how the teenage boys in the boarding school were proud of the pottery ornaments they created as presents for their mothers. They had achieved something that was important to them. Creating art can bring higher self-esteem and self- actualisation especially if achievements are recognized and appreciated. Julie describes the difference the opening of a gallery at Bolton Station Community Centre, made to amateur artists. She noted how they displayed their work with pride and gained confidence from the compliments and praise they received in discussing their exhibits with other artists and visitors. Self-actualization and the motivations of intrinsic values are described by Ken Heathcote, in his account of the contribution of George Sheehan to the exercise of running. George saw the value of running as a struggle of one's self, the challenge of being the person you wanted to be (self-actualization). His published work setting out his values encouraged people to take up running for serious sport or simply as fun exercise, whatever their choice.

Paul Dolan identifies happiness as pleasure and purpose over time (Dolan, 2014), and George's running as a challenge could be identified as such. For Bill Pearl, another of Ken Heathcote's inspiring individuals, a purpose could be comprised of goals and activities from several sources, in his case, body-building, vintage cars, philosophy and writing poetry and books. Ken himself found a purpose not only in setting up a new Health Club in Bolton, but also in his training and competitive running and swimming.

Baumeister et al, (2013) maintain that although having meaning in life and happiness overlap, indeed some theorists describe eudemonia to incorporate positive feelings with purposefulness and meaning, there are differences (Deci and Ryan, 2008). Baumeister and colleagues argue that although happiness and meaning are interrelated they are different; meaningfulness is both a cognitive and emotional assessment of the value and purpose of life. They also maintain that although having a meaningful life may contribute towards happiness, having a highly meaningful life is not necessarily a happy one for example a religious missionary or a political activist. However, Reginald suggests in Chapter 9 that forgiveness has a positive association with happiness as both are involved in human development. Forgiveness may help in the search for meaning.

We do not contend to estimate the happiness of our authors, but there are plenty of examples of meaningfulness being an integral component of their experience. Mohammed Sadiq found profound meaning through faith and a way to personal happiness. Elisabeth Long's work with Relate and her foundation of 1point at Silverwell House has provided much needed support and services to many people in Bolton. Julie Levy in her employment at the Devon boarding school and her development of the Nurture Group for Special Needs pupils in a Wigan school made a positive difference to those involved. The Hummingbird School project described by Ian Platt and colleagues has already measured improvements in well-being, resilience, and optimism for the school students involved in the study. All indications are that future delivery will improve flourishing and reduce mental ill health in participants. The volunteers working with the three community groups in Bolton described in Kathryn's chapter would be able to find meaning from their work with these disadvantaged women. Chris described how Dad and Grandad were proud of their work, believing that they were doing something valuable and essential. Dad worked at Liverpool in the war, repairing damaged ships, and Grandad was a prize winning drayman taking great care of his dray horses and delivering beer to pubs. They both found meaning and a sense of pride not only in their world of work, but in their leisure sphere of life. Grandad grew vegetables on his allotment, partly to augment the family's food budget, but very importantly to win prizes at the local show. It was a matter of honour to gain first prize for marrows or other vegetable exhibits. Dad was a keen cyclist, not just for enjoyment, but also to win races.

If some people can find meaning and purpose in life and this enhances their happiness, and others cannot, is there anything special about them that explains this difference? Is there a personality trait that makes it easier to be happier? According to Veenhoven, there is not, as happiness is not temporally stable, situationally consistent, nor completely dependent on internal characteristics, the three elements he maintains are indicative of personality traits (Veenhoven, 1994). Some people may have a more naturally optimistic outlook, where the glass is always half full and never half empty, and hence happiness comes easier to them. Later research reported by Veenhoven (1997), indicated that happiness was often accompanied by social assertiveness and empathy and was found more amongst people who had a tendency towards what he called, 'internal control beliefs', whereas unhappier people tended to feel they were at the mercy of fate. Having goals, finding a purpose and engendering pride in achievements as we have seen in examples in the chapters of this book all support this suggestion.

Is it possible that higher optimism may be connected to genetic makeup? Frey maintains that a person's genetic inheritance has a strong influence on happiness. He states that psychological studies have attributed genetic inheritance to 40-60% of the differences (Frey, 2018). Sgroi et al (2017), estimate that genetic factors can explain about one-third of a person's well-being. They refer to Iacono and McGue's (2002), twin studies. They also suggest that genetic make-up can affect the happiness levels of nations citing research with Danish people which show a higher tendency for them to be happier, than many other European countries. It is possible that genetic influences may be connected to the neurotransmitter serotonin, considered to be a contributor to happiness by affecting mood. They cite their research showing a link with second generation American immigrants whose well-being levels were similar to the European country of origin of their parents. (Sgroi et al, 2017). Although there appears to be a link with genes and happiness, whatever the percentage effect is accepted, this is a complex interaction, and there is a considerable portion left to be explained by other influences.

We have already discussed above the importance of human basic needs. Our physical and mental health profoundly affects happiness experiences. People's circumstances, their opportunities for personal development matter. An interest in the disparities between the North and South of England has generated much recent research (see our Chapter 13) and one of the key messages of the 2019 General Election was to level up opportunity in all regions (Rawnsley, 2020). Whatever policies are implemented, there is much that people can influence themselves, like finding meaning or a purpose. The Dali Lama purports that 'Happiness is not something ready-made. It comes from your own actions'. With 40% available to come from our daily actions and conscious choices, people can enhance their happiness (Action for Happiness, 2020). We consider that our authors' inner motivations and values explain their achievements and their experiences of happiness.

As humans are social animals, relationships with others are part of everyday life. To Richard Layard, friendships are very important, with family, social and community relationships enhancing happiness (Layard, 2005). Our own research illustrated this. The analysis of the frequency of words used to describe happiness in 1938 and 2014, revealed the importance of time spent with friends and family. In 1938 the second and third most frequent cause of happiness was family and home and helping and giving to other people. In 2014 after activities, happiness was defined as time spent with family and friends. Kathryn has given details of the results from the coding of the Focus Group discussions with community groups. Across the community groups the most significant factor for experiencing happiness was family and friends. Bob Snape in his chapter on the role of leisure in happiness has drawn our attention to the importance of the Worktown local pub described by Spender as 'having a community feeling......people who knew each other and were happy to know each other'. The pub was a communal meeting place in a neighbourhood, a 'home from home'. Elisabeth has described the concept of a supportive community bound together by humour in Bolton; this she argues is part of an ongoing positive community spirit that has been evident in the town throughout the centuries.

At the end of our chapter 2 we indicated the way we would like our future research to develop with different projects. There is still much to understand about human happiness, and perhaps its essence will change over time. The present Coronavirus 19 pandemic with all its ramifications of home working, restricted travel and so on may influence values and attitudes towards life and happiness. It is hoped that Positive Psychology will continue to develop its wellbeing aids so that people can experience higher levels of happiness and wellbeing when possible (Ackerman, 2020). We hope that this book will have made a contribution to this endeavour.

References

Ackerman, C.E. (2020) *What is Positive Psychology and why is it important?* [Accessed 18th August 2020 at https://positivepsychology.com/what-is-positive-psychology-definition/]

Action for Happiness *About Us* [Accessed on 29th April 2020 at https://www.actionforhappiness.org/about-us]

Baumeister, R.F., Vohs, K.D., Aaker, J.L. and Garbinsky, N. (2013) Some Key differences between a happy life and a meaningful life. *The Journal of Positive Psychology*, 8, 6, 505-516

Brandon, D. (1982) *The Trick of Being Ordinary*. London: Mind Publications

Dolan, P. (2014) *Happiness by Design. Finding pleasure and purpose in everyday life*. London: Penguin

Deci, E.L. and Ryan, R.M. (2008) Hedonia, Eudaimonia and well-being: An introduction. *Journal of Happiness Studies*, 9, 1-11

Frey, B.S. (2018) *The Economics of Happiness*. Cham, Switzerland: Springer

Guest, H.S. (2014) Maslow's Hierarchy of Needs – the sixth level. *The Psychologist*, 27, 12, 982-983

Helliwell, J., Layard, R. and Sachs, J. (2017) *World Happiness Report 2017*. New York: Sustainable Development Solutions, Network

Iacono, W.G. and McGue, M. (2002) Minnesota Twin Family Study. *Twin Research and Human Genetics*, 5, 5, 482-487

James, C. (2009) The Blaze of Obscurity: The TV Years. London: Picador

Jarrett, C. (2013) The Psychology of stuff and things. *The Psychologist*, 26, 8, 560-564

Jobs, S. (2005) Commencement address at Stanford University. www.youyube.com/

watch?v=UF8uR6Z6KLc

Kierkegaard, S. (1843) *Journalen* JJ, 167, Soren Kierkegaard's Skrifter, Research Center, Copenhagen. Vol 18, p.306

Layard, R. (2005) *Happiness.* New York: Penguin Group

Maslow, A.H. (1943) A theory of human motivation. *Psychological Review* 50, 4, 370-96

Mass Observation (1987) *The Pub and the People.* London: The Cresset Library

Rawnsley, A. (2020) *It won't be easy for Boris Johnson to keep his pledges to his new friends in the north.* The Guardian. [Accessed 18th August 2020 at https://www.theguardian.com/commentisfree/2020/jan/19/it-wont-be-easy-for-boris-johnson-to-keep-his-pledges-to-his-new-friends-in-the-north]

Sgroi, D., Hills, T., O'Donnell, G., Oswald, A. and Proto, E. (2017) *Understanding Happiness. A CAGE Policy Report,* edited by K. Brandon. London: Social Market Foundation

Veenhoven, R. (1994) IS HAPPINESS A TRAIT? Tests of the theory that a better society does not make people any happier. *Social Indicators Research, 1994, 32,* 101-160

Veenhoven, R. (1997) Advances in understanding happiness *Revue Québécoise de Psychologie, 1997, 18,* 29-74

Index

Note: Page locators in *italic* refer to tables.

Lightning Source UK Ltd.
Milton Keynes UK
UKHW021037221121
394391UK00013B/868